OUR CENTURY

"To those wishing to enjoy life to its utmost,
in the most perfect climate on earth,
midst the most beautiful environments,
we would say come to this Heaven-blessed land.
Come once and the fascination will enthrall you . . ."
— *The Weekly Lake Worth News, 1900*

Published by Mega-Books/Progressive Publishing
240 East 60th St.
New York, NY 10022

Printed in the United States of America

1st printing 2000

Library of Congress Catalog Card Number: 00-190376

ISBN: 0-9657200-3-9

This book was printed by Mega-Books/Progressive Publishing

ON THE COVER: *A South Florida family mantle. Portraits, from left: developer John D. MacArthur, midwife Millie Gildersleeve, Seminole educator Louise Gopher, Henry Morrison Flagler, farmer George Morikami, architect Addison Mizner. Photographed at the Addison-Mizner-designed home of Cathleen McFarlane, Villa des Cygnes (House of Swans), in Palm Beach.*

Cover design by Sarah Franquet
Photograph by Richard Graulich

ON PAGES 2 AND 3: *A Palm Beach afternoon, shortly after the turn of the 20th century.*

OUR CENTURY

featuring

THE PALM BEACH POST 100

The people who changed the way we live

Edited by Jan Tuckwood

Chronology text by Eliot Kleinberg

Design by Daniela Dornic Jones

Portraits by Richard Graulich

THE PALM BEACH POST

Mega-Books/Progressive Publishing

'CIVILIZATION IS A STREAM WITH BANKS.
The stream is sometimes filled with blood from people killing,
stealing, shouting and doing the things historians usually record,
while on the banks, unnoticed, people build homes, make love,
raise children, sing songs, write poetry and even whittle statues.
The story of civilization is the story of what happened on the banks.'
— *U.S. historian Will Durant*

George Washington didn't sleep here. But Henry Flagler did. So did Hernando de Soto and Osceola, Napoleon Bonaparte Broward and E.R. Bradley.

And so did millions of people you never heard of. They hooked grouper, planted pineapples, cut cane and nailed railbeds. They fled frost or despots or poverty or the law. They built ragtag settlements in one of the last frontiers in America — a wilderness both beautiful and cruel.

Our history is what happened on the banks. Of the Atlantic, the Indian River, Lake Worth.

As histories go, the saga of Palm Beach, St. Lucie and Martin counties is remarkably new: Some early witnesses are still alive to tell it. But it is an unprecedented mix of scrappy pioneers and enterprising tycoons.

In *Our Century*, we salute 100-plus people who played important roles this past 100 years. Through their stories, we come to understand the stories of the millions who walked alongside them.

— ELIOT KLEINBERG

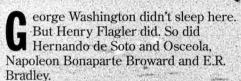

CONTENTS

Introduction, *page 8*

INTRODUCTION

'The history of a place is the history of the people who lived there'
— Judge James R. Knott

WEST PALM BEACH pioneer Roslyn Anthony Anderson once told me, "It's the intangible things in life that are permanent — honesty, compassion, love."

All the tangibles — the old buildings, the scrapbooks, the photographs in this book — are simply the record of the fascinating people who came and went and made their mark and deserve to be remembered.

In this book, we tell the stories of people who brought their honesty and goodness and a few other intangibles, including greed and grit, to South Florida and changed our century.

Our "Palm Beach Post 100" features people great and small who had an influence on Palm Beach, Martin and St. Lucie counties and the cities around Lake Okeechobee. This is not intended to be a list of the "most influential" people — that's simply too subjective. Instead, we've chosen a range of folks — some famous, some unknown, some beloved, some reviled.

It wasn't enough to be powerful or to be first. Many of our 100-plus people were chosen because they represented others like them, or they had one crowning achievement that affected the whole community.

We began this project in February 1999, when we asked *Palm Beach Post* readers to submit names for consideration. We also invited a panel of local historians to contribute. Finally, long-time editors and reporters debated and honed the list. Once we began poking our nose into local history, it was clear we could barely scratch the surface of our remarkable past.

By JAN TUCKWOOD
Associate Editor of
The Palm Beach Post

Our modern history is young — just 140 years old if you start counting from the lighting of the Jupiter Lighthouse — but deep. If you think everybody in South Florida arrived yesterday, you don't know South Florida.

"We've been around a long time," says Dr. Reggie Stambaugh, whose family has lived for five generations in Palm Beach. "The only people who think this place is transient are the people who just moved here."

Dr. Stambaugh made our list because he cared so much about his alma mater, Palm Beach High School, that he led a charge of alumni to save it.

He remembers all the intangibles of his youth: The taste of the brownies at the Campus Shop, the feeling of dropping a fishing line into a crystal-blue Lake Worth, the pain of sending his high-school pals off to World War II.

He knows how glorious it is to spend your childhood in bare feet and a bathing suit.

He knows that history is what makes a town a *home* town.

Stuart author Ernie Lyons wrote it best: "Florida is for amazement, wonder and delight, and refreshment of the soul. It may take a little more time to hunt out and enjoy the real Florida, but you will be well repaid.

"We are lucky, lucky people to have a home like this."

Historical Society of Martin County

FROND FROCK, 1930s:
Edith Coventry, a Stuart photographer, frolics at the beach.

The Barefoot Mailman: Land, sea and legacy

In the 1880s, with no railroad or regular ship service, a letter from Miami to Jupiter would make a six- to eight-week odyssey via Key West, Havana and New York. So between 1885 and 1893, 11 rugged pioneers traversed the 136 miles, 56 in small boats and 80 on foot, between Palm Beach and Key Biscayne. The grueling trip took three days each way.

One of the 11, James E. "Ed" Hamilton, never completed his round.

On Oct. 9, 1887, at the Hillsboro Inlet near Pompano Beach, he saw someone had stolen his boat. He tried to swim to the cove. The next day, mail contractor George Charter and others went looking for Hamilton. They found only his bag, and Charter concluded he was drowned, or killed by sharks or alligators.

Picking up Hamilton's route were Andrew W. Garnett, who homesteaded at Hypoluxo in 1885, and Charles W. Pierce, who wrote *Pioneer Life in Southeast Florida.*

Margaret Garnett Harris, who is 91 and lives in Tennessee, said: "It's hard now to imagine no one living between Lake Worth and Biscayne Bay except at the two houses of refuge built by the government to help shipwrecked people. One was at present-day Delray Beach and the other at New River (Fort Lauderdale). My father and fellow pioneer Charles Pierce fulfilled Ed Hamilton's contract to carry the mail. When a wagon road was completed, the era of the Barefoot Mailman came to an end. I still find it hard to believe that there was a time when my father knew every one, at least by name, from Palm Beach to Miami."

Andrew Garnett's son, Roy (1901-1992), became influential in Lake Worth. He was president of the First National Bank of Lake Worth for 31 years, and he and two colleagues were the force behind the city's purchase of beach south of the casino. Because of them, Lake Worth boasts a large public beach today.

Garnett family

Andrew Garnett with his wife, Lillie, and their children in 1907, from left: Lewis, Irl, Leland and Roy.

The barefoot mailman (top), perhaps the most colorful of South Florida's pioneer characters, as pictured by Connecticut artist Steven Dohanos. Dohanos' murals from the 1930s hang in the main U.S. Post Office on Summit Boulevard in West Palm Beach.

Gen. George Meade, who would later win the battle of Gettysburg, designed the Jupiter Lighthouse to guide mariners over the treacherous shallows.

Wilderness and War

REMEMBER LOCAL HISTORY THIS WAY: The 20th century really started with the Jupiter Lighthouse in 1860.

Before that, South Florida's natural wilderness daunted all but the Indians — and the soldiers who showed up three times to fight them. These wars forced the Seminoles and Miccosukees out of Florida or deep into the Everglades.

It would take the Jupiter light to lure groups of white settlers south of Titusville.

Most, like Marion Dimick Geer's family, came south "determined to colonize and seek that flowery land where Ponce de Leon so faithfully sought the fabled spring of eternal youth."

Her family settled along a body of water the Indians had called "Hypoluxo" — "water all around, can't get out." By the time she arrived in 1876, the closed-in lagoon and the surrounding region were called "Lake Worth."

She sought a Garden of Eden but found an earthly hell: "Oh, desolation! What a place to travel weary days and nights to find!" she wrote in 1896. "There seemed absolutely nothing to build our hopes upon, surely not the thin soil with the coquina rock cropping out everywhere."

America's last frontier east of the Mississippi was a tough beast to tame — as treacherous and wild as the Wild West.

Historical Society of Palm Beach County

Seminole Indians were frequent visitors to the Jupiter Lighthouse. These photos were taken in 1879 by Mel Spencer, who was assistant light keeper for a time.

FLORIDA'S MANY MASTERS

Spain: 1513 to 1763
England: 1763 to 1783
Spain: 1783 to 1821
United States: 1821 to present

Ponce de Leon

APRIL 21, 1513: Juan Ponce de Leon plants cross at Jupiter Inlet.

SEPT. 8, 1565: St. Augustine founded.

SEPT. 23, 1696: Jonathan Dickinson shipwrecked near Jupiter Island. Journal of his two-month walk to St. Augustine is first detailed account of region.

JULY 31, 1715: Spanish silver fleet sinks, giving Treasure Coast its name.

MARCH 1803: James A. Hutchinson receives grant for land between Fort Pierce and Jensen Beach. After his death, grant moves to what is now Hutchinson Island.

JULY 6, 1815: Florida's Spanish governor grants Don Eusebio Gomez 12,180 acres. "Gomez Grant" covers present-day Jupiter Island and Hobe Sound.

1818: First Seminole War.

1835-1842: Second Seminole War.

1838: Tennessee Volunteers carve supply trail (the future Military Trail) through Palm Beach County.

1838: Fort Floyd built west of Fort Pierce. Fort McRae built on eastern shore of Lake Okeechobee.

JAN. 2, 1838: Construction begins on Fort Pierce, named for Lt. Col. Benjamin Kendrick Pierce, a brother of the president.

JAN. 26, 1838: Fort Jupiter established 3 miles west of Jupiter Inlet; abandoned in May 1838.

1840-1842: Soldiers discover waterway and name it Lake Worth for William Jenkins Worth, leader of U.S. forces in Second Seminole War.

AUG. 4, 1842: At least 21 settlers use Armed Occupation Act to get 160 acres each and settle region around Lake Worth. They are gone by the early 1870s.

MARCH 3, 1845: Florida becomes 27th state.

JUNE 1848: First major survey of Everglades.

Maj. Gen. William Jenkins Worth

1850: Fort Drum built.

1853-1858: Third Seminole War.

FEB. 21, 1855: New Fort Jupiter established 2 miles east of old fort, at present site of Jupiter Plantation development.

1858: Fort Van Swearingen established 6 miles east of present-day Okeechobee City.

JULY 10, 1860: Jupiter lighthouse begins operation. First families settle around lighthouse.

1861-1865: Florida joins Confederate states. State sends 15,000 soldiers; one-third die.

APRIL 15, 1861: Augustus Lang, assistant keeper of Jupiter Lighthouse and believed to be area's first settler, seizes lighting mechanism to help Confederate blockade runners. He hides it until after war.

MAY 20, 1866: U.S. flag again flies over Tallahassee.

JUNE 28, 1866: Jupiter Lighthouse relighted.

Augustus Lang

11

in Lake Worth

Frontier Days

1876, along the shores of Lake Worth

"**T**O BE SURE, there were many things connected with this pioneer life that were hard to endure. With St. Lucie the nearest post office, 65 miles north, and Miami 75 miles south, with no carrier between, and our grocery and dry goods store at Titusville, 130 miles away, our mail came by whomsoever chanced to be coming our way. The news of President Garfield's death came in a paper thrown by a passing steamer to one of our boats.

"But no steamer could throw us a can of kerosene, baking powder or other housekeeping necessities. They came, though, most bountifully, and we grew to depend upon the ocean as our carrier, looking upon that restless body as the servant of Him whose promise to provide we had not doubted.

"Sometimes the generosity of the waves appalled us; we needed lard and seven barrels came, 2,800 pounds! We needed kerosene and cans of it were washed ashore. Along with it came boxes of bacon and tobacco, and cans of turpentine. . . .

"In one hurricane . . . everything from pins and needles to a saw mill came. . . . Trunks containing ladies' clothing, too — and Mr. Charlie Moore assured us he wore trimmed underclothes for some time, having no wife to utilize them."

> — *Marion Dimick Geer, writing in an 1896 issue of* The Lake Worth Historian. *Mrs. Geer, sister of influential pioneer E.N. "Cap" Dimick, arrived in 1876.*

PARADISE OF PALMS: *(preceding pages) On Jan. 9, 1878, the 175-ton brig Providencia wrecked on Palm Beach with a load of 20,000 coconuts. By 1885, when this photo was taken, the island was lush with palms. Dr. Richard Potter is the first man on the left, and the woman at right is his sister Ellen.*

LEGACY OF SKETCHES: *(facing page) George Potter sketched this pioneer woman and Seminole Indian on the western shore of Lake Worth. The first Bethesda-by-the-Sea Church, built in 1889, is behind them.*

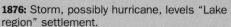

JULY 28, 1873: First homestead claim in Lake Worth region filed by H.F. Hammon. Second homestead claim filed by Hannibal Pierce.

APRIL 1876: U.S. government opens nine houses of refuge for mariners in Florida, including Gilbert's Bar on Hutchinson Island and Orange Grove in Delray Beach, which settlers call Zion.

1876: Storm, possibly hurricane, levels "Lake region" settlement.

H.F. Hammon

1878: Frank Prescott, believed first settler in what is now Martin County, settles about 11 miles southwest of present-day Stuart.

JAN. 9, 1878: The brig Providencia wrecks in Palm Beach with 20,000 coconuts. Palm trees lead to town's name.

1880: E.N. "Cap" Dimick opens Lake region's first hotel, the Cocoanut Grove House. First settlers in Potsdam, later Stuart. Danish settler John Lawrence Jensen sets up pineapple farm in what will become Jensen Beach.

'Cap' Dimick   *John Jensen*

1881: "Lake region" gets first doctor, Richard Potter. Charles Jackson of Ohio believed to be first settler of Jupiter Island.

JUNE 1881: Hamilton Disston buys 4 million acres of Central and South Florida and begins state's first large drainage effort.

1884: First settlers in what is now the Glades.

1885 TO 1893: "Barefoot Mailman" route established from Palm Beach to Miami. Eleven rugged pioneers traversed the 136 miles (56 in boats and 80 on foot), which took three days each way.

1886: Indian River House of Refuge established on Hutchinson Island. First school in Fort Pierce opens.

MARCH 1886: Dade County's first schoolhouse opens in Palm Beach.

Historical Society of Palm Beach County

PALM BEACH SCHOOLHOUSE: *First schoolhouse in Dade County, which then extended north to Stuart, built in 1886 along Lake Worth. Teacher Hattie Gale stands in the door.*

JUPITER: *The family of Mel Spencer (left) around 1898. Spencer came to South Florida in 1875 and homesteaded 123 acres in Palm Beach. His father, V.O. Spencer (with cane), became the first postmaster of Palm Beach.*

HUTCHINSON ISLAND: *The wife and sister of Hubert Bessey at the Gilbert's Bar House of Refuge, where Bessey was the keeper. Bessey arrived in what would become Martin County in 1883. He owned the Danforth House, Stuart's first hotel, and hosted actor Joseph Jefferson and President Grover Cleveland. The house of refuge is the oldest building in Martin County.*

BOCA RATON: *Capt. Thomas Moore Rickards, a land surveyor for the railroad, was Boca's first settler in the 1880s. Rickards (center, with crew) did the first Boca survey and built Boca's first house, near the site of today's Palmetto Park bridge.*

Letters from a pioneer
1880, along the Indian River:

"Well, I'm finally here — but what a disappointment! This is not the Eden I expected, but a wild and primitive place, and we are truly pioneers ...

"All I could see ... was a dock that looked like some planks fastened between two row of palm stumps. ... At the top of the steps in a clearing are two palmetto huts with a big table between them. Everywhere else was jungle ... The whole place seemed so menacing, I wanted to go back out in the middle of the river and feel safe again. Father was saying, 'I know it doesn't look like much, Lue, but wait until we have the pineapples planted as far as you can see both ways. We'll have the fine Eden Inn set back from the bank with gardens, and a fine wide wharf where guests can land their boats. ... It will all be fine, Lue. You'll see."

— written by Lucie Richards, 20, whose father, Capt. Thomas E. Richards, started a pineapple plantation north of the Jupiter Inlet in a place they called Eden. Her 1880-88 letters to best friend Mary Webb of Newark, N.J., are in a volume called Memories of Eden, *collected by Mary's great-grandson, Raymond Richards Brown*

April 1882, to Mary:

"Did you ever see a turtle ready for the pan? Well, they never die, I guess. They almost jump out of the frying pan. I would not eat a piece for the world. I fry some of it, and the boarders just rave over it, and my turtle soup they say is wonderful. One gentleman came to the kitchen and complimented me. He said, 'I have eaten turtle soup twice, once at Delmonico's and here on your table today. You are a wonderful cook." I will be so glad when the season is over. I am tired, and I want to go sailing and boating."

Historical Society of St. Lucie County

Lucie Richards in her later years.

1888, to Mary:

"Our inn has become quite renowned as a winter resort, and we have so many interesting guests. . . so many of the things Father only dreamed of have come true. We have the long wide dock where the sternwheelers land to bring our guests. The ladies in their pretty hats and fine clothes walk up to the inn on our wide path bordered by flowering hedges. The view from the inn is so lovely that newcomers stand in awe. . . The pineapple business has been very successful, too. Last year, Father cleared $14,000 on pineapples alone and will probably do better than that this year ... We have neighbors now up and down the river from Stuart-Jensen all the way to Titusville, so we have enough social life to keep Mother happy ... You will like it here now, Mary, and it really has become an Eden — complete with serpents..."

> *— from Lucie to Mary, who had just agreed to marry Lucie's brother, Harry. Lucie spent the rest of her life along the shore of the Indian River and died in 1934.*

FEB. 24, 1887: Melbourne-based *Indian River News* begins.

1888: Caloosahatchee Canal connects Gulf Coast with Lake Okeechobee.

JAN. 9, 1889: Lake Worth region gets first church, Bethesda-by-the-Sea.

FIRST CHURCH: *Bethesda-by-the-Sea Episcopal Church was founded in 1889. This building, the church's second, was built in 1894. It's now a private home.*

FEB. 18, 1889: Dade County seat moves from Miami to Juno.

JULY 4, 1889: Jupiter and Lake Worth (Celestial) Railway, first in South Florida, opens, spanning 7.5 miles from Jupiter to Juno.

CELESTIAL RAILWAY: *Engineer Blus Rice (center) rode with his hounddog and even rented the dog out to riders who wanted to hunt along the route.*

NOVEMBER 1889: Henry E. Sewall settles plantation home at tip of what will become Sewall's Point.

1890: First Baptist Church of Fort Pierce, believed to be the first church in St. Lucie County, founded.

MARCH 18, 1891: *Indian River News* moves from Titusville to Juno, becomes *Tropical Sun.*

1892: First schoolhouse in Potsdam (later Stuart) opens. St. Lucie Inlet opened.

DECEMBER 1892: First road to Biscayne Bay region opens from Lantana to North Miami.

1893: Henry M. Flagler visits Palm Beach and buys land on both sides of Lake Worth for $170,000.

AT WHITEHALL: *(preceding pages) A 1904 party at Henry Flagler's mansion, which he built for his third wife, Mary Lily, in 1901. The ballroom was decorated in the style of Louis XV, with a white and gold color scheme.*

IN THE COCONUT GROVE: *Henry Flagler and friends at the Royal Poinciana Hotel around 1900. Flagler, born in 1830, opened the fabulous Hotel Ponce de Leon in St. Augustine in 1888 and the Royal Poinciana in 1894.*

The Flagler Years

H ENRY MORRISON FLAGLER opened up the Florida frontier — and fast.

The Standard Oil tycoon, who had already turned St. Augustine into a winter resort by 1893, declared Palm Beach "a veritable paradise" and pushed his railroad southward.

On Jan. 29, 1894, Flagler's Florida East Coast Railway reached Fort Pierce, and it made it to West Palm Beach two months later. The town of Linton (soon to be Delray) got its first post office the next year, and by 1896, Flagler's railroad reached Miami.

With the train came a rush of newcomers, enterprising young men such as the Anthony brothers, who launched a retail empire in West Palm Beach. And a young doctor, Dr. Clyde Phillip Platts, who moved to Fort Pierce in 1895 and served families from West Palm Beach to Melbourne and west to Kissimmee. And Ransom Ren Ricou, who followed the railroad down to Jensen, where he built up a large fish business, with fish houses from Titusville to Fort Lauderdale.

Their descendants live here to this day.

20

Henry M. Flagler Museum

The Royal Poinciana

Nothing represented the dramatic change in Palm Beach more than this Flagler hotel, which opened in mid-February 1894. A month later, Flagler's railroad reached West Palm Beach, opening it to the world.

The Breakers

The original Breakers opens in 1896 as the Palm Beach Inn but burns in 1903. The second Breakers, pictured above, opens a year later but burns in 1925.

Whitehall

Flagler's mansion for his third wife opened for its first season in 1902. It is preserved today as the Henry Morrison Flagler Museum.

Rolling along the Waterway

JOSEPH JEFFERSON: *The famed actor of the late 1800s owned $200,000 in real estate in early West Palm Beach, including the first electric plant. Here, he gets a ride from his man Friday, Carl Kettler. Kettler's son, Carl Jr., opened the Bijou and Kettler theaters in West Palm Beach.*

Florida State Archives

PALM BEACH WHEELCHAIRS: *Wheelchairs powered by bicycles were the main means of transportation in Palm Beach since Flagler allowed no automobiles. The vehicles, usually pedaled by blacks, were at first called Afrimobiles and later Afromobiles.*

BRADLEY'S BEACH CLUB: *E.R. Bradley's Beach Club casino opened in 1898 and attracted society's brightest stars. When it closed in 1945, Joseph P. Kennedy lamented that Palm Beach had "lost its zipperoo." Bradley, a Kentucky colonel, died in 1946, and the club was torn down.*

Florida State Archives

INTRACOASTAL WALKWAY, 1900s: *(above)*
Novelist Henry James, who visited the Royal Poinciana just after the turn of the century, was taken by the beauty of the hotel grounds. For James, "the gardens of groves, the vistas and avenues between alignments of palms, the fostered insolence of flame-colored flower and golden fruit" were the resort's greatest charms.

BOAT RACES AT THE ROYAL POINCIANA, EARLY 1900s:
(left) The white peak of Flagler's mansion, Whitehall, can be seen in the background.

On Palm Beach, 1905

TOURIST'S CHOICE: *Palm Beach visitors could walk to Alligator Joe's (left) or take the Jungle Trail. Joe Frazier kept almost 100 alligators and crocodiles in a pen on land that is now the Everglades Club golf course. Tourists watched him wrestle the reptiles daily. The Jungle Trail (present-day Worth Avenue) was a long, winding road through a literal jungle. It was one of Palm Beach's biggest tourist attractions — particularly when a snake or alligator would cross the path.*

1905 E. W. Hazard photographs courtesy of Flagler Museum

ROOT TRAIL: *This neighborhood of hotel workers was located along a narrow road north of the Palm Beach resorts. Today, it is still home to artists, and the road, which runs from County Road to the ocean, is considered one of Palm Beach's best-kept secrets.*

BREAKERS BEACH: *Bathers relax on the beach in front of The Breakers hotel. Many came to the beach fully — even formally — clothed, and women who dared to wear bathing suits faced inspection by a censor. "The censor determined if her hose were dark enough so it didn't look like she was bare-legged," says historian Jim Ponce. The censor's famous cry upon seeing bare skin was, "Ladies! Rules is rules!"*

The Styx in 1900—Looking North on County Road—Palm Be...

1905 E.W. Hazard photo courtesy of Flagler Museum

SHANTYTOWN: *The neighborhood known as the Styx sprang up at North County Road and Sunrise Avenue in the 1890s to house the more than 2,000 black workers employed at Palm Beach hotels.*

What happened to the Styx?

THE CIRCUS came to town, and the Styx burned. Or did it?

The black shantytown known as the Styx sprang up on North County Road, north of the Royal Poinciana Hotel, in the 1890s to house the more than 2,000 black workers at Palm Beach's hotels.

Over the years, a legend developed that Henry Flagler was eager to oust the blacks so he could develop the land. He had the Styx condemned on health grounds. Then, he hired a circus to come to West Palm Beach, gave black residents passes, and while they were there, burned their homes down.

Another legend places the incident on Guy Fawkes Day, Nov. 5, 1906. It says the blacks were at celebrations in West Palm Beach, and when they returned the next day, their homes were burned.

"I don't remember any fire," Inez Peppers Lovett, born in 1895, says. "Maybe they did burn the shacks, but if they did, it was after everyone had already moved away."

In February 1994, T.T. Reese Jr., of the pioneer Dimick/Reese family, wrote to *The Palm Beach Post* "to lay these questions to rest."

First, Flagler didn't own the property. The Bradley brothers, who owned the Beach Club casino, bought the 30 acres around 1910 and by February 1912 had cut the land into 230 residential lots for the Floral Park development.

In 1912, Reese says, Bradley ordered his father to move the residents out. He says his father gave them at least two weeks.

"I remember watching the squatters and their belongings going across the old wooden bridge with hand carts and other carriers," Reese says. "After everyone had vacated the property, my dad brought in gardeners from the Beach Club and cleared the land, piled up the trash and burned it on the spot."

The pioneers' pride, early 1900s

JENSEN BEACH: *Jensen Beach was originally settled by John Lawrence Jensen of Wheeling, W.Va. Jensen, who came to the area in the early 1880s, immediately began clearing land to grow pineapples. Within a few years, the community became the hub of the pineapple industry on the east coast. The Al Fresco Hotel — the first hotel south of St. Augustine — opened in 1895. The hotel, at the far right of this picture, burned in 1910.*

WEST PALM BEACH: *In this photo of the city's skyline, taken about 1908, West Palm Beach's first library, the "free reading room," is the two-story house at the base of the pier. Left of it stands the Salt Air Hotel, and to its left, the Holland Hotel. The Holland stood on the site where the Pennsylvania Hotel, a longtime city landmark, was built in 1925 (and demolished in the mid-'90s). The Palms and Seminole hotels are to the right of the reading room, and behind it is City Park. The park, at the foot of Clematis Street, was the center of activity for early West Palm Beach and the scene of concerts and impromptu ball games.*

LAKE WORTH: *A view of Lake Avenue, the city's main street, in the 1920s. Water mains were laid on the avenue in 1914 and electric current was turned on for the first time on May 18 of that year. The lights operated from 6 p.m. to midnight. Those residing in the city that day and their descendants are considered pioneers of Lake Worth.*

PACKING ORANGES, 1908: *These workers at George Long's packing house in Boca Raton were shipping oranges up north. Long was the local agent for Florida East Coast Railway and its Model Land Co. He installed a power plant, and his packing house became the unofficial community center.*

Boca Raton Historical Society

Historical Society of Martin County

LOADING PINEAPPLES, 1902: *A worker prepares pineapples for transport at the H.W. Kling Pineapple Plantation. Picking and shipping was done mainly during the month of June, and Baltimore was the big pineapple mart.*

Stuart's first promoter

Ernest Stypmann, a German immigrant, became the first person to buy land along the St. Lucie River when he picked up 40 acres for $50 (now most of downtown Stuart) in 1882. He married widow Frances Hunter and built a shack from palmetto fronds; the couple's child, the first born on the river, drowned in it.

The Stypmanns grew pineapples, caught turtles and became partners in the first commercial fish house. He called the settlement Potsdam, for the German town of his birth, but the name was changed to Stuart in June 1895 because "Potsdam" sounded like "damn pots" when called out by the railroad engineer.

Stypmann sold a riverfront tract to President Grover Cleveland and sold his downtown holdings in 1911. He died in 1917.

1893: Barefoot mailman service ends. West Palm Beach gets first newspaper, *The Weekly Gazetteer*. Tabernacle Missionary Baptist Church and Payne Chapel A.M.E. founded in the Styx, a black area of Palm Beach.

MAY 11, 1893: Dade County State Bank, first in region, established on Palm Beach.

AUGUST 1893: Henry Flagler lays out 48-block town site of West Palm Beach.

JAN. 29, 1894: Flagler's Florida East Coast Railway reaches Fort Pierce.

FEBRUARY 1894: Flagler's Royal Poinciana Hotel opens in Palm Beach.

MARCH 22, 1894: Railroad reaches West Palm Beach.

MAY 1, 1894: Railroad crosses the St. Lucie River at Potsdam (Stuart).

NOV. 5, 1894: West Palm Beach incorporated.

The Dade County State Bank, founded in 1893, was moved to West Palm Beach, where it was an office, then a novelty shop. The city's oldest building is now the Palm Beach High museum.

1894: *The first building on Clematis Street in West Palm Beach was Otto Weybrecht's hardware store. Billy Bowlegs attended the opening.*

1895: West Palm Beach's first power plant begins operation.

JANUARY 1895: *Tropical Sun* newspaper moves from Juno to West Palm Beach.

NOV. 16, 1895: First bridge across Lake Worth, a railroad spur from around Banyan Street in downtown West Palm Beach, opens.

1896: Maps first use spelling of "Boca Raton." Original plat recorded for town of Linton, now Delray Beach.

JAN. 16, 1896: Flagler opens the Palm Beach Inn, which becomes The Breakers.

SPRING 1896: Linton School opens at site of present Old School Square.

APRIL 21, 1896: Railroad reaches Miami.

OCTOBER 1896: Raulerson family becomes Okeechobee County's first settlers.

NOV. 25, 1900: First library building in West Palm Beach opens.

1901: New bridge, at site of present Flagler Memorial Bridge, built.

1903: Fort Pierce reading room becomes first library in St. Lucie County.

WOODLAWN CEMETERY, early 1900s: *The inscription on the iron gate says: "That which is so universal as death must be a blessing." Flagler had planned to be buried here until he became angry when West Palm Beach tried to annex Palm Beach in 1911. He is buried in St. Augustine.*

JUNE 9, 1903: The Breakers hotel in Palm Beach burns.

SEPT. 11, 1903: British steamer Inchulva sinks off Delray Beach in hurricane. Wreckage now a diving spot.

DEC. 11, 1903: *Fort Pierce News,* a weekly, begins publication.

1904: Anti-alcohol crusader Carry Nation crusades along Banyan Street in West Palm Beach.

LATE 1904: Yamato Colony founded near Boca Raton; the colony disbands by the beginning of World War II.

Boy from Yamato Colony

1905: Telephone company set up in West Palm Beach.

JAN. 3, 1905: Napoleon Bonaparte Broward elected governor on a promise to drain the Everglades.

1907: *Daily Lake Worth News* becomes *Palm Beach Daily News.*

Broward

1908: Central school built on "the hill" at Hibiscus and Georgia streets, west of downtown West Palm Beach. Site will later house Palm Beach High School. First schools open in Boca Raton and Stuart.

Central School "on the hill" (right) had its tower knocked down in the '28 hurricane. The building at left became the junior high school by the 1920s.

1909: *Palm Beach County,* weekly forerunner to *The Palm Beach Post,* founded.

1911: Bridge to Jupiter Island opens. Royal Park Bridge, a wooden trestle from Lakeview Avenue in West Palm Beach to Royal Palm Way in Palm Beach, opens. First airplane flies over area.

1912: First bridge across Intracoastal Waterway at Delray opens.

JAN. 12, 1912: Flagler opens railroad link to Key West.

MAY 23, 1912: *Lake Worth Herald* begins publication. (It will become the oldest continuous business in Lake Worth.)

1913-27: State builds network of canals along Lake Okeechobee, creating farm land.

APRIL 11, 1913: First library in Delray opens.

APRIL 18, 1913: *Stuart Times,* later the *Stuart News,* publishes first edition.

MAY 20, 1913: Henry Morrison Flagler dies in Palm Beach.

SEPT. 8, 1913: Boynton Beach's first school opens.

Historical Society of Palm Beach County

33

WHAT A SIGHT: *James McCurdy, test pilot for Curtiss Aircraft, flew his plane over Lake Worth (with the Royal Poinciana Hotel in the background) in 1911. The Wright Brothers had considered opening a flying school here in 1910.*

PLEASURE PALACE: *The Lake Worth Casino opened in 1922 with a saltwater pool (below) and diving towers, shops, restaurants and a tunnel walkway to the ocean (right photo, at left). The casino attracted people from miles around for the dances and the diving contests. It was described as "a pleasure palace, the like of which is not to be found from Jacksonville to Key West."*

Museum of the City of Lake Worth

LAND FOR SALE: *Many early arrivals to Lake Worth came from the Midwest, lured by the Chicago team of Harold J. Bryant and William F. Greenwood. Some of Bryant & Greenwood's earliest brochures stated: "Lake Worth is the only city in Florida without negroes. There are none there. No property is sold to colored people." But in fact, Bryant & Greenwood had purchased 187 acres from Fannie James, a woman of mixed race who was the area's first postmistress, in 1910. When Fannie died in 1915, she still owned 40 acres, which today boasts some of the city's most historic, Spanish-style homes. Fannie is buried next to her husband Samuel in what is now the yard of a home on South L Street. Bryant & Greenwood sold land for a bargain price in 1912: For $250, one could buy a contract, which included one tract of farmland and one townsite in Lake Worth.*

'HERE IS A CITY of the sun. Here is a city of summer breeze, an environment of Eden. And here is health and happiness and prosperity for those who listen to its call. And this city's people, content in the pure joy of living, bid you come and make your home among them.'

— *Introduction to a special West Palm Beach edition of* The Palm Beach Post, *October 1922*

The Boom

FOR SALE: SEA, SUN, LAND. As much paradise as the market can stand. So many people flocked to Florida in the '20s that one northern newspaper claimed: "Entire populations are moving away bodily."

One promoter even used the Bible to lure visitors to Florida: "Arise, and go toward the south."

Neighborhoods sprang up, and so did a few skyscrapers. Downtowns from Fort Pierce to Boca Raton were lined with real-estate offices and tents selling lots. Property values artificially doubled, then tripled in the frenzy of demand.

One January 1925 copy of *The Palm Beach Post*, 150 pages fat, contained 12 full-page advertisements in a row for developments.

This was the era of the grand hotels: The El Verano (1923, later the George Washington and now the Helen Wilkes in West Palm Beach), The new Breakers hotel (1926), Mizner's Cloister Inn (forerunner to the Boca Resort and Club, 1926), the Gulfstream in Lake Worth (1925), the Pelican in Stuart (1925).

And new schools, new hospitals, new theaters, new roads.

Property values in West Palm Beach increased from $13.6 million to $61 million in just five years, from 1920 to 1925.

But by the end of 1925, runaway real-estate speculation promised an end to the boom. And soon, two hurricanes would seal South Florida's fate.

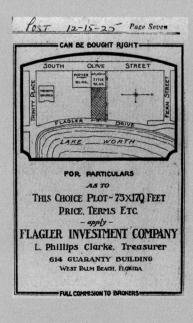

REAL ESTATE FOR SALE: *In the early 1920s, South Florida's hottest commodity was land.* The Palm Beach Post *grew fat with ads.*

SUNDAY OUTING, 1916: *The Myrick family of Boca Raton and friends enjoy a day of sun at the Hillsboro Light Station in Broward County. William and Mamie Myrick built their home in Boca Raton around 1914. George and Nellie Race bought the Myrick house in 1917, and their only child, Lillian Race Williams, named it Singing Pines because of the Australian pines on the property. In 1975, it was moved from S.W. First Avenue to Crawford Boulevard, where it is now the Children's Museum.*

During Boca's boom years, another prominent family was the Long family. George Long settled in Boca Raton in 1902 and became the local agent for the Florida East Coast Railway and its Model Land Company in 1906. Long built a power plant and a packing house, which became the unofficial community center.

Boca Raton Historical Society

Boca goes to school

Boca Raton got its first formal school in 1908, a one-room schoolhouse on N.W. Second Avenue, north of Palmetto Park Road. The teacher was Laurence Gould, 18, who taught grades one through eight. In 1923, the Roadman Elementary School for the town's black children was opened by Alex Hughes.

Boca Raton Historical Society

SCHOOL BUS, AROUND 1915: *Frank Chesebro's Model T Ford, Boca Raton's first automobile, was used to take children to and from school. Sand roads made driving a challenge.*

SCHOOL, EARLY 1920s: *Big bows and a couple barefoot boys stand out in this class, taught by Clementine Brown, wife of John Brown, who became Boca's first mayor.*

39

WHAT A WAY TO GO: *Yachts, ferry, cars, train. This view of the West Palm Beach yacht basin (above) shows the twin-towered Alba Hotel (now the Biltmore), which was built in the mid-'20s, in the background. The railroad bridge is also visible. A favorite way to get from West Palm Beach to Palm Beach was still the ferry.*

Courtesy South Florida Rail Sales

A wider shot (left) shows more of Palm Beach, and the palm-tree-lined Flagler Drive in West Palm Beach. This photograph was taken from the roof of the "new" Pennsylvania Hotel in 1926. The Pennsylvania was demolished in the mid-1990s. On the Palm Beach side to the right is the Whitehall Hotel. Henry Flagler's home, Whitehall, had a hotel addition on the back of it from the '20s until the '50s. In the middle is the sprawling Royal Poinciana Hotel, which was demolished in the mid-1930s.

"Would you rather live in the north, in ice and snow, or come to Lake Worth and watch us grow?"
— *Boom-era slogan for Lake Worth, "The Wonder City"*

The original SunFest

From 1916 to 1950, no March was complete without the Seminole Sun Dance, a three-day festival that brought everyone to downtown West Palm Beach. It was an early version of today's SunFest — a party designed to keep tourists here past the usual winter season. "Barco Motors (then on Third Street between Dixie and the F.E.C. tracks) donated cars, which were decorated with crepe paper. High school students rode in and on the cars, and each year, a king and queen were featured in the parade," Helen Hopkins Ryan recalled in 1994. She came to West Palm Beach in 1928. Seminoles performed sun-worshiping ceremonies, residents dressed in Seminole costumes, and there was even a baby contest (above in 1917). South Floridians have always loved a parade. A float in a Lake Worth parade in the 1920s boasted a banner that proudly stated: "Lake Worth has the only coconut lamp factory in the U.S." Heady stuff.

41

*While Palm Beach attracted the Vanderbilts, hotels popped up
on the west side of the Intracoastal to serve the middle class.*

Where summer spends the winter...
and so do the tourists

GULFSTREAM HOTEL: *Lake Worth's
pink princess (above) was built
in the boom '20s and is now run
by Holiday Inn, which completed
a superb renovation in 1999.*

BEACH CASINO: *In the Palm Beach
of the early 1900s, lounging at the
beach was the big pastime, though
women bathers were clothed from
neck to toe.*

HOTEL SALT AIR: *Built on the waterfront in West Palm Beach, it was a premiere middle-class hotel in the early 1900s. Later, a Holiday Inn was built on this site, and it was imploded on Jan. 1, 1994.*

THE PALMS: *At the corner of Clematis and Narcissus (where the Cuillo Theatre is now), The Palms, built in 1896, featured stores on its first floor and views of City Park and the Intracoastal. The "temperance hotel" was torn down in 1926.*

THE PENNSYLVANIA: *The boom-era hotel was built on the West Palm Beach waterfront in 1925 on the site of the old Holland Hotel. In 1964, the Pennsylvania became a residence hotel run by Carmelite nuns. It was torn down in 1995.*

FOR THE UPPER CRUST, the social schedule stayed rigid until the '30s: A trolley car pulled by a mule took visitors from the Royal Poinciana, on the Intracoastal in Palm Beach to The Breakers and its beach casino. From 11 a.m. to 1 p.m. — and only at those times — guests far too dressed for bathing lounged at the beach, while a beach censor made sure women's legs were covered. Then it was back to the hotel for an eight-course lunch. At 4 p.m. came afternoon tea at the Coconut Grove of the Royal Poinciana, a lush garden of palms on the hotel's southwest side. In the evening, the Vanderbilts, Phippses and Astors dressed full-tilt to watch black employees dance the cakewalk, a furious tap-dancing competition. Some dinner guests at The Breakers and the Boca Raton Resort still dress to the nines, but as late as the 1970s, high style was required.

"AS A WINTER RESORT, West Palm Beach is surpassed only by her sister, Palm Beach, while for the moderately wealthy she is, perhaps, the more desirable of the two. Her streets, her avenues and her sidewalks are models of cleanliness; her stores are filled with the latest and most popular goods, in every line, of the very best quality; she has her own gas works, her own water works, and only recently agreed by ballot to bond herself for the purpose of putting in a system of sewerage; a number of churches invite her visitors to worship, while a well-stocked free reading room affords a place of rest and quiet… More than half a score of first-class hotels are open for the reception of visitors, with rates from $1.50 to $3 per day, while there are numerous smaller boarding houses and restaurants where board can be had for less. The Florida East Coast Railway's foot bridge connects this city with Palm Beach, and the Lake Worth Ferry has several splendid launches… All this and much more has West Palm Beach, and the roses are so plentiful and so lovely, and the thorns so few, that people are coming every day to pluck the flowers by the wayside. And they remain for a season and the next year, behold, they return again, and the number of them is increasing daily."
— *From* The Weekly Lake Worth News, *December, 1900*

IN STUART, the first real hotel was the Danforth House, owned by Hubert Bessey, who had been the keeper of the Gilbert's Bar House of Refuge on Hutchinson Island. The Danforth House hosted distinguished guests such as actor Joseph Jefferson and President Grover Cleveland, who came to fish. In West Palm Beach, the Holland at Evernia and the lakefront and the Hotel Salt Air at Datura and the lakefront welcomed visitors around the turn of the century. The mid-'20s brought several fancy, bigger hotels — including the Gulfstream in Lake Worth, now run by Holiday Inn after a superb renovation, the Pennsylvania Hotel in West Palm Beach (demolished in the mid-'90s), the El Verano in West Palm Beach (later called the George Washington, and now the Helen Wilkes Residence Hotel), The Colony in Delray Beach and the Alba Hotel in Palm Beach (now the Biltmore).

43

FLAMBOYANT PIONEER: *In this era of aviation, Stuart resident Hugh Willoughby was a colorful character. He was already internationally known when he came to Sewall's Point in 1908 looking for a site for a southern station of the New York Yacht Club. In 1909, his bi-plane, War Hawk, became the first plane designed for military use. He also built seaplanes on Sewall's Point, where he had an estate, Mandalay. He was an all-around interesting guy. He drove a car in the first race ever held on a circular track, and his 60-foot boat, Sea Otter, was the first motor boat to be equipped with a wireless telegraph.*

Historical Society of Martin County

Florida's first planned community

KELSEY CITY, the dream town of Massachusetts restaurateur Harry Kelsey, incorporated Nov. 16, 1923, as the state's first planned community. It was designed by the Olmstead brothers, the landscape architects of Central Park.

A gate over Old Dixie Highway that would last for decades welcomed visitors to the "World's Winter Playground." A 1922 newspaper ad featured this boastful acrostic: "Kelsey City. Elevation. Location. Scenery. Efficient management. Yacht basin. Causeway to ocean. Industries. Telephone exchange. Year round CITY."

At his peak, Kelsey owned 120,000 acres and 14 miles of oceanfront between Miami and Jupiter. But the crash sent Kelsey to the canvas.

In 1939, his town became Lake Park.

Kelsey died in 1957.

Glades County, Florida

FIRST FEMALE MAYOR: *Moore Haven incorporated on June 8, 1917, and elected Marian Newhall Horwitz O'Brien its first mayor — three years before women could vote nationwide. Moore Haven was one of three Florida cities at that time to allow women to vote and hold office.*

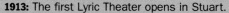

1913: The first Lyric Theater opens in Stuart.

1914: "Emergency Hospital," forerunner to Good Samaritan, founded in West Palm Beach.

JULY 1, 1915: *Okeechobee Call,* the first newspaper in the Glades, begins; it later becomes *Okeechobee News.*

1915: Florida East Coast Railway spur opens to Okeechobee.

JULY 1, 1915: State creates Lake Worth Inlet District, later Port of Palm Beach.

JANUARY 1916: *Palm Beach County* becomes *The Palm Beach Post.*

APRIL 15, 1916: Pine Ridge Hospital for blacks opens at Fifth and Division Streets in West Palm Beach.

1917: Industrial High School for blacks opens in West Palm Beach.

JAN. 19, 1917: Stuart gets electricity.

APRIL 1917: New Palm Beach County courthouse opens in West Palm Beach.

JUNE 8, 1917: Moore Haven incorporated. Marian Newhall Horwitz O'Brien elected first mayor — three years before women's suffrage.

JAN. 31, 1918: First bridge over St. Lucie River in Stuart opens.

1919: Bridge to Lake Worth opens. First air field opens in Fort Pierce.

FEB. 2, 1919: Wooden bridge linking Stuart and Palm City opens.

JAN. 18, 1920: Port of Palm Beach opens.

MARCH 1, 1920: Forerunner to *Fort Pierce Tribune* created. It begins daily publication in 1922.

MAY 19, 1920: Good Samaritan, area's first permanent hospital, opens in West Palm Beach.

Good Samaritan Hospital in 1920.

MAY 9, 1921: Fort Pierce Inlet cut through to ocean.

1922: *Clewiston Progress* begins publication. Becomes *Clewiston News* in 1928.

SEPT. 8, 1922: *The Palm Beach Times* founded.

CLEMATIS STREET LOOKING EAST, 1920s:
West Palm bustled with people, boasting every kind of store (including a Victrola shop) and cafes, plus "fireproof" hotels.

KETTLER THEATRE: *Carl Kettler's Kettler Theatre in West Palm Beach, which opened in 1924, was hailed as the "finest structure south of Atlanta." This site is now the parking lot south of the Centennial Fountain.*

Historical Society of Palm Beach County

CARL KETTLER AND FAMILY: *Kettler's wife, Maude, was the daughter of pioneer L.W. Burkhardt. Their son Ralph was born in 1908.*

Elmer Upthegrove

Workers load sugar cane at First Glades' Canal Point mill about 1925.

MARCH 1923: First Glades sugar mill opens in Canal Point.

JUNE 13, 1923: Saint Lucie Canal opens.

AUG. 11, 1923: *Delray Beach News* founded.

OCT. 27, 1923: First synagogue in West Palm Beach, Temple Israel, founded.

MARCH 14, 1924: *Everglades News,* forerunner to *Belle Glade Sun,* founded.

JULY 24, 1924: Connors Highway (now State Road 80) opens, connecting West Palm Beach and Glades and creating first cross-Florida route.

AUG. 11, 1924: Royal Park Bridge, rebuilt after first one collapsed in 1921, opens.

1924-1925: Height of real estate boom in South Florida. Some lots leap in value from $250 to $50,000.

1925: Jensen Bridge opens. Bridge to Singer Island opens. West Palm Beach's two tallest buildings constructed: the Comeau, on Clematis Street, and the Harvey building, on Datura Street.

JAN. 25, 1925: Seaboard Coast Line opens to West Palm Beach.

MAY 24, 1925: First offering of lots in Boca Raton sells for $2.1 million, a one-day record.

DECEMBER 1925: Steamship service established at Port of Palm Beach.

1925-1926: West Palm Beach Canal opens from Lake Okeechobee.

1926: Boynton Inlet opens.

FEB. 6. 1926: Addison Mizner-designed Cloister Inn, forerunner to the Boca Raton Resort and Club, opens.

Florida State Archives

The Lyric Theater

MARCH 15, 1926: Current Lyric Theater opens in Stuart.

THE BREAKERS BURNS: *The Breakers fire of March 18, 1925, lit up the whole island of Palm Beach, and flying embers burned down several other buildings. It was started by a "new-fangled curling iron" used by the wife of the mayor of Chicago to pretty herself for the St. Patrick's Day ball. Escaping that day: Margaret Tobin Brown, the "unsinkable Molly Brown" of Titanic fame, and actress Billie Burke.*

The three Breakers

1903: The first Breakers burns

Henry Flagler opened the Palm Beach Inn, the forerunner to The Breakers, in 1896. This building, notable for its dormer windows, burned down in 1903.

1904 to 1925: The second Breakers hotel

This hotel soon overtook Flagler's Royal Poinciana in popularity because of its ocean location. It burned down in 1925.

1926-today: The famous twin towers

The Italian Renaissance-style hotel was built in record time after the 1925 fire, and its fabulous Circle Dining Room was added in 1928. Until 1971, it was open only from mid-December until mid-April. A $100 million renovation in the '90s helped The Breakers win back its five stars from Mobil in 1998. The hotel is owned by the Kenan family, the descendants of Flagler's third wife, Mary Lily.

DOG TRICK: *Beachgoers needed a laugh in Lake Worth in 1940.*

The Bust

WHY DID the South Florida Boom go bust? The list is long. Railroads and ships couldn't get building materials down fast enough. The law was catching up with the con artists, and the nation's stock market was shaky.

Nervous speculators, in a bit of self-fulfilling prophecy, began to take the money and run. Then came the killer hurricanes of 1926 and 1928.

In one awful year, from 1929 to 1930, West Palm Beach's total property value dropped more than half.

PANIC ON CLEMATIS: *The corner of Olive Avenue and Clematis Street is packed with people trying to get their money out of the bank. By 1933, more than 200 Florida banks had closed, some of them in West Palm Beach.*

Winds rip Mar-a-Lago in Palm Beach during the storm.

Bodies are stacked in Belle Glade. About 2,000 died.

Memories of the '28 hurricane
Written by historian Bessie DuBois in 1968

"There was a time when just the word 'hurricane' could tie my stomach up in a hard knot like a rock, but I had my wits completely scared out of me in 1928 ...

"Our home on Jupiter Inlet across the river from the old red brick lighthouse, was right at the edge of the river ... the winds galloped over us like a thousand freight trains accompanied by that high-pitched whine that beggars description ... Papa made a macabre joke by shaving so he would make 'a handsome corpse.' ... About all that held our house together was the chimney and the concrete back porch. I found myself praying over and over again that the tide would change, the center of the storm would pass ... We did not know how well we had fared until the reports began to come in ...

"First, one of the neighbors came to tell us that John's sister's house had been completely destroyed and their baby, a beautiful little girl less than a year old, had been killed, and her father, from whose arms she had been blown, was terribly injured ... The funeral of the baby was sad indeed, with not a flower for the little casket. Every green thing was stripped bare."

G.J. BENDER, CHIEF.

M.W. STOKES ASST. CHIEF

JOHN LA MONT DRIVER B...

J.K. McCLINTOCK, CAP...

LOCAL HANGOUT: *The Palm Garden Drug Store at Third Street and Rosemary Avenue, West Palm Beach, in the early 1930s.*

BOCA BOYS: *Chief G.J. Bender and the crew of The Boca Raton Fire Department, Aug. 27, 1927.*

JUNE 1926: Closing of Palm Beach Bank and Trust sparks run on banks; by April 1930, 11 Palm Beach County banks will fail.

SEPT. 17, 1926: Hurricane kills 392 in Miami; it breaks Lake Okeechobee dike and kills 300 to 400 in Moore Haven.

DEC. 29, 1926: The Breakers reopens with the famous twin towers.

1927: Boynton Beach High School opens.

FEB. 5, 1927: WFLA-AM, "The Voice of Tropical America," operated by Addison Mizner, goes on the air. It shuts down within a year.

FEB. 8, 1928: *Clewiston News* begins publication.

MARCH 1, 1928: Krueger Field, Stuart's municipal airport, opens.

SEPT. 16, 1928: Hurricane crumbles dike around Lake Okeechobee, drowning 1,800 to 3,000. Third-deadliest disaster in U.S. history.

1929: West Palm Beach's property value at boom high of $89 million.

THE EVERGLADES CLUB: *While the Depression raged, high society partied on in Palm Beach. Over at Flagler's Royal Poinciana Hotel, however, a glamorous era was ending. The hotel, once the largest wooden structure in the world, was torn down by 1936.*

FEB. 21, 1930: Port of Fort Pierce opens.

JULY 4, 1930: President Herbert Hoover approves construction of the dike around Lake Okeechobee.

FEB. 17, 1932: Palm Beach Kennel Club opens.

DEC. 13, 1932: John Demarest of Hypoluxo sells 440 acres of land for a new air terminal in West Palm Beach.

SEPT. 3, 1933: Hurricane damages the Treasure Coast; two die.

OCTOBER 1933: Palm Beach Junior College, first in state, opens.

1934: "South Bridge" from Fort Pierce to Hutchinson Island opens. Casino magnate E.R. Bradley buys *The Palm Beach Post* and *The Palm Beach Times*.

JAN. 9, 1934: Roosevelt Bridge dedicated.

1934-35: Flagler's Royal Poinciana Hotel is razed.

1935: West Palm Beach's property value hits bottom at $18.2 million. Seminoles establish Brighton reservation in Glades County. West Palm Beach-based *Photo News* black newspaper begins publication.

SEPT. 2, 1935: "Labor Day Storm" kills 400 to 600 and sweeps away Flagler's "Overseas Railroad" through the Keys.

1936: Everglades Memorial Hospital opens in Pahokee.

THE SUNSET LOUNGE: *"Have you ever heard of the Cotton Club in Harlem?" said Nat Lane of West Palm Beach in 1990. "That's how this place used to be." From the '30s through the '50s, the Sunset Lounge attracted musical greats such as Duke Ellington and Ella Fitzgerald. At right, the original lounge at 8th Street and Henrietta Avenue, with roof garden, service station and garage.*

Savior of the Cloister Inn

Clarence Geist bought Addison Mizner's Cloister Inn in Boca Raton in 1927, when the Mizner Corporation went bankrupt. Geist planned a $2 million addition, and his Boca Raton Club opened in 1930, the same year Geist decided to revive the faded real estate market of Boca Raton. This photograph was taken as Clarence and Florence Geist arrived in Boca for the opening of the club season. Geist was the town's largest landowner, and he hired Palm Beach architect Maurice Fatio to design four grand homes in 1935. Geist died in 1938.

J. Meyer Schine bought the Boca Raton Club in 1944, Arthur Vining Davis bought it in 1956, and today it is owned by H. Wayne Huizenga's Florida Panthers Holdings.

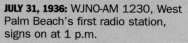
JULY 31, 1936: WJNO-AM 1230, West Palm Beach's first radio station, signs on at 1 p.m.

FALL 1936: Industrial High School football team in West Palm Beach wins area's first state sports championship.

DEC. 19, 1936: New West Palm Beach airport is dedicated; named Morrison Field in honor of secretary Grace K. Morrison.

1938: Belle Glade Memorial Hospital opens in Belle Glade. New bridge from Lake Worth to beach opens.

JULY 1, 1938: Flagler Memorial Bridge from West Palm Beach to Palm Beach replaces wooden bridge.

Aviation pioneer Grace Morrison was the first woman in the area to fly solo.

NEW BRIDGE: *This view of Lake Worth from the top of the Gulfstream Hotel shows the new bridge (1938) leading to the Lake Worth Casino.*

MARCH 8, 1939: Martin Memorial Hospital opens in Stuart. St. Mary's Hospital opens in West Palm Beach.

FEB. 8, 1941: Norton Gallery and School of Art opens.

FEB. 29, 1940: The Lake Theater opens on Lake Avenue in Lake Worth. It's now the Palm Beach Institute of Contemporary Art.

AUG. 20, 1941: Airport opens at Lantana.

The Lake Theater in Lake Worth

BY AIR: *About 45,000 fliers trained at or left from Morrison Field, and about 6,000 planes passed through in the eight months before D-Day.*

BY SEA: *German submarines were active in shipping lanes off the coast. During a 10-day stretch in May 1942, seven ships were torpedoed between Fort Pierce and Boca Raton.*

OFFSHORE HEROICS: *Lt. Gleason Stambaugh (left) led the recovery effort when the Gulf Bell collided with the Gulfland during a blackout and burned.*

FEAR, INTRIGUE AND ROMANCE: *Thousands of GIs poured into South Florida bases. Canteens (such as this one in Palm Beach) and U.S.O. clubs entertained the troops.*

The War Years

WORLD WAR II was right off the shore of Palm Beach County and the Treasure Coast. Close enough to feel the heat and see the flames of ships being picked off night after night by the Third Reich's *Unterseeboots*.

South Floridians went to bed in fear every night, their windows and headlights blackened.

"We couldn't go up on the oceanfront after dark," remembers Bobby Riggs, who grew up in West Palm Beach. "I was sitting at The Hut (a hangout on Flagler Drive) one night and the whole sky lit up. The Germans had sunk a tanker off Palm Beach."

Germans sank 16 ships from Cape Canaveral to Boca Raton between February and May of 1942.

Rationing was tough, recalls Riggs, who graduated from Palm Beach High School in 1943, but leaving for war was tougher. On graduation night, he and some friends went out to the Palm Beach Pier one last time and started to cry. Their carefree boyhood was over; in days, they'd be overseas.

For those who stayed home, memories are bittersweet. Canteens and U.S.O. clubs entertained the thousands of GIs stationed here. The intensity of war made even the simplest pleasures grand.

WAR ENTRANCE: *Grace Frost England in front of Wert's restaurant in Palm Beach, now Charley's Crab. (Their slogan: "Everyone goes from bad to Wert's.") The entrance was moved from the oceanfront to the side to prevent light from shining out at sea. It remains on the side today.*

BREAKERS HOSPITAL: *The Breakers hotel became Ream General Hospital during the war. One of the glamorous ballrooms was transformed for a holiday prayer vigil (left).*

BOCA AIR FIELD: *The Boca Raton Army Air Field was set up as an Army Air Corps training site and radar training base. The property was later split; half became a municipal airport and the other half Florida Atlantic University. Edith Jackson Mize trained there, then flew to the front lines.*

MORRISON FIELD: *Taken over by the Army in 1941, it was the forerunner of Palm Beach International Airport. It was home base to 3,000 personnel during the war.*

DECEMBER 1941: Gilbert's Bar House of Refuge reassigned as wartime patrol station.

DEC. 7, 1941: Morrison Field Army Air Force Command activated.

1942-1945: Military bases and personnel fill Florida. Among them: Morrison Field (PBIA), Boca Raton Army Air Field (Boca Raton Airport/FAU), Camp Murphy (Jonathan Dickinson State Park), Hutchinson Island Navy Base, Fort Pierce Amphibious Training Base. The Stuart airport becomes a U.S. Navy base named for Paul Homer Witham, a Stuart man who was killed in action in 1942.

FEBRUARY-MAY 1942: German U-boats sink 16 ships between Cape Canaveral and Boca Raton. Local Coast Guard Reserve, headed by Gleason Stambaugh, aids in saving crew members from burning ships.

DEC. 11, 1942: The Breakers hotel becomes Army's Ream General Hospital.

MAY 28, 1943: U.S. government builds St. Lucie County airport as a military base.

FEBRUARY 1944: Liberty Point prisoner-of-war camp for Germans opens near Clewiston. It closes in September 1945.

NOV. 30, 1944: Camp Murphy closes.

MARCH 1945: Belle Glade prisoner-of-war camp for Germans opens. It closes in December.

BY 1947: Most military sites returned to local governments.

HOMEFRONT HEROES: *Civilians helped the war effort through war stamps and war savings bonds.*

AT LAST: *Miss West Palm Beach of 1945, Frances M. Stambaugh, shows soldiers the good news — peace — as reported by* The Palm Beach Times.

GO WILDCATS! *In 1948, happiness meant a letter sweater, a best girl or guy and a winning team. Top all that off with a Coke and a hamburger C.K. (clean kitchen, or with everything) or a Coney Island Cheesit (a hot dog filled with cheese) from The Hut, and you have a teen dream, Palm Beach-style. These Palm Beach High School cheerleaders from the Class of '48 had a lot to cheer about.*

GIVE ME THAT OLD EAGLE SPIRIT: *The Eagles of Carver High in Delray Beach proudly wore their blue and white. Coach Spencer Pompey's football team had an unbeaten record for five years: 1949, 1950, 1961, 1962 and 1963. This cheerleading squad, from 1962, was key: "We didn't move without the cheerleaders," Pompey said. A favorite cheer: "Give me that old Eagles spirit, it's good enough for me ..." The Eagles played on Thursdays, and their games attracted both blacks and whites (white high schools played on Fridays). Though they sat on different sides of the field, the games proved a place for both races to join together.*

A home in the sun

COME TO PARADISE: *General Development Corp. began luring Northerners to what would eventually become Port St. Lucie with sales poster like this one in the late 1950s. The company began offering 80-foot by 125-foot lots in St. Lucie County for $10 down and $10 a month. A one-bedroom house cost $9,995.*

ON CLEMATIS: *(preceding pages) The street was still bustling in the 1940s, but by the 1970s, downtown was in decline.*

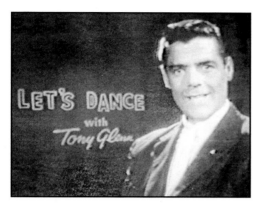

LET'S DANCE: *Channel 5 weatherman Tony Glenn hosted* Let's Dance, *a teen dance party broadcast from venues such as bowling alleys and car lots.*

Prime Time

S OUTH FLORIDA'S confidence was back. Buoyed by military dollars during World War II and an influx of veterans moving south, Palm Beach County and the Treasure Coast entered a new era of progress.

Ads in *The Palm Beach Post* touted "new prestige neighborhoods" of concrete block homes in "suburban community villages." What could be finer than a three-bedroom swimming pool home with central air — for just $14,950?

And then, to top it all off, a set of rabbit ears and a television.

TV came to town in 1953. Before long, everyone was getting their news from Bill Gordon on WPTV, and Tony Glenn's *Let's Dance* show tapped into the rock 'n' roll craze.

But locals didn't stay glued to their sets — not with the piers, the baseball diamonds and hangouts like The Hut in West Palm Beach and Frances Langford's Outrigger Resort and Restaurant in Jensen Beach.

Most of our happy days, as always, were spent out in the sun.

GROWING PLACES:
Advertisements from The Palm Beach Post *in the 1950s. The West Palm Beach metropolitan area was the fourth fastest growing place in the country between 1950 and 1960. Development spread west past Military Trail and south to Lake Clarke Shores.*

LAKE WORTH LANDMARK: *Musical groups sing at the Lake Worth Bandshell in 1953 to raise money for the Salvation Army. After years at various sites in Lake Worth, the bandshell was brought to its current lakefront location in the 1930s. It became part of Bryant Park when the park was officially named for Harold J. Bryant — Lake Worth's first and biggest promoter — in 1937.*

1946-1963
Prime Time

PALM BEACH PIER: *In the '40s, Worth Avenue extended right out over the water, thanks to the Palm Beach Pier. The pier was damaged in a 1966 storm and later torn down.*

MAY 18, 1946: WIRA-AM 1400 in Fort Pierce becomes first radio station on the Treasure Coast.

FEB. 17, 1947: John H. Perry buys *The Palm Beach Post* and *Palm Beach Daily News*.

OCT. 12, 1947: Second hurricane in a month causes worst flooding ever in South Florida.

DEC. 17, 1947: Palm Beach International Airport terminal opens.

1948: Okeechobee General Hospital opens.

1949: Seacrest High in Delray Beach, now Atlantic High, opens. Airport opens in Pahokee.

New airport terminal, 1947.

APRIL 5, 1949: Estelle Murer is elected West Palm Beach's first female commissioner.

JUNE 10, 1949: Flood control district formed; later becomes South Florida Water Management District.

AUG. 26, 1949: Last big hurricane to hit region last century.

JULY 16, 1950: Southeast Florida State Sanatorium (later A.G. Holley Hospital), for tuberculosis, opens in Lantana.

FALL 1950: Industrial High School for blacks in West Palm Beach absorbed by Roosevelt High.

SEPT. 15, 1950: Southern Boulevard bridge to Palm Beach opens.

1951: Paul Dreher, West Palm Beach's director of parks, stocks a 108-acre park with some trees and a few animals. In 1957, this becomes the Dreher Park Zoo. It's now called the Palm Beach Zoo at Dreher Park.

APRIL 1, 1951: Hendry General Hospital opens in Clewiston.

JUNE 8, 1951: Loxahatchee National Wildlife Refuge established.

NOV. 10, 1952: New Atlantic Avenue bridge opens in Delray Beach.

SEPT. 13, 1953: WIRK-TV, Channel 21, area's first television station, signs on; it closes Feb. 29, 1956.

1954: John D. MacArthur spends $5.5 million for 2,600 acres in what is now Palm Beach Shores, Lake Park, North Palm Beach and Palm Beach Gardens.

CAREFREE THEATRE: *A 1951 ad called the Carefree Center the "Playhouse of the Palm Beaches." It opened in 1939 as the Carefree Bowlaway in the heart of the Flamingo Park business district on Dixie and Flamingo. The Carefree Theatre featured the premiere of* Portrait of Jennie *in 1948.*

A ZOO IS BORN: *West Palm Beach parks director Paul Dreher stocked a 108-acre park with trees and animals in 1951. In 1957, it became the Dreher Park Zoo, now the Palm Beach Zoo at Dreher Park.*

AFRICA, U.S.A.: *Palm Beach County's first big animal attraction, based in Boca Raton, closed in September 1961. Walt Disney considered land in Palm Beach County for a new theme park, but he went to Orlando instead.*

FEB. 2, 1954: WDBF-AM 1420 is Delray Beach's first radio station.

AUG. 22, 1954: WJNO-TV, Channel 5 (NBC), signs on. It becomes WPTV in 1956.

DEC. 9, 1954: WSTU-AM is Stuart's first radio station.

JAN. 1, 1955: WEAT-TV, later WPEC, Channel 12 (ABC), signs on.

SEPT. 2, 1955: *Boca Raton News* begins publication.

NOV. 30, 1955: West Palm Beach buys water plant from Flagler estate.

1956: Arvida buys 850 acres in Boca Raton, including Boca Raton Resort and Club.

JAN. 25, 1957: Sunshine State Parkway, now Florida's Turnpike, opens.

OCT. 3, 1957: *Jupiter Courier* begins publication.

JAN. 3, 1958: Ernest Lyons Bridge, from Stuart to Sewall's Point, and Evans Crary Bridge, from Sewall's Point to Hutchinson Island, open.

MAY 27, 1958: Pratt & Whitney opens plant in northwest Palm Beach County.

AUG. 13, 1958: Beeline Highway opens.

SEPTEMBER 1958: Roosevelt Junior College for blacks opens.

DEC. 1, 1958: West Palm Beach police hire first female officer, Winifred H. Moree.

1959: Indian River Junior College formed in Fort Pierce. Lincoln Junior College, for blacks, formed at the same time.

WHITEHALL TURNED INTO MUSEUM: *Flagler's mansion, Whitehall, which had become a hotel in 1926, is saved by his granddaughter in 1959. She has the addition torn down and opens the Flagler Museum in 1960.*

JAN. 1, 1959: Cuban revolution; Glades sugar production increases sixfold in '60s.

FEB. 9, 1959: Bethesda Memorial Hospital in Boynton Beach opens.

MAY 16, 1959: New Royal Park Bridge (middle bridge) to Palm Beach opens.

1960: Harmon Elliott opens the Elliott Museum on Hutchinson Island. His father Sterling's inventions are among the museum's treasures.

SAFE HARBOR: *The Port of Palm Beach in 1957. Today, about 3 million tons of freight are shipped each year through the port, which opened in 1920.*

THE ULTIMATE HANGOUT: *The Hut was so all-American that* The Saturday Evening Post *featured it in its June 22, 1946, issue. "Those were the days of convertibles and cruisin' around," Dick Hall recalled in 1994. His father, Harold, opened The Hut in 1930 between Flagler Drive and Holy Trinity Church in West Palm Beach. The Hut made way for the Phillips Point office tower in the early '80s.*

Saturday Evening Post

'There was a richness to it all. I don't think there is anything like it now, short of living in a small town in Iowa. There was no violence, no drugs. Something as weird as the *a capella choir* — the men's glee club — was a big thing to get into. People just laughed and smiled and joked. It was *Happy Days.'*

— *Actor Monte Markham, president of Palm Beach High School's Class of 1953*

1961: U.S. Army Corps of Engineers begins cutting canal across Kissimmee River to improve flood protection.

MAY 24, 1961: RCA opens $4 million plant in Palm Beach Gardens.

SEPT. 11, 1961: Lake Worth High School and Palm Beach Junior College get first black students.

OCT. 21, 1961: South Florida Science Museum in West Palm Beach opens.

NOV. 12, 1961: Former President Herbert Hoover dedicates Herbert Hoover Dike around Lake Okeechobee.

APRIL 1962: WTVX-TV, Channel 34 in Fort Pierce, signs on.

MARCH 9, 1963: West Palm Beach Municipal Stadium opens with the Milwaukee (later Atlanta) Braves as the first spring training tenant.

APRIL 25, 1963: Professional Golfers Association moves its national headquarters to Palm Beach Gardens.

NOV. 16-17, 1963: President John F. Kennedy spends last weekend of his life in Palm Beach.

President Kennedy at St. Ann Church on Nov. 17, 1963.

Welcome to the Sprawl...

I T WAS THE DAWN of so many big changes: Suburbia, integration, big industry (Pratt & Whitney, IBM, RCA). And new problems.

The old downtowns lost their identities as residents spilled west to developments like the General Development Corp.'s Port St. Lucie and Louis Perini's Palm Beach Lakes development in West Palm Beach.

The Palm Beach Mall lured shoppers from Main Street.

And then came the condos — a bonanza for developers. Century Village broke ground west of West Palm Beach in 1971, with another following in suburban Boca Raton in 1979.

Apartment buildings dotted the oceanfront.

While the retirees played cards (and politics, with their powerhouse voting block), the young got restless. They protested for peace and proclaimed love.

The uncertain times helped birth a new college in downtown West Palm Beach — Palm Beach Atlantic, dedicated to the teachings of the Bible.

The Palm Beach County Development Board touted "a new, uncomplicated way of life" in a 1969 ad. But for the region's old communities — once simple, carefree places where neighbors knew each other — the complications of growth had just begun.

.. and the Mall

PALM BEACH MALL, 1968:
The height of shopping chic at the time, the mall brought shoppers out west, away from downtown shops.

I-95 completed at last

MISSING LINK: *The completion of Interstate 95 between Palm Beach Gardens and Miami on July 3, 1976, made it a lot easier to get around. Here's how the Okeechobee Boulevard interchange appeared, looking south, in 1970. "Today, you can drive down to Delray for lunch," said former state Sen. Phil Lewis. "But in those days, you wouldn't have thought about doing that unless you had a gun to your head."*

Under the teepee...   and out in the bush

SEPT. 3, 1967: *The West Palm Beach Auditorium opens on Palm Beach Lakes Boulevard.*

AUG. 20, 1967: *Lion Country Safari, a 659-acre jungle park, opens west of West Palm Beach.*

REP. PAUL ROGERS:

As Palm Beach County's congressman from 1955 until 1979, Rogers (above right) was known as 'Mr. Health' for pioneering health legislation. Surely, the new Lake Worth pier, which opened in 1972, provided a dose of healthful tourism.

FIRST MOBILE PHONE?

Royal Palm Beach Police Chief Bob V. Horn takes a call on his patrol car phone, possibly the first law enforcement vehicle in Palm Beach County equipped with both two-way radio and phone service. The date: Nov. 30, 1968.

1965: New Jensen Bridge opens.

APRIL 9, 1965: St. Lucie Inlet State Preserve opens.

APRIL 12, 1965: *Stuart News,* then a weekly, is bought by the Scripps-Howard newspaper chain.

JUNE 4, 1965: Roosevelt Junior College for blacks becomes branch of Palm Beach Junior College.

JULY 1, 1965: Indian River Junior College and Lincoln Junior College for blacks become Indian River Community College.

FEB. 17, 1966: John F. Kennedy Memorial Hospital opens in Atlantis.

OCT. 29, 1966: A five-building terminal opens at Palm Beach International Airport, featuring all the modern conveniences.

Palm Beach International Airport in 1968. Today, the airport serves almost 6 million passengers each year.

DEC. 14, 1966: First part of Interstate 95 in Palm Beach County, a 3.6-mile stretch from Okeechobee Boulevard to 45th Street, opens. Completed north to Palm Beach Gardens in 1969.

JULY 15, 1967: Boca Raton Community Hospital opens.

SEPTEMBER 1967: IBM opens in Boca Raton.

SEPT. 3, 1967: West Palm Beach Auditorium opens.

OCT. 26, 1967: Palm Beach Mall opens.

SEPTEMBER 1968: Palm Beach Atlantic College opens in downtown West Palm Beach with 88 students.

OCT. 6, 1968: Carver Hospital, for blacks, opens in Belle Glade.

DECEMBER 1968: Palm Beach Gardens Medical Center opens.

JULY 1, 1969: Publisher John H. Perry sells his 27 newspapers, including *The Palm Beach Post* and *Evening Times,* to Cox Enterprises.

SEPT. 30, 1969: Hobe Sound National Wildlife Refuge established.

MAY 4, 1970: *The Palm Beach Post* is awarded a Pulitzer Prize in feature photography for photos of the poverty and poor working conditions of farm workers in the Glades.

FALL 1970: Palm Beach High and Roosevelt High combine into Twin Lakes — and the old Palm Beach High name is covered over.

JULY 19, 1971: *National Enquirer* tabloid moves to Lantana.

NOVEMBER 1971: Scientists find first Florida cases of lethal yellowing, a plant disease that nearly wipes out Palm Beach County's coconut palms.

Palm Beach High School's name is covered when the school becomes Twin Lakes in 1970.

1967 VIEW: *Landfill widened Flagler Drive in West Palm Beach. The towering Phillips Point and Esperante buildings would not arrive until the '80s.*

DIALING FOR DOLLARS: *Dave Davis hosted the popular game show on WPTV in the 1970s. During the afternoon movie, he would call residents at random. If they were watching, they won cash.*

Champion of the underdog

Percy Lee became president of the Palm Beach County Urban League in 1974 and built the first Urban League local office in the country. Pictured here in 1976, Lee became the voice of the disadvantaged and disenfranchised for 18 years, helping kids get jobs and minority contractors get work. He died as he lived: He was pushing for West Palm Beach to hire a black city attorney when he had a heart attack outside commission chambers in 1992.

Boat-building dynasty

John Rybovich

John and Anna Rybovich started their boat yard along the Intracoastal near 45th Street, where it stands today. Later, Rybovich and Sons made Palm Beach County famous with their sport fishing boats, considered the industry's best.

Brothers John Jr., Tommy, and Emil, and daughters Ethel and Irene, worked at the yard, and the brothers took over from John Sr. in 1946. The family sold the company in 1975. Rybovich Marine merged with Spencer Boat Co. in 1991. Emil, Ethel and Irene still live in Palm Beach County.

FEB. 17, 1972: Palm Beach County Commission approves first tract for what will become Wellington.

JAN. 22, 1973: Doctors Hospital, later Palm Beach Regional Hospital, opens in Lake Worth.

JULY 9, 1973: Federal judge rules that Palm Beach County schools are integrated.

JULY 11, 1973: New bridge opens over Lake Worth.

AUG. 10, 1973: Fort Pierce Inlet State Recreational Area opens.

AUG. 30, 1974: "South Bridge" from Fort Pierce to Hutchinson Island opens.

1975: Caldwell Theatre Company opens in Boca Raton under the direction of Michael Hall. It's named for James Caldwell, founder of the Rubbermaid Corp. and avid theater lover and benefactor.

DECEMBER 1975: Portions of Interstate 95 between Lake Worth and Hypoluxo and between Boynton Beach and Miami open.

JULY 3, 1976: Interstate 95 is completed between Palm Beach Gardens and Miami.

A helicopter carrying dignitaries arrives for dedication of the Blue Heron Bridge in June 1976.

JUNE 6, 1976: The Blue Heron Bridge opens.

DEC. 21, 1976: St. Lucie Nuclear Power Plant on Hutchinson Island opens. Second plant opens Aug. 8, 1983.

JAN. 19, 1977: First-ever recorded snow in West Palm Beach.

APRIL 25, 1977: Savannas State Preserve opens.

JULY 17, 1978: *Stuart News* begins publishing *St. Lucie News*.

FEB. 14, 1979: Palm Beach-Martin County Medical Center opens. Changed to Jupiter Medical Center in September 1984.

FEB. 9, 1979: H.H. Raulerson Jr., Memorial Hospital opens in Okeechobee, replacing Okeechobee General Hospital.

SEPT. 3, 1979: Hurricane David slides up Palm Beach County coast.

HURRICANE DAVID, the last hurricane to strike Palm Beach County and the Treasure Coast, ruined the 1979 Labor Day Weekend and collapsed the Palm Beach Jai Alai Fronton, but that was about it. This area has not had a major hurricane in 50 years.

WOODSTOCK SOUTH: *From Nov. 28 to 30, 1969, 40,000 teenagers wallowed in mud and music at the Palm Beach International Music and Arts Festival at the Palm Beach International Speedway (now Moroso Motorsports complex). The concert featured the Rolling Stones and Janis Joplin. The festival had many powerful opponents, including Sheriff William Heidtman, who was accused of planting red ants on the concert field. "If I had to do it over again, I'd try to stop it again," said Heidtman, whose deputies made about 120 arrests during the event, most involving drugs.*

Two places to learn

SEPTEMBER 1964: *Florida Atlantic University opened in Boca Raton, thanks largely to the efforts of banker Thomas Fleming Jr. Fleming, who founded two banks in Boca Raton and was a city councilman and mayor, helped push politically and financially for the college. He poured in his own money and raised it by using slogans such as "Boca U in '62; open the doors in '64."*

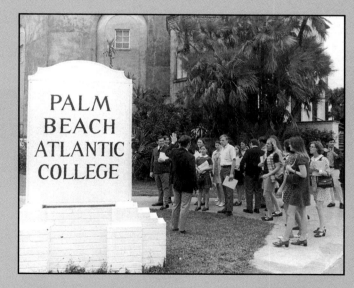

SEPTEMBER 1968: *Palm Beach Atlantic College in downtown West Palm Beach opened its doors with 88 students. The school was founded by Palm Beach County cardiologist Donald Warren and the Rev. Jess Moody, using the First Baptist Church as a base.*

77

DOWNTOWN WEST PALM BEACH 1962

The old Holiday Inn, foreground, was imploded at midnight on New Year's Eve as 1993 gave way to 1994, symbolizing new downtown growth. The old Pennsylvania Hotel, to its left, was torn down later that year.

DOWNTOWN WEST PALM BEACH 1999

The Meyer Amphitheater replaces the Holiday Inn. It opened July 4, 1996. The Palm Beach Post park is to the left, and the new residence for the Carmelite nuns is behind the park. The downtown of 1999 recalls the City Park of 1899 — a green space where neighbors can gather.

LIFT OFF: *(preceding pages) Space shuttle Discovery is seen taking off on Dec. 19, 1999. The launch was the last shuttle mission before 2000. Post photographer Stuart Thurlkill took this time exposure from the Southern Boulevard causeway in West Palm Beach. The shuttle was on its way to repair the Hubble telescope.*

Poised for a New Century

ONE HUNDRED YEARS of change. And yet two things have come full-circle: We've come back to our historic downtowns. And we're trying to fix decades of mistakes along the Kissimmee River, Lake Okeechobee and the Everglades.

We've learned the price of growth. And also its certainty.

This era marked dramatic milestones: Palm Beach County's population reached 1 million, and in 1999, the suburban sprawl of Port St. Lucie eclipsed West Palm Beach as this region's biggest city.

The industries that spurred growth in the 1950s — Pratt & Whitney and IBM — left Palm Beach County, and Internet businesses sprang up.

A rush of private donations created a culture boom: The Kravis Center for the Performing Arts, the expanded Norton Museum of Art, the International Museum of Cartoon Art in Boca Raton.

Our residents became more diverse. One of every eight students in Palm Beach County's schools speaks English as a second language, and half the students are non-white. In 25 years, Hispanics will be Palm Beach County's largest ethnic group, growing from 7.7 percent in 1990 to 44.9 percent in the year 2025. In Martin and St. Lucie counties, Hispanics will grow from around 4.5 percent of the population in 1990 to around 25 percent in 2025.

As always, newcomers seek their fortunes in our land, our sun and our sea.

As always, change comes as surely as the next hurricane season, the next housing development, or the next arrival of tomorrow's tycoons.

1980-1999

1980: Town Center at Boca Raton opens on Glades Road. By the end of 2000, it will be the second largest mall in South Florida.

JAN. 14, 1980: New West Palm Beach City Hall opens at Dixie Highway and Second Street.

MAY 7, 1980: *Town-Crier* newspaper opens in Wellington.

MAY 7, 1980: West Palm Beach jail closes for good. All prisoners now go to county jail.

Town Center at Boca Raton

JULY 7, 1981: John D. MacArthur Beach State Park opens.

JUNE 1982: Palm Beach Junior College opens Palm Beach Gardens campus.

JULY 8, 1982: Public station WWPF-TV, Channel 42, signs on. It becomes WXEL on Jan. 1, 1985.

OCTOBER 1982: WFLX-TV, Channel 29, signs on in West Palm Beach.

OCT. 4, 1982: Delray Community Hospital opens.

DEC. 1, 1982: Jail complex opens in West Palm Beach.

MAY 6-15, 1983: First SunFest in West Palm Beach.

MARCH 1984: Northwood College opens in suburban West Palm Beach. It becomes Northwood University in 1994.

APRIL 20, 1984: *Stuart News* becomes a daily newspaper.

JUNE 13, 1985: Port St. Lucie annexes St. Lucie West, a 4,600-acre development.

DEC. 12, 1985: Avalon State Recreation Area opens in St. Lucie County.

FEB. 2, 1986: West Boca Medical Center opens.

FEBRUARY 1986: Columbia Palms West Hospital opens.

AUGUST 1986: St. Lucie Medical Center opens, Port St. Lucie.

OCT. 1, 1986: Wellington Regional Medical Center opens.

NOVEMBER 1986: $25 million post office opens on Summit Boulevard in West Palm Beach.

MAY 4, 1987: *The Evening Times* merges into sister paper *The Palm Beach Post.*

DEC. 19, 1987: Missing link of Interstate 95, from Palm Beach Gardens to Stuart, opens, completing 1,894-mile expressway from Miami to Maine.

MARCH 5, 1988: New York Mets start spring training at St. Lucie County Sports Complex in St. Lucie West.

APRIL 16, 1988: Area code 407 established from Boca Raton to Orlando.

MAY 31, 1988: West Palm Beach annexes about 1,500 acres near Beeline Highway.

JUNE 7, 1988: Delray Elementary School closes after 75 years; building becomes part of Old School Square complex.

JUNE 15, 1988: Palm Beach Junior College renamed Palm Beach Community College.

OCTOBER 1988: The Gardens mall opens in Palm Beach Gardens.

The Gardens in Palm Beach Gardens

81

CLEAR LAKE, WEST PALM BEACH late '50s

Connie Mack Field, where Babe Ruth and other greats once played, still stood next to Palm Beach High. In Palm Beach, The Breakers welcomed guests, as did Flagler's mansion, White-hall, then a hotel (a multi-story addi-tion had been built onto the mansion). Okeechobee Road was built out west to Military Trail in 1909.

Atlantic Ocean

The Breakers

Whitehall

Old Okeechobee Rd.

Palm Beach High School

Connie Mack Field

N

Clear Lake

CLEAR LAKE, WEST PALM BEACH 1999

The Kravis Center for the Performing Arts stands on the former Connie Mack field; and CityPlace, a shop-ping/entertainment complex, is being built east of the Kravis Center. CityPlace is sched-uled to open in the fall of 2000. A much bigger Okeechobee Boule-vard connects Palm Beach to Interstate 95. Palm Beach High has undergone a splendid renova-tion and is now the Alexander Dreyfoos School of the Arts.

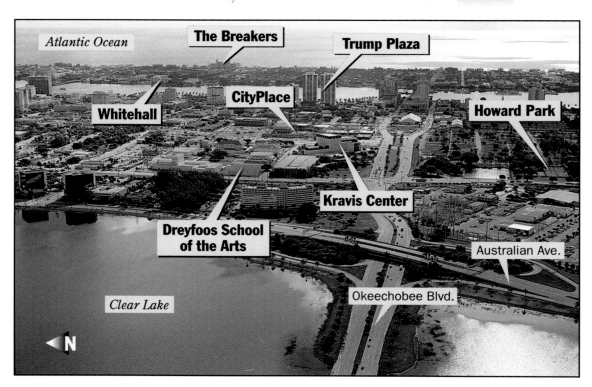

Atlantic Ocean

The Breakers

Trump Plaza

CityPlace

Whitehall

Howard Park

Kravis Center

Dreyfoos School of the Arts

Australian Ave.

Okeechobee Blvd.

Clear Lake

N

The deal maker

Pat Pepper, West Palm Beach mayor from 1988 to 1989, was instrumental in bringing the Kravis Center to its current site after deals fell through with Palm Beach Community College.

"It's a miracle the Kravis is in West Palm Beach," she said.

During her first visit to the hall in 1992, "I was moved to tears by the beauty of the place, the aesthetics and the whole ambience," Pepper, 53, said. "Just to enjoy that scene and know I had the privilege of helping to make it possible ... I don't think I ever had a feeling like that."

Pepper moved on from West Palm Beach, first becoming director of housing for the state, then heading a community partnership for the homeless in Miami. She now lives in New York.

The Kravis Center for the Performing Arts boosted West Palm Beach's downtown revitalization, but the city almost lost its showpiece. "It's a miracle the Kravis is in West Palm Beach," said Pat Pepper, mayor from 1988-89. She helped bring the Kravis to its current location after deals fell through.

NEW PBIA: *The first aircraft scheduled to take off from PBIA's new $62 million terminal sit at their gates on October 24, 1988. The terminal was named for World War II ace and Palm Beach County resident David McCampbell. He is best known for his heroism during air-to-air combat against Japanese aircraft over the Pacific in 1944. McCampbell received the Congressional Medal of Honor after shooting down nine Japanese planes and forcing 60 enemy aircraft to abandon the attack during the Battle of Leyte Gulf. Jim Gregory, one of the men McCampbell commanded, pushed the County Commission to honor the captain.*

OCT. 24, 1988: New terminal opens at Palm Beach International Airport; named for World War II ace David McCampbell.

SEPT. 19, 1988: WAQ-TV, Channel 19 (independent) signs on.

JAN. 1, 1989: WPEC-TV, Channel 12, switches from ABC to CBS; WPBF-TV (ABC), Channel 25, signs on; and former CBS affiliate WTVX-TV, Channel 34, becomes an independent.

JAN. 9, 1989: Tri-Rail commuter train, a 70-mile line from West Palm Beach to Miami, begins service.

JAN. 10, 1989: Martin County courthouse complex completed. Three years later, it's evacuated because mold makes employees sick. Employees will not move in until 1996.

APRIL 6, 1990: Port St. Lucie's developer, Miami-based General Development Corp., files for bankruptcy protection.

JAN. 11, 1991: Mizner Park, Boca Raton's 28-acre shopping and entertainment complex, opens, signaling a rebirth of the city's downtown.

MARCH 9, 1991: Old School Square, comprising three restored buildings of the former Delray High School, opens.

APRIL 1991: A Jupiter woman, Patricia Bowman, accuses William Kennedy Smith of raping her behind the Kennedy estate in Palm Beach. The trial lures world press to downtown West Palm Beach. Smith is acquitted on Dec. 11.

SEPT. 20, 1991: College of Boca Raton becomes Lynn University.

OCT. 20, 1991: Abandoned burial ground behind Tamarind Avenue home, believed to contain about 674 black victims of 1928 hurricane, is rededicated.

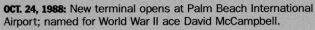

KENNEDY ON TRIAL: *William Kennedy Smith at his trial. His mother Jean, aunts Ethel Kennedy and Eunice Shriver, cousin John F. Kennedy Jr. and other family members came to court to support him.*

OCT. 22, 1991: Seabranch State Preserve in St. Lucie County opens.

JAN. 6, 1992: Indian River Community College opens St. Lucie West campus.

AUG. 27, 1992: Black-oriented *Courier* newspaper in Fort Pierce begins publication.

SEPT. 19, 1992: Raymond F. Kravis Center for the Performing Arts in West Palm Beach opens.

APRIL 22, 1994: North County Airport in Gardens opens.

MAY 16, 1996: Fifty acres in St. Lucie County placed in trust for Florida's sixth Seminole reservation.

FEBRUARY 1995: New West Palm Beach police station opens.

Making their mark

Mort and his museum

Cartoonist Mort Walker, far more genial than "Sarge" in his beloved comic strip Beetle Bailey, put his reputation and his money behind the $15 million International Museum of Cartoon Art in Boca Raton. The museum opened in Mizner Park on March 8, 1996. It holds one of the largest cartoon collections in the world.

Johnny Jones, from plumber to political ramrod

Jones, director of the Florida Wildlife Federation from 1971 to 1986, figures he's lobbied dozens of bills — all about lake cleaning, land buying, wetlands protection and Everglades fixing. The former plumber could summon legions of hunters and fishermen to support his environmental causes. His creed: "Never lie. Make friends. If they vote against you, don't hold it against them. Deal with those who have the clout, even if you don't like their politics. Do your crying behind closed doors and come out smiling." The West Palm Beach resident drafted the Kissimmee River restoration bill with Art Marshall.

TV network in West Palm Beach

On Aug. 31, 1998, Lowell "Bud" Paxson of Palm Beach launched Pax TV, the first network based in West Palm Beach. The born-again Paxson fills the airwaves with family programming. In September 1999, he announced that General Electric's NBC would pay $415 million for 32 percent of his Paxson Communications, its 72 stations and Pax TV.

Serena and Venus

The Williams sisters — at home on the world's center courts and in Palm Beach Gardens — are ready to join the new century's list of great athletes. Serena won the U.S. Open in 1999 at age 18, and both won more than $1 million in 1999. Dad Richard Williams predicts they'll have more endorsements than Michael Jordan one day. Few dispute they already are on the verge of becoming the richest black female athletes in history.

Palm Beach County Courthouse

APRIL 20, 1995: New Palm Beach County Courthouse opens.

JUNE 26, 1995: New VA medical center opens in Riviera Beach.

AUGUST 1995: Palm Beach County's first mosque opens in West Palm Beach.

FALL 1995: Florida Atlantic University opens Treasure Coast campus at St. Lucie West.

MARCH 3, 1996: Area code 941 is created for central and southwest Florida, including Okeechobee, Glades and Hendry counties.

APRIL 26, 1996: Coral Sky Amphitheater opens west of West Palm Beach. Renamed the MARS Music Amphitheater in January 2000.

MAY 13, 1996: Area code 561 is created for Palm Beach, Martin, St. Lucie and Indian River counties.

DEC. 31, 1996: Wellington incorporated as Palm Beach County's 38th city.

1997: Stuart begins annexing more than 1,200 acres, increasing its size by 40 percent.

FEB. 8, 1997: WHDT-TV, Channel 55, goes on the air.

MAY 2, 1997: *Stuart News* begins publishing *Fort Pierce News.*

AUG. 31, 1997: West Palm Beach Municipal Stadium hosts Expos minor-league game, its last league baseball game.

NOV. 1, 1997: New high-span Roosevelt Bridge opens in Stuart.

FEB. 28, 1998: $28 million Roger Dean Stadium complex in Jupiter opens.

MARCH 7, 1998: WPXP-TV, Channel 67, goes on the air.

APRIL 7, 1998: Everglades Regional Regional Medical Center closes after 60 years.

SEPT. 1, 1998: 61-year-old Palm Beach County town of Golfview bought out for airport property, goes out of existence.

The opening of the new Roosevelt Bridge attracted old-timers who also saw the dedication of the old bridge in 1934, (from left) Morris and Rose Walton, Toley Engebretsen and Vee Chambers.

JUNE 10, 1999: Work begins on restoring Kissimmee River.

AUG. 12, 1999: Pratt & Whitney and partner Sikorsky Aircraft announce they will close most of their Palm Beach County operations.

WELLINGTON 1956

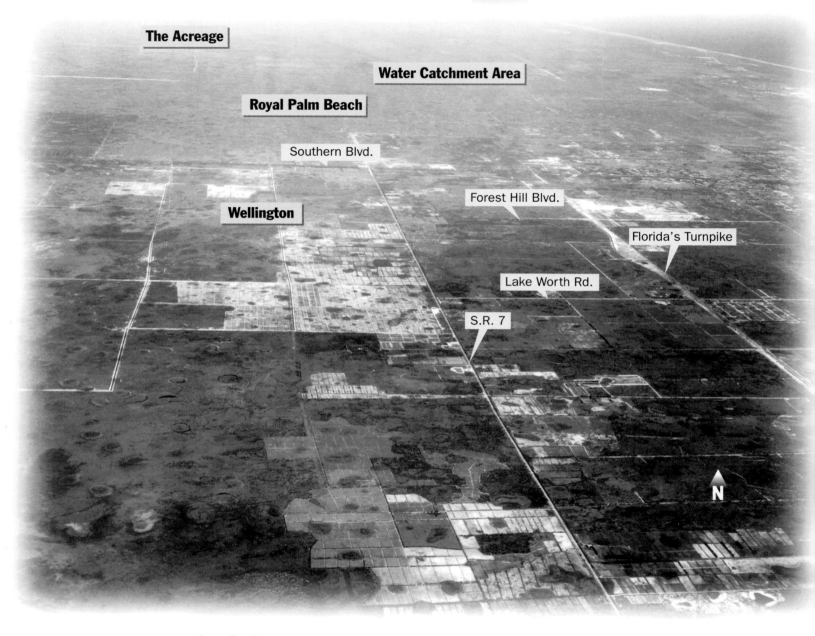

Actually, there was no town of Wellington in 1956 — there was just land owned by C. Oliver Wellington, a wealthy Boston accountant, who bought 18,000 acres of swamp here after World War II. He named the area Flying C.O.W. Ranch (C.O.W. for his initials, flying because he was a pilot). In the early '70s, Fort Lauderdale developer Jim Nall planned the community, and Palm Beach County officials approved it, believing no one would want to live that far west. (There was no Acreage or Royal Palm Beach then, either; this photo shows their future sites.)

WELLINGTON 1999

The Acreage

Water Catchment Area

Royal Palm Beach

Okeechobee Blvd.

M1 Canal

Breakers West

Southern Blvd.

S.R. 7

Wellington

Forest Hill Blvd.

C8 Canal

Mall site

N

Dillon-Reynolds Aerial Photography Inc., Fort Lauderdale

Today, the village of Wellington (incorporated in 1996) is home to 31,000 people, and approximately 58,000 more live in Royal Palm Beach and The Acreage to the north. Construction on the Wellington mall (this 1998 photograph shows farmland on the mall site) began in February, and the mall is expected to open by Christmas 2001. This western corridor is poised to nearly double in population in the next 50 years.

BOCA RATON 1961

Yamato Rd.

E3 Canal

Future
St. Andrews Blvd.

Military Trail

Boca Raton
Bath and Tennis

L45 Canal

University Park

Former Polo grounds

Future site of
Town Center mall

N

Glades Rd.

In 1956, Arthur Vining Davis of Arvida spent $22.5 million for the Boca Raton Resort and Club and surrounding land, the largest land deal in Florida at the time. He moved the polo fields from just south of the resort out west to Glades Road and started plotting the subdivisions of west Boca. In this photo, land had just been cleared for the University Park neighborhood and Boca Raton Bath & Tennis Club.

Clint Moore Rd.

Military Trail

Yamato Rd.

Timber Creek

Powerline/Jog Rd.

**Boca Raton
Bath and Tennis**

St. Andrews Blvd.

I-95

L45 Canal

University Park

E3 Canal

Glades Rd.

N

Town Center mall

Wall-to-wall development. By the end of 2000, Town Center mall will be South Florida's second largest mall, after Sawgrass Mills. It's also one of the top malls in sales, no doubt because of the expensive subdivisions around it. Arthur Vining Davis died in 1962; John Temple presided over Arvida during its boom period of the 1980s.

PORT ST. LUCIE 1958

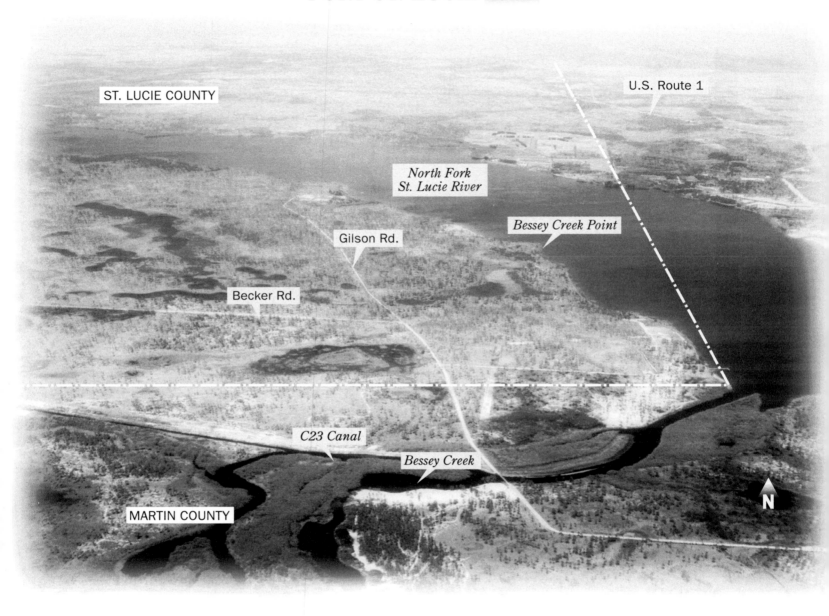

There's nothing but a developer's dream in this photo of the North Fork of the St. Lucie River. It was taken as General Development Corp. first contemplated the city of Port St. Lucie, which by 1999 would be more populous than any city in Palm Beach County or the Treasure Coast.

PORT ST. LUCIE 1999

Port St. Lucie Blvd.

U.S. Route 1

Ballantrae Golf and Yacht Club

Club Med Sandpiper

ST. LUCIE COUNTY

Harbour Ridge Country Club

North Fork St. Lucie River

Bessey Creek Point

Southbend Blvd.

Gilson Rd.

Becker Rd.

MARTIN COUNTY

C23 Canal

Bessey Creek

N

The river remains at the center but the city around it grew to 83,000 residents. Experts expect another 50,000 people in 20 years. Mainly a bedroom community that flourished after Interstate 95 was built in the late 1980s, the city in recent years made progress in attracting industry.

NORTH PALM BEACH 1969

The Post *ran this photograph in 1969 because insurance magnate and developer John D. MacArthur was beginning to dredge the North Palm Beach site for homes. But the MacArthur land remained fallow for decades, while subdivisions sprang up in Palm Beach Gardens to the west.*

Burns Rd.

Prosperity Farms Rd.

Garden Ln.

Prosperity Harbor

Future Harbour Isles

North Palm Beach Waterway

North Palm Beach Country Club

N

NORTH PALM BEACH 1999

Most of the land to the west is developed — and Watermark Communities is building 105 waterfront homes, called Harbour Isles, on the former MacArthur land. MacArthur's foundation sold its last 15,000 acres in 1999, spawning a land rush among developers.

Burns Rd.

RCA Blvd.

Prosperity Farms Rd.

Harbour Isles

Prosperity Harbor

North Palm Beach Country Club

N

Dillon-Reynolds Aerial Photography Inc., Fort Lauderdale

94

MIDNIGHT! AND THE CROWD GOES WILD! *At the Century Village clubhouse in West Palm Beach, the revelers know how to party — they've been at it for most of the 20th century. Who gets the first kiss of the new millennium from Selma Lichten (right)? Husband Milton, of course. They've been married (and sharing New Year's smooches) for 55 years. The year 2000 dawned with celebration and hope. The one constant for South Florida is growth, as new residents continue to flood in. For many retirees, the second life they find in Florida at Century Village is a wonderful surprise. "I felt like I started my life over here," said Esther Kanterman, who met her second husband at the condo. "People on the outside have no idea what it's like here. When they call it Century Village, it's because you can live to be 100 years old here."*

The people who changed THE WAY WE LIVE

the firsts • the architects • the politicians • the symbols • the environmentalists • the artists • the healers • the inventors • the merchants • the dynasties • the farmers, planters and ranchers • the educators • the developers • the champions of a cause • the sports figures • the personalities • the believers • the stars • the historians and storytellers

The ultimate developer

HENRY FLAGLER
Jan. 2, 1830 — May 20, 1913

Henry Morrison Flagler's fortune started with a pocketful of coins he carried the rest of his life, a reminder of the lesson in a biblical parable: no risk, no gain.

He built one fortune, saw it collapse, and within five years was the second-in-command at Standard Oil and on his way to becoming one of America's wealthiest men. He was private, aloof and vain: Even when he was nearly blind, he was never photographed wearing his glasses. He was abundant in his charity but judged every penny spent or donated on how it would help his business.

The son of a minister, he was a man of strict morals who profited early in his career from the brokering of grain to whiskey makers. He closed his operations on Sundays but ignored the casino gambling going on under his nose. He was an honorable man but spent $300 to buy his way out of the Civil War and helped Standard Oil build a reputation for ruthless monopoly.

His successes were tempered by personal tragedies. Of his three wives, he buried one and institutionalized another. He was estranged from his son for nearly two decades.

He made more money than he would ever need but still sought immortality. So, at an age when most people retire, he began a second career that made him the pivotal person in Florida's modern history.

Henry Morrison Flagler brought the railroads and hotels to Southeast Florida. He put Palm Beach on the map and founded West Palm Beach "for my help." By the time he died in 1913, he had changed Florida forever.

— ELIOT KLEINBERG

Henry Flagler spent his childhood in upstate New York, then went to Ohio, where the family of his first wife, Mary Harkness, provided him with his first successes in their country store. Mary died in 1881 and Flagler married Ida Alice Shourds. They honeymooned in St. Augustine, where Flagler's Florida dream was born. Flagler divorced Ida and married Mary Lily Kenan, 34, in 1901, when he was 71. He built Whitehall in Palm Beach for Mary Lily.

The Vanderbilts arrive at Flagler's Royal Poinciana Hotel in 1896, the year his rail spur to Palm Beach was completed.

The first hotel on Palm Beach, Cap Dimick's
Cocoanut Grove House, shown here in a sketch
by George Potter. The hotel burned in 1893.

ELISHA NEWTON 'CAP' DIMICK
April 29, 1849 — Jan. 6, 1919

Colorful pioneer

*Cap Dimick:
First hotelier and
first mayor of
Palm Beach.*

Cap Dimick, named for his favored white hats, never skippered a ship, but he did steer early Palm Beach.
His family came to the island in 1876 and soon had lush crops of sweet potatoes, pumpkins and pineapples. In 1880, Dimick added eight rooms to his home and opened the first hotel, the Cocoanut Grove House.

By 1899, Cap owned 136 acres of Palm Beach, then just a patch of jungle and swamp from lake to ocean.

He built a wooden bridge himself in 1911 and called it the Royal Park Bridge. He charged a quarter per car and a nickel per pedestrian. In 1919, Palm Beach County bought Dimick's bridge for $40,000.

Cap became Palm Beach's first mayor when the town incorporated in 1911. He also was a state representative in 1890 and state senator in 1896, and he helped start the region's first bank, the Dade County State Bank.

His grandson, Claude Dimick Reese, served 56 years in Palm Beach government, 18 as mayor and 38 as a council member. He died at 87 in 1984.

Today, a statue of Cap Dimick, holding his cap, stands on Royal Palm Way and welcomes visitors to Palm Beach.

— ELIOT KLEINBERG

THE SUNDYS: DELRAY BEACH'S FIRST FAMILY

One day in 1898, John Sundy stepped off the Florida East Coast Railway track in what would become Delray Beach. Henry Flagler told him, "There's nothing here." Sundy retorted: "There will be." Sundy was right. He would be the first mayor of Delray Beach and be elected eight times. His family business, Sundy Feed and Fertilizer, became a landmark, and so did his Queen Anne-style house. The Sundys had eight children. Ben Sundy served on the Palm Beach County Commission. His wife, Elizabeth, was chairwoman of the town's first board of education and taught Latin. In 1990, Daisy Sundy Meehan sold the home. It's now a restaurant. Meehan died Jan. 5, 2000, at 91.

1981 file photo of Sadie and Addie Sundy, daughters of John Sundy

Album of the Late 20th Century

*Nancy Graham celebrates the heart of downtown West Palm Beach — the fountain that bears
her name. When it opened in November 1994 for the city's centennial, she danced through
the water with Gov. Lawton Chiles. "The fountain has been the great equalizer," she said.
"Once I got a letter from a welfare mother who wanted to tell me how much that fountain
had meant to her. 'I can't afford to take my kids to the pool or slide,' she wrote, 'but I can pack
a sandwich and we can come to the fountain and play and be just like everybody else who is there.'"*

Mayor of West Palm Beach,
November 1991 to March 1999

NANCY GRAHAM
Born June 5, 1946

The city's spark plug

Because she told an all-male commission that "government cannot work when people don't have the balls to stand up for something." And, as West Palm Beach's first strong mayor, she did.

Because she decided the city needed a real downtown where people buy latte instead of crack cocaine.

Because, as she promoted herself to anyone who would listen, she also promoted that vision — that downtown could give people a sense of place where poor and rich children played in the same fountain.

Because even those who resented her acknowledged the city is a better place because she challenged them. Events like Clematis by Night made West Palm Beach such a hot destination even Donald Trump called Clematis "the hottest street in Florida." In one year — from 1996 to 1997 — downtown tax rolls jumped 13 percent, nearly three times the rate of growth for the rest of Palm Beach County.

Because she's now a developer for WCI (Watermark Communities Inc.), feeling the tension between the ideals of downtown living she promoted and the realities of a company that builds golf course communities in the suburbs.

Because she opened her mouth more than one too many times, and kept talking.

Because people called her the "iron lady," but she insists she's "very mushy on the inside."

Because she worked a 52-cents-an-hour job to support herself when she was 12, felt the pain of watching her disabled son die when he was a teenager and conquered the skin cancer that was threatening her life.

Because those experiences made city battles seem inconsequential.

Because sometimes she did cry, feeling the wounds of public life. And sometimes she would drive the streets of West Palm Beach feeling overwhelmed. But she persisted. "I have an incredibly strong commitment inside and belief that it can be done."

Because as mayor, she told her staff "Just do something. If it's wrong, you can try something else."

Because even though her big projects like CityPlace — the shopping/entertainment complex now being built near the Kravis Center — got most of the attention, her proudest accomplishments, she says, are the quieter ones: Helping 150 people buy their own homes through her Renaissance Fund, which teamed needy people with banks willing to lend money at cost. Building a community center in Pleasant City. Buying book bags for hundreds of schoolchildren. And just getting neighbors downtown.

Because she gave West Palm Beach back its pride. "I wanted to give the city a positive attitude, that they could do something and it could be great. I hope my legacy is that I gave them back a sense of community spirit."

— NOAH BIERMAN

C.E. and Marjorie Chillingworth

THE CHILLINGWORTHS

The murder and the law

The double murder of Palm Beach Circuit Judge Curtis Eugene Chillingworth and his wife Marjorie in 1955 was horrific in itself. What made it the local crime of the century was the prominence of the judge and his pioneer family.

Chillingworth's grandfather, Richard, moved to the region from New York in 1893, a year before the railroad arrived. He was a mayor of West Palm Beach and the sheriff of Dade County, which then included present-day Palm Beach County. Curtis Chillingworth's father, Charles, was the first West Palm Beach city attorney.

Like many early settlers, Charles invested in land. His Palm Beach Land Company purchased 12,000 acres in Palm City in 1910. He called it Palm City Farms and advertised it up north for its "healthfulness."

Curtis Chillingworth spent two years in the U.S. Navy before joining his father's law firm. He married the daughter of his father's closest friend and they had three daughters. He was the youngest circuit judge in Florida history, elected in 1920 at age 26. He would serve on the bench for three decades. In 1955, he began closing in on the corrupt ways of another judge, Joseph Peel Jr.

On June 15, 1955, two henchmen hired for $2,500 by Peel forced the Chillingworths from their seaside Manalapan bungalow, took them 2 miles out at sea, weighed them down and threw them overboard.

The bodies of Chillingworth, 58, and his wife, Marjorie, 47, were never found, but five years later, one of the thugs bragged to friends, and the law pounced on Peel and the killers, Floyd "Lucky" Holzapfel and Bobby Lincoln.

Peel spent 21 years in prison; he was paroled in 1982 and died nine days later. Lincoln went to Chicago, became a black Muslim and later returned to Palm Beach County, where he still lives. Holzapfel died in prison in 1996.

"You and your cohorts participated in a crime or crimes which were gruesome, vicious, cold-blooded, premeditated in design, and the likes of which the history of Florida has not seen," Judge Russell O. Morrow told Holzapfel at sentencing.

"It was not just a man's life that was taken. It was Judge Chillingworth that was taken. ... He was a man of honor and, in sense, a bulwark in this county and state against the unlawful."

— ELIOT KLEINBERG

Okeechobee Historical Society

Peter and Louisiana Raulerson, Okeechobee's first white settlers.

THE RAULERSONS

Big family

In 1896, Peter Raulerson and his wife, Louisiana Chandler Raulerson, became the first white settlers on the northern side of Lake Okeechobee.

The Raulersons were first to do just about everything in Okeechobee County and city. First county commissioner, first mayor, first banker, first merchant.

Peter was the first county commissioner and the first mayor of Okeechobee City (originally called Tantie). Louisiana was the first postmistress, and school was held in her home.

Their son Lewis opened a general store in 1905, and by 1923, his son Hiram had a thriving men's clothing store. Hiram's wife, "Miz Annie" was a volunteer in Okeechobee until her death in 1997 at 91.

Today, there's a pawn shop where the old Raulerson department store was, and a different attitude downtown.

"It used to be you waved to everyone," said O.L. Raulerson, Okeechobee's former sheriff. "Now you wave, and they say, 'Who's that?' "

— JERI BUTLER

In this Chillingworth family portrait, the future judge is 17 and standing in the back row at right. Also pictured (from left): his sister, Margarita Chillingworth; a brother, Walter Seabrook Chillingworth; his father, Charles Curtis Chillingworth, first city attorney of West Palm Beach; his mother, Jennie Dietz Chillingworth; his grandfather, Richard Jolley Chillingworth, a pioneer who became sheriff of Dade County; and another brother, Richard.

Museum of the City of Lake Worth

When Lillian Fulton (left front) preached, the crowd at First Congregational Church frequently overflowed into the street.

LILLIAN BRITTON FULTON

May 15, 1881 — July 1939

Pioneer pastor

Lillian Fulton traveled the country preaching with Billy Sunday and Gypsy Smith. In 1920, she was ordained into the ministry of the Congregational Church and became the first female minister of any faith in Florida. In 1928, she became the first woman in America to receive a doctor of divinity degree.

Fulton served as pastor of Lake Worth's First Congregational Church from 1924 until a few weeks before her death in 1939. She told her congregation: "I have been with your loved ones in their last hours, buried your dead, baptized your babies, married your children — and there's been a heap of living going on in this church family."

REUBEN CARLTON

Born Nov. 3, 1920

Living off the land

Reuben Wright Carlton, grandson of a St. Lucie County pioneer, built a cattle business that straddles the Martin-St. Lucie county line. He's been involved in banking, water management and other businesses.

He shares some of the family stories with a sharp memory, a sense of humor and a twinkle in his eye:

"My grandfather, also named Reuben Carlton, brought his family here from Fort Meade (south of Bartow) in 1874," Carlton said. "He brought the first herd of cattle into St. Lucie County, also the first school teacher.

"She lived with the family on the bank of the Indian River, then moved out to Ten Mile with them."

Ten Mile, dubbed that because it was about 10 miles from Fort Pierce, was Carlton's home from birth until age 13, when the family moved into town.

Farm life at Ten Mile was typical for families of that era.

"All of us had certain chores to do," Carlton said. "I milked two cows and fed the horses and chickens.

"I had to walk a quarter-mile to the bus stop, then rode the Model T school bus 10 miles into town. I got home about 4 p.m. and had to do those same chores all over again."

They used kerosene lamps, outdoor toilets, hand-operated pumps and a cypress tank to collect rainwater.

Carlton's grandmother had a 3-acre citrus grove at Ten Mile, and his father took care of it.

"Dad picked the fruit, wrapped it with thin paper and put it in wooden barrels to take by ox cart to Fort Pierce," Carlton said. "Capt. Johnson's steamer carried it up the river to Jacksonville."

Carlton got into cattle in a big way after graduation from the University of Florida and World War II service in the U.S. Air Force.

"I bought a tract of land southwest of Fort Pierce," Carlton said. "Then I got an opportunity to buy some land in Martin County and I've been at it ever since."

Today, Ru-Mar Inc., a family corporation, owns or leases thousands of acres in Martin and St. Lucie counties.

Among Ru-Mar's holdings is what's believed to be the oldest citrus grove in St. Lucie County.

"The old-timers said the Indians got the seed from Spaniards in St. Augustine," Carlton said. "They didn't plant nice neat rows like we do today. The grove is still producing."

Some land that the Carlton family once owned has been converted into Port St. Lucie home sites.

"My brother was an attorney and they contacted him about buying the land," Carlton said. "He called us in and told us they wanted to build a subdivision.

"I said, 'Who's going to live way down there? They'll be trying to give the land back to us in a year."

Does Carlton wish he had been right?

"Yes and no," Carlton said. "If they had built better roads, provided water and sewer and put in bigger, finer houses, I would have liked it better."

— JIM REEDER

The death of Daniel Carlton, St. Lucie's first sheriff

The Carlton family provided St. Lucie County's first elected sheriff, cattle and citrus men, attorneys and saloonkeepers.

Daniel S. Carlton, uncle of Reuben Wright Carlton, was elected St. Lucie County's first sheriff in 1905. He was killed 10 years later — May 22, 1915 — during a Saturday night shootout on Pine Street (now Second Street). The shooter: D.J. Disney, a night watchman paid by merchants to patrol the downtown area.

Some say the assassin was a hired gunman, paid by a member of a prominent family. But newspaper accounts of the day report a coroner's conclusion that the sheriff was the aggressor.

Disney reportedly said he accidentally bumped into Carlton while talking with someone, but the sheriff accused him of striking him deliberately.

Whatever the cause, bullets started flying. The sheriff was hit in the head near the right eye and twice in the chest. Disney was shot in the right eye, arm, leg and side. He suffered a broken leg when townspeople dragged him off a train that was to take him to a hospital in Miami.

The first jury to hear the case deliberated 40 hours but was unable to reach a verdict. A re-trial in Orlando ended with Disney convicted of manslaughter and sentenced to five years in prison.

Reuben Carlton in one of his citrus groves in Fort Pierce. A B-17 pilot in World War II, he once watched over his vast land holdings by flying over them in his own plane.

105

The political precedent setters

Catherine Strong began working at Delray Beach City Hall as a clerk and became a commissioner in 1953. Because she got more votes than any other candidate, she was named mayor.

The New York native also was the first woman called for jury duty in the county, in January 1950.

She served on the council until 1957.

Strong died at 52 in December 1963 at Bethesda Memorial Hospital in Boynton Beach, where she had served on the founding board. A hospital wing was named

CATHERINE ELIZABETH STRONG
1911 — Dec. 23, 1963
Palm Beach County's first female mayor

for her in 1966 and a Delray Beach city community center in March 1964.

Strong is remembered as a civil rights advocate.

In 1956, she used her influence with former Florida Gov. LeRoy Collins to help ease racial tensions at Delray Beach beaches.

F. Malcolm Cunningham Sr. became the first black to hold office in a city with white residents since Reconstruction. He was elected to the Riviera Beach city council in 1962, and he received 299 white votes, or 18 percent of the white turnout — pretty significant in a city where just six years previously someone had burned a cross outside the black polling place.

Cunningham, a Plant City native, attended Florida A&M University but had to go to Howard University for his legal training because no Florida law school was open to African-Americans.

He came to Palm Beach County in 1953 and opened his law office in West Palm Beach. He retired from city office

F. MALCOLM CUNNINGHAM SR.
Jan. 27, 1927 — Feb. 28, 1978
First black elected to Riviera Beach city council

after three Riviera council terms, during which the city undertook a major expansion of water and sewer service, but continued his law practice.

"He always wanted to go to law school to learn to fight the obstacles that he encountered," said his brother and law partner, T.J. Cunningham, upon his death from cancer at 51.

"He never gave up. He was always optimistic."

The county's bar association for African-Americans bears his name.

"I am not proud of the fact that I am the first black mayor of West Palm Beach," Eva Williams Mack said when other city commissioners elected her mayor in 1982. She and Ruby Bullock had become the first black city commissioners in 1978.

"As I think back over the years, I remember the many black men and black women who tried and failed in their attempts to win election to this commision," she said.

Mack came to West Palm Beach in 1948 and worked as a public health nurse for 26 years, then as a Florida A&M

EVA MACK
Feb. 19, 1915 — June 3, 1998
First black mayor of West Palm Beach

University instructor, then as the first health specialist for the Palm Beach County School Board.

She lobbied for health classes in all grades, including courses in sex education, and she helped change the policy of expelling pregnant students. She also founded the Sickle Cell Disease Foundation of Palm Beach County.

— Stories by ELIOT KLEINBERG

LOUISE JONES GOPHER

Born May 25, 1945

First Seminole woman to get
a four-year degree

Seminole storyteller

Because she personifies Florida's native culture. She was born in a chickee in a Fort Pierce Seminole camp, and her grandfather was DeSoto Tiger, a Seminole leader and the first murder victim of notorious gangster John Ashley.

Because when she was 6, her father, Willie Jones, a worker for a western St. Lucie County farmer, decided he wanted his three children to get an education. They were con-sidered neither black nor white, so Jones pleaded with St. Lucie County Schools Super-intendent Ben L. Bryan to allow Louise and her older brother and sister to attend the Fairlawn School, a school west of Fort Pierce for farming families.

Because she spoke no English when she went to school — but she ended up going to the University of Florida and Florida Atlantic University. She became the first Seminole woman to graduate with a four-year college degree, in 1970.

Because she has dedicated her career to preserving Seminole culture. The Seminoles' native languages, Creek or Mikasuki, are spoken only by older tribe members, so she transcribes Mikasuki teachings. "We were losing our culture and language, and needed to reinforce it," she said.

Because she became director of cultural education for Florida's five Seminole reserva-tions and is now an education liaison for the Brighton reservation near Moore Haven.

Because she appreciates her history, and she shares it.

— ELIOT KLEINBERG

"My grandfather was a medicine man, and we were the only Indian family that went to school in Fort Pierce," said Louise Gopher, who grew up in a chickee hut similar to this one on the Brighton reservation. Now an education leader for her tribe, Gopher wears a traditional Seminole ceremonial robe.

107

ADDISON MIZNER
Dec. 12, 1872 — Feb. 5, 1933

Society's stylist

The ultimate society architect, Addison Cairn Mizner created the Palm Beach look and built Boca Raton.

His client list: Vanderbilts, Warburtons and Wanamakers. He had no university training as an architect — just an eye for high style.

While building country homes on Long Island, Mizner met Paris Singer, 24th child of sewing machine magnate Isaac Merritt Singer. Singer brought Mizner to Palm Beach in 1918.

Paris Singer

Eventually, Singer decided to build a hospital for war veterans that could later be a social club. Mizner's Spanish-style Everglades Club — with tiles hand-crafted by his own Mizner Industries — became the toast of the town in 1919, a romantic departure from Flagler's wood-frame hotels.

Soon, society matrons came calling.

For Eva Stotesbury, who ruled Palm Beach from 1918 to 1938, Mizner built the 40-room El Mirasol, the pinnacle of his style: rough stucco walls, hand-made barrel-tile roofs, archways and loggias and rooms that opened up to the sea.

His grandest mansions, such as El Mirasol, were torn down in the 1950s, but his crown jewel of resorts, the Cloister Inn, lives on as the much-expanded Boca Raton Resort and Club.

Mizner wanted a hotel in Boca Raton to help lure land investors for his planned housing developments there. But by the time the Cloister Inn opened in 1926, the Florida boom had busted.

In all, Mizner would design or build 67 structures in Palm Beach, five in West Palm Beach, one in Belle Glade, one in Manalapan, three in Boynton Beach, one in Gulf Stream and 27 in Boca Raton.

Mizner, his pet monkey Johnnie Brown on his shoulder, was not even the most eccentric Mizner. He was the artist; his brother Wilson the consummate salesman. It was Wilson who said, "Copy from one, it's research; copy from two, it's plagiarism," "The second hundred years are the hardest" and "Be nice to people on the way up; you'll see them on the way down."

At its peak, the brothers' real-estate enterprise was making $2 million in sales a week. But the bust killed their business. Addison Mizner was dead by February 1933, Wilson two months later.

Singer's Blue Heron hotel, a Mizner-designed $4 million resort on what became Singer Island, was never finished. Singer died in 1932. The shell of his Blue Heron hotel stood for 14 years until it was razed in the early 1940s.

— ELIOT KLEINBERG

He was born in California, but Addison Mizner became famous for the look that defines Palm Beach and Boca Raton. The 9,300-square-foot home he built for Philadelphia magnate Rodman Wanamaker II became the Kennedy compound. At right is the interior of the Everglades Club.

Florida State Archives

THE EVERGLADES CLUB: *In the early '20s, Mizner would load prospective land buyers into buses parked in front of the Everglades Club (on Worth Avenue) and drive them to Boca. At right: interior of the Everglades Club.*

Boca Raton Historical Society

THE CLOISTER INN: *Completed in 1926 for $1.25 million, the inn was called the most expensive 100-room inn ever built. The interior was adorned with intricate wrought-iron chandeliers and stained-glass windows, all made at Mizner's West Palm Beach factory.*

Historical Society of Palm Beach County

The original beauty of the El Verano Hotel, built in 1922, can still be glimpsed if one looks to the upper floors, but the ground level of the hotel (now the Helen Wilkes) has been changed dramatically. Note how the Intracoastal Waterway came up close to the hotel in this 1920s shot (before Flagler Drive was widened).

A talent lost too soon

HAZEL AUGUSTUS
Died in 1926

Palm Beach Post file photo

Built in 1924 in the Gothic revival style, the Payne Chapel A.M.E. church is a West Palm Beach landmark.

Architect Hazel Augustus designed three of the boom-era's most distinguished, most enduring buildings: The El Verano Hotel (now the Helen Wilkes Residence Hotel), and the Payne Chapel A.M.E. and Tabernacle Baptist churches in West Palm Beach.

Little is known of Augustus' life. He was born in Florida and moved to Palm Beach County early in the century, according to an account given to *The Post* by his goddaughter, Hazel Augustus Driskell, in 1990. He served in World War I, then went to the University of Pennsylvania, said Preston Tillman, a leader of the Black Historical Preservation Society.

Augustus, the area's first black architect, was a tall, lanky man who spoke softly, even when correcting a construction worker, Tillman recalled. He designed many of the grandest homes in the black neighborhoods of West Palm Beach. His El Verano Hotel, designed in 1922 in the Spanish Colonial Revival style, has been drastically modernized and only glimpses of its original glamour can now be seen.

Augustus' career was cut short in 1926, when he died in a traffic wreck. His home, an impressive columned structure on Division Street, was to have been restored as a centerpiece of African-American heritage, along with the Augustus-designed Gwen Cherry house next door, but it was so run down it had to be demolished in 1987.

— ELIOT KLEINBERG

Sherman Childs designed the Lake Worth City Hall, shown here in 1938, with distinctive minarets. It's been renovated many times over the years, but still looks the same. Childs also designed two of Lake Worth's most memorable homes, the Birthday Cake Castle and the Lakeside Castle. He moved to Lake Worth from Minnesota in 1912, along with James Love, who became the first elected mayor.

DESIGNER OF LAKE WORTH LANDMARKS: *G. Sherman Childs, an associate of Addison Mizner, built the Lake Worth City Hall, the original Lake Worth Casino and several notable homes. His daughter, Jean, was the first girl born in the city.*

Black Historical Preservation Society

Hazel Augustus stands on the porch of his majestic home in the Northwest neighborhood of West Palm Beach. It was torn down in 1987.

Photos provided by Alexandra Fatio Taylor

MAURICE FATIO
March 18, 1897 - Dec. 2, 1943

Style and substance

The elegant Maurice Fatio became Addison Mizner's successor as Palm Beach's favorite society architect. He danced the tango with the Sanfords, sipped champagne with Astors, vacationed with Mellons, dined with the Prince of Wales, and created designs for the Vanderbilts, Rockefellers, Phippses and even the son of Theodore Roosevelt.

"Connections are everything in this country; talent comes afterwards," the Geneva-born Fatio (pronouced Faah-see-o) wrote in 1921. "I realize the only way to succeed is to make oneself known and to go out as often as possible."

Fatio often got jobs after sketching ideas on dinner napkins. In 1923, Fatio's firm, Treanor & Fatio, was among the 10 busiest architectural firms in New York. In 1924, Fatio opened an office in Palm Beach, and by 1925, he prompted the town government to adopt rules restricting the height and size of buildings.

He designed in many styles, including Mediterranean, Georgian and modern, and his public work includes the First National Bank and the Society of Four Arts in Palm Beach.

One of his notable homes, built for Mortimer Schiff in 1927, is known as the "ham and cheese" house because of its mix of pink and white coquina and brick. In February 2000, it sold for $13 million, a Palm Beach County record for a home on the west side of State Road A1A with an ocean view.
— AVA VAN DE WATER

Above, Fatio's "ham and cheese" house" at 920 S. Ocean Blvd., in Palm Beach. At left, Maurice Fatio in Palm Beach in 1921.

Below, Fatio (left) loved flying and joined the party making the first landing at the airstrip at Morrison Field, forerunner to Palm Beach International Airport, which was named after his secretary, Grace Morrison (see page 55).

Photos provided by the Volk family

Volk designed the 300 block of Worth Avenue, called the Everglades Arcade (from the pink building to the right in this photo) in 1965. Volk's important Palm Beach buildings include the Royal Poinciana Plaza and Theatre, a section of Town Hall, the Beach Club and the golf terrace and orange gardens of the Everglades Club.

Volk's 1950 design for Clark-Warwick Oldsmobile (below), at Lakeview and Olive Avenue in West Palm Beach, was the height of hip: This was the first open-air automobile showroom in America. It's been changed many times over the years, but the basic lines of Volk's designs can still be seen.

JOHN L. VOLK
Oct. 15, 1901 — Feb. 20, 1984

Prolific classicist

John Volk belonged to an exclusive club of early Palm Beach architects: Mizner. Fatio. Wyeth. Urban. The men whose vision of grand Mediterranean-style villas and lush tropical gardens became the trademark look for one of America's toniest towns.

But Volk was one of the few who churned out designs well into his later years, more than 1,000 by his own estimate.

"From the inlet, all the way down to the south end of the island, there's hardly a street in Palm Beach that doesn't have something to show for more than 50 years of work."

That work includes some of the area's most notable landmarks: Good Samaritan Medical Center, the Royal Poinciana Plaza and Playhouse, the 1944 redesigned Bath and Tennis Club and the Parker Playhouse in Fort Lauderdale.

He designed homes for the rich and famous — George Vanderbilt, Nicholas DuPont, Henry Ford II — as well as the no-so-rich. Over the years, his work encompassed Spanish, Italian, Classical, Oriental and British Colonial styles. He championed preservation, despised condominiums, and always looked back fondly on the splendor of the '20s.

"It was a happy era back then."

— HEATHER GRAULICH

Florida State Archives

McCarty arrives for his inauguration with his family in 1953.

DANIEL THOMAS McCARTY JR.

Jan. 18, 1912 — Sept. 28, 1953

Native son

As the first governor raised in southeast Florida, Daniel Thomas McCarty Jr. represented the dramatic power shift of the 1950s as the state became bottom heavy in population. But his tenure was brief.

The Fort Pierce citrus grower and cattleman came from a family that had been in the area 65 years. Calm but gregarious, McCarty was elected to the Florida House of Representatives at 24 and became the youngest-ever speaker at 29.

He landed at Normandy on D-Day and was an Army colonel at 33. In 1948, still in his 30s, he had a failed run for governor. Four years later, only 40, he won — the youngest governor in a half century.

The athlete, sportsman and horseman seemed perfect to lead a burgeoning state. His top platform: Restoring trust in a state where gambling was rampant and officials were linked to corruption.

But on Feb. 25, 1953, only seven weeks in office, McCarty suffered a heart attack. He died in September after seven months in office.

— ELIOT KLEINBERG

LAKE LYTAL

Aug. 26, 1906 — April 29, 1992

'What a public official should be'

While the rest of the South fought the unstoppable train that was civil rights, one simple act helped change Palm Beach County.

One weekend in the early '60s, county workers, summoned by then-Commissioner Lake Lytal, quietly came into the county courthouse and painted over signs at drinking fountains that said "white" and "colored."

Just like that, the county's offices were integrated.

"When everyone came to work on Monday, this miraculous change had occurred," Circuit Judge Marvin Mounts recalled.

Lytal served 32 years on the commission, longer than anyone.

"He set an example of what a public official should be all about," said his son, Lake Lytal Jr. "He was a champion of the little guy and felt the government should help people who needed to be helped."

Lytal moved from Louisiana at 12 in 1918 and graduated from Palm Beach High in 1924.

As a commissioner, he fought for zoning laws to control growth and the rights of women and minorities. In 1974, he became the first man in Palm Beach County to join the local chapter of the League of Women Voters. And he lobbied for recreational facilities.

"Every school campus should have a swimming pool," Lytal said in 1991. "Every park should have a swimming pool and a shuffleboard court. It makes me cringe every time I drive down Gun Club Road and see the millions of dollars they're spending on prisons, when they could probably spend half as much

114

on parks and playgrounds and do a lot more good. Nothing causes more trouble than a lack of something to do."

Lytal worked full time on the county commission in the days when the salary didn't encourage such devotion.

He and his wife, Ruth, a schoolteacher, lived in a modest home in Lake Clarke Shores.

With a drawl left over from his Louisiana childhood, he said he hated the wealthy who considered themselves above the regulations of others. In 1964, land baron John D. MacArthur lost a slander suit against Lytal, who had said a north county road project was going to unduly benefit MacArthur.

In 1975, Lake Lytal Park in West Palm Beach was named for him. Then 68, he leaped from the high-dive to celebrate.

"I'm 52 and people are just now starting to forget that I'm Lake Lytal's son," Lake Lytal Jr. said when his father died at 85 in 1992. More than 400 people came to the funeral.

"He was interested in those who could not fend for themselves," former Florida Senate President Phil Lewis eulogized. "Ethics in government he spelled out, and he lived it."

— ELIOT KLEINBERG

Palm Beach Post file photo

"He was interested in those who could not fend for themselves," former Florida Senate President Phil Lewis said.

A. O. KANNER
Nov. 2, 1893 — April 13, 1967

'Most respected judge' of the Treasure Coast

Abram Otto Kanner served in all three branches of government. But long-time lawyers in the Treasure Coast remember him best as the area's most influential judge and personal role model.

"He trained all the Treasure Coast lawyers of his time," said Senior Circuit Judge C.P. Trowbridge, and his time spanned nearly half a century. "He was the only judge in the Treasure Coast when I came to practice law in 1956, and he was the most respected and revered judge of the century."

Respected because Kanner was known throughout the state for his honesty; revered because he brooked no nonsense.

"He was like Judge Chillingworth," recalled Bill Oughterson, lifelong Stuart resident, attorney and friend of Kanner. "You stood up when he walked in a room, and you said 'Yes, sir' and 'No, sir.'"

Kanner was born in Sanford, and began his law practice in Jacksonville with John W. Martin, who would become governor of Florida and namesake of Martin County. When the county was formed in 1925, Gov. Martin appointed Kanner state attorney of the then-21st Judicial Circuit. The next year, Kanner was elected to the Florida House of Representatives, where he served until heading to the Florida Senate in 1935. In 1941, he became judge of what was then the 9th Judicial Circuit, serving the seven-county area that included Martin County.

Collection of Sandra Thurlow

A.O. Kanner in the 1930s, when he formed deep friendships with young lawyers such as T.T. Oughterson and Evans Crary.

Continued on next page

115

'Most respected judge' of the Treasure Coast

Continued from previous page

As a legislator, Kanner fought for roads. State Road 76, now the A.O. Kanner Highway, was the result of his effort to get good roads to the Glades. He also pushed for construction of Roosevelt Bridge, long the only one spanning the St. Lucie River in Stuart. His Kanner Act, which allowed Florida counties to use gas tax money to avoid bankruptcy, helped lift the state out of the Depression.

When Bill Oughterson's father, T.T., came to Stuart in 1925, he formed a kinship with Kanner, as did Evans Crary Sr., who arrived in 1927. (Crary became an influential state senator and Martin County attorney.) Kanner personally presided when "little Billy Oughterson" took the oath to become a lawyer in 1950.

"Before he got married (in 1949), Judge Kanner was a regular at breakfast at Chisholm's Restaurant on Federal Highway, which was *the* eating place back then," Oughterson recalled. "He would allow an attorney to get the court file and bring it to Chisholm's, and he would sign orders."

After Judge Kanner died, the Martin County Commission passed a resolution honoring him.

His good works, they said, "are a tribute to the principle that good government does not just happen but is the result of dedicated leadership."

— JAN TUCKWOOD

KAREN MARCUS

Born April 15, 1952

Palm Beach County commissioner, 1984 to present

Because in a land of transients, her managed-growth political philosophy is rooted in the fact that she has lived 42 of her 47 years in Palm Beach County.

Because after 15 years on the commission and the previous eight years as a commission aide, she has become the commission's institutional memory.

Because she has no intention of going to Tallahassee or Washington or anywhere else.

Because as a 5-foot-9½ 20-year-old with long legs and blond hair, she spent eight months modeling in New York City — and the next 20 years trying to live down what she calls the "modeling stigma."

Because she wore fake glasses for her first campaign in 1984 to look less like a model.

Because the modeling stigma was erased in 1992 when one of the most powerful figures in Palm Beach County — megadeveloper E. Llwyd Ecclestone Jr. — tried to topple her and her slow-growth views.

Because despite raising the scarlet M of modeling from Marcus' past, Ecclestone failed to oust her.

Because four years later, nobody ran against her and she got a $500 if-you-can't-beat-them-join-them contribution from Ecclestone.

Because her fingerprints are on virtually every significant local growth-control measure since the mid-1980s, plus $250 million worth of bond issues to buy environmentally sensitive lands and limit development in the Agricultural Reserve.

Because she was the driving force behind the Juno Pier and a key player in keeping spring training baseball in Palm Beach County.

Because she also stays determinedly close to home when venturing thoughts on her legacy: "I'm a local girl who tried to make her community a better place."

— GEORGE BENNETT

CLIFF BARNES

Born Aug. 11, 1956

St. Lucie County commissioner, 1992 to present

Because he ran for office as an environmentalist when his friends said he could never win on that platform. Eventually, more candidates followed him down the path of slower growth, changing the course of St. Lucie County politics.

Because he helped win the support of 67 percent of the voters for higher taxes to buy environmental lands when others said voters would never approve.

Because he challenged supporters of an industrial seaport and regional jetport to look at other quality-of-life issues.

Because he got fellow commissioners to limit future construction of high-rises on Hutchinson Island.

Because he thought growing up on North Hutchinson Island was boring, but he returned from college with a new appreciation and determination to preserve the county's water, and blue skies.

— JIM REEDER

The hometown commissioners

Karen Marcus on the $2.5 million Juno Beach Fishing Pier, which opened in January 1999, thanks to the work of tackle shop owner John Lott, who gathered signatures for a new pier, then went to the county commission. Marcus and fellow commissioners Warren Newell and Carol Roberts went to Tallahassee to lobby for the pier. The old Juno pier was blown down on Thanksgiving 1984.

Cliff Barnes at Spruce Bluff, a nature preserve west of Port St. Lucie that the county purchased.

117

RICHARD GRAULICH/Staff Photographer

Confronting the struggles of his small town

CLARENCE ANTHONY

Born Oct. 10, 1959

Mayor of South Bay, 1984 to present

Clarence Anthony outside City Hall. His son, Reidel, plays football for the Tampa Bay Buccaneers. "He is a tremendous source of pride for me," the mayor says.

By the time Clarence Anthony was elected mayor of South Bay, he had earned a master's in public administration, headed the Palm Beach County Housing Department and worked for both the South Florida Water Management District and the Treasure Coast Regional Planning Council.

He was only 24.

Last year, he celebrated his 40th birthday on a plane returning from one of the monthly meetings he makes as president of the National League of Cities.

But Anthony doesn't forget where he came from. He's the sixth child of migrant farmers who picked celery, beans and corn up the east coast. His first priority in office 15 years ago was better housing for farm workers. Second priority: Education.

The library in South Bay bears his name because he fought to bring it to his city. Education made the difference in his life, he tells students.

In 1994, Anthony faced his biggest challege when South Bay Growers closed its vegetable processing plant, putting 1,300 people out of work. Although the town of 4,000 had been lukewarm to the notion of a prison in town, it needed the jobs. Anthony persuaded state officials to build a prison.

Like his town, Anthony's a "survivor," he says. "I know what my blessings are."

— ANGIE FRANCALANCIA

118

Mr. Republican and Ms. Democrat

TOM LEWIS
Born Oct. 26, 1924

U.S. congressman,
1983 to 1995

He was "Mr. Republican" in northern Palm Beach County for more than 30 years — and he never lost an election.

Tom Lewis, a respected voice of moderation and compromise, began his political career in 1964 with his election to the North Palm Beach village council. In 1972, he moved up to the state House, eight years later was elected to the state Senate, and in 1983, he went to Washington to represent Palm Beach County and the Treasure Coast.

A veteran of both World War II and the Korean War, Lewis had been a gunner aboard a B-25 bomber. After a decade in the Air Force, Lewis moved to North Palm Beach to become an aircraft testing specialist for Pratt & Whitney.

He became an advocate for airline safety, helping to pass a series of bills forcing airlines and the Federal Aviation Administration to try to improve the survivability of plane crashes.

He never wanted to become a national leader, preferring to focus on issues important to the folks back home. One of those was the building of a Veterans Affairs Hospital in Riviera Beach. He also fought the Pentagon plans to eliminate a squadron of WC-130 planes — the "hurricane hunters" that provide data on storms.

"When I retired, I knew it was time to give someone else a chance to pick up the torch," he said. "Now I spend the time enjoying my wife and family, traveling and working on a few charity boards. I'm not too involved in politics anymore, but I'm glad I was able to do some good."

LOIS FRANKEL
Born May 16, 1948

Florida House of Representatives,
1986 to 1992, 1994 to present

Frankel's most important legislative mission: taking care of women and children.

She has been recognized repeatedly for her work in legislation involving AIDS, domestic abuse, sex education, school clinics, tougher laws against selling tobacco to children, abortion rights and the Healthy Families program.

She talked about reducing teen pregnancies and improving child care before those causes were fashionable.

When one group of child and family advocates honored her, they wrote: "She has taken on and won many of the most difficult and volatile issues in health care and social services."

She wins because she's persistent — even when she goes up against powerful lobbyists.

"People like me get reputations as hell on wheels or pit bulls because we will not sit down and be quiet," she said. "But I can't give up. I'm motivated to be the voice of people who can't afford to hire a gun. I always felt like I had this burning fire in me, always. It represents having to fight for justice, for the underdog."

Born in New York City, Frankel got her law degree from Georgetown University in 1973 and came to Florida in 1974 to work for the Palm Beach County Public Defenders Office. Now, she is a leader among House Democrats and, if the party takes control in 2000, she could become House speaker.

Her biggest reward: "Just being stopped in the hallway by somebody who says 'Thank you, thank you for fighting for me' or going to a day care and seeing the faces of the children. That's when I realize I've got to keep doing this. People are counting on me."

— Stories by BRIAN E. CROWLEY

BILLY BOWMAN

Third generation dairyman, 61, on his land west of Jupiter

*For 25 years, he has elevated the backwoods barbecue to a sophisticated money-raising vehicle,
parlaying grilled pork and black-eyed peas into thousands of dollars for charities and political candidates.
His cause is his land: He is one of the largest landowners in southern Palm Beach County, and he is among
the farmers in the county's Agricultural Reserve who want development rights that will raise the value
of their land. He sees development not as an end to agriculture, but as a vital source of cash
that will allow farmers like him to keep working the land — albeit somewhere else. "We'll go farther
up the line," he says. "Probably to Martin County." Though he's been behind the scenes in political deals,
he says he'll never run for office. Why? "Too many skeletons, and too many good times."*

'Cows, cash and condos'

A ndre Fladell describes the Palm Beach County political game of the 1980s with the three C's: Cows, cash and condos.

Rancher Billy Bowman, famous for his money-raising barbecues, represented the cowboys. Developer E. Llwyd Ecclestone Jr. (page 176) represented the cash. And chiropractor Fladell represented the condos.

"If cows could vote or cash could vote, they would have had control," Fladell said in 1999. "But condos could vote, so I did."

In Fladell's glory days in the mid-'80s, he claimed his South County Political Cooperative controlled 28,000 votes — and politicians believed him. The Palm Beach County commission actually signed a proclamation in 1985 declaring him "unofficial prince of Palm Beach County" — and he celebrated by getting a necklace of gold and pave diamonds that spells out "Prince Andre."

His idea of princely raiment is a T-shirt, denim shorts and sneakers. On formal occasions, such as a meeting with the attorney general of Florida, he makes sure the T-shirt has sleeves.

Fladell, representing what he called "quality of life and home," agitated so many developers with his anti-growth stance that one, the developer of Mission Bay west of Boca Raton, complained in 1988 that he "had to pray at the altar of Andre Fladell and the condos."

Fladell's monarchy was rocked in 1988 when a drive for single-member districts, initiated by businessmen seeking to contain the influence of Fladell and other south-county power brokers, passed. The Palm Beach County Commission went from a panel of five elected at large to a panel of seven, one from each district.

"Now cash can vote," Fladell mused in 1999.

Even though his clout isn't what it once was, candidates, commissioners and other operatives still call him regularly.

Also on their speed-dial: Murray Kalish, head of the United South County Democratic Club.

Central Casting could not have produced a more authentic-looking embodiment of that stock South Florida character, the condo commando.

Kalish's political saga is the story of late-20th century Palm Beach County Democratic politics: retiree (in his case, from the garment business) from up north (New York) is stirred from his quietude (in Delray Villas) by a nearby zoning petition (trailer homes for "wayward boys," as he recalls it). He fights, wins, takes on similar causes, builds power.

He built so much power that he runs the largest Democratic club in Palm Beach County, and politicians ask to be included in his coffee klatches. They also covet a spot on Kalish's election day "palm cards" — printed lists of his preferred candidates that go out to 60,000 voters each election day. The palm cards helped Robert Wexler topple incumbent Don Childers in a 1990 Democratic state Senate primary. Kalish helped Ron Klein beat incumbent Steve Press in a 1992 state House primary, and he helped Burt Aaronson defeat incumbent Carol Phillips in a 1992 county commission primary.

"If you ask, 'Would I rather have the endorsement of *The Palm Beach Post* or Murray Kalish?' I'd pick Murray Kalish," Wexler said in 1996.

— GEORGE BENNETT

ANDRE FLADELL

52-year-old chiropractor and kingpin of condo voters, pictured in his Delray Beach office.

His legacy: "Putting South County on an even measure with West Palm Beach. The person in the back row has to yell louder. We yelled louder."

MURRAY KALISH

Retiree and condo commando

"If you want to run for office in Palm Beach County, you must go to Murray Kalish early, among your very first calls," said state Rep. Suzanne Jacobs, D-Delray Beach. He is one of about a dozen senior citizens who play the political scene as if it were a chess board.

HARRY JOHNSTON III

Born Dec. 2, 1931

U.S. congressman, 1989-1997
Senate president, 1985-1986
Florida Senate member, 1974-1986

As a fifth-generation Floridian, he championed growth management: "I do not want South Florida to be another Southern California." He recalls the West Palm Beach of his youth as "a great small town. There were all these big theaters downtown, and downtown was very bustling. Everything west of West Palm Beach was still under water." His father, Col. Harry Johnston, a Palm Beach County attorney for 30 years, was a devout Christian Scientist and disciplinarian who expected his three children to excel in everything they did. "The colonel was something to be seen," Phil Lewis said of Harry's dad. "You talk about a dedicated public servant, he was it. Harry got his early training from that tough old man of his."

JERRY THOMAS

April 30, 1929 — July 29, 1980

Senate president, 1971-1972
Florida Senate member, 1965-1972

Born and raised in West Palm Beach, Thomas was "a man for all seasons," said Phil Lewis when Thomas died of cancer at 51. The banker-turned-politician wrote or co-sponsored hundreds of laws, including the Florida Sunshine Law. Today, the bridge from mainland Riviera Beach to Singer Island and a Jupiter elementary school are named for him.

PHIL LEWIS

Born Sept. 27, 1929

Senate president, 1979-1980
Florida Senate member, 1970-1980

"He's Christianity in action," says state Rep. Ed Healey, D-West Palm Beach. "He is deeply religious, but he doesn't wear it on his shoulder. He doesn't preach; he just lives that life." Former state Senate President Dempsey Barron put it another way: "Phil's strong as a bear's breath, but you wouldn't know it … He is so thoughtful and caring that he can bring you over to his side without having to be too mean to you. He's strong because he's philosophically so strong." Lewis, who has a Riviera Beach real estate office, credits his mother, Julia, for his upbeat demeanor: "My mother could look at the devil himself and say, 'He's got nice ear lobes.' A positive outlook pays off. I tell you, you continue to look at the best side of people, you're going to bring the best side out of them."

Deans of the Florida Senate

Because these three childhood friends from West Palm Beach dominated Florida politics from the mid-'60s through the mid-'80s.

Because Jerry Thomas was "probably the most significant environmental law-changer in the history of this state," according to Lewis. "He was years ahead of everybody else."

Because the first time Phil Lewis' son, Neil, saw his dad cry was the day Jerry Thomas died. "My father told me then," Neil said, " 'Don't ever be afraid to tell someone you love them.' "

Because the love these three lawmakers had for their hometown led them to make important changes: Thomas was known as Mr. Conservation because he helped stop the dumping of untreated sewage into Lake Worth. In 1970, Lewis launched the campaign to complete Palm Beach County's last stretch of Interstate 95. Governors, both Republicans and Democrats, called on him to be the peacemaker. He has served on dozens of education boards, including the Board of Regents. Johnston sponsored legislation to start the first Children's Services Council in the state and made sure it passed. During his Senate presidency, the Growth Management Act passed. In August 1999, President Clinton named him special envoy to the Sudan because of his role as chairman of the House Foreign Affairs African subcommittee.

Because when a new technology building was named for him at Palm Beach Community College's north campus, Lewis said, "The next building here should be named The Taxpayer. He has made a tremendous sacrifice to make education possible." And, when asked why he likes public service, Lewis replied: "I consider it fundamentally an honor to serve the public. I learned early on that one person can make a difference."

— JAN TUCKWOOD

Harry Johnston and Phil Lewis in front of the mariner statue at Phil Foster Park.
The statue once stood in front of Jerry Thomas' First Marine Bank.

CONNOR MORAN

April 27, 1990 — Feb. 21, 1992

The toddler's death from a brain tumor spurred his mother, Teri Moran, to start Connor Moran Children's Cancer Foundation.

CONNOR CRAY

Oct. 9, 1961 — May 19, 1988

Just before he died from AIDS, his uncle, Charlie Cray, raised money to start Connor's Nursery for babies with AIDS.

The two Connors

In a world with too few heroes, here are two: Teri Moran and Charlie Cray.

Strangers, really. Except each loved a boy named Connor, who came in and out of their lives, touched their souls and changed them forever.

Teri Moran's second baby, Connor, was diagnosed with a brain tumor when he was just 8 months old. He hung on for another 14 months, long enough to learn to laugh and crawl and give his family a love they will forever cherish.

After Connor died in 1992, Moran knew she couldn't sit and do nothing. So she took her grief and her pain, and she started the Connor Moran Children's Cancer Foundation to help mothers like her. Today, the West Palm Beach-based foundation has an annual budget of $250,000 and helps more than 150 families a year with everything from paying the electric bill to accepting the emotional panic of loving and living with a dying child. From baby Connor came this good that families rely on day after day,

month after month, year after year.

And then there's Charlie Cray. Cray's life-changing loss came in 1986, when he found out that his nephew — his happy, healthy, go-get-'em nephew — had AIDS. Connor Cray was 24 and engaged to be married when he was diagnosed with HIV.

Just before Connor's death in 1988, Charlie Cray, a financial adviser from Tequesta, got drafted to sit on the board at The Children's Place, a local social service agency. And that's when he heard about the nursery they wanted to start, the nursery for babies with AIDS.

"What's the hold-up?" Cray remembers asking.

"Money," they told him.

The next day, Charlie Cray showed up with a check from his brother, his sister and himself. He won't say how much, but it was enough to get things rolling.

Connor's Nursery, the loving place named after a grown man who died too soon, celebrated its 10th anniversary in February 2000.

— EMILY J. MINOR

KIMBERLY BERGALIS
Jan. 19, 1968 — Dec. 8, 1991

'She left behind courage'

— sister Allison Bergalis

Kimberly Bergalis became a national symbol of the AIDS crisis. She was the first person believed to have contracted the AIDS virus from a health professional — her dentist, Dr. David Acer.

"If it can happen to me, it can happen to anyone," the 23-year-old Fort Pierce woman had said. "If I can save one person, I won't die in vain."

Acer removed two of Bergalis' molars in December 1987 and later two wisdom teeth. The University of Florida student became sick in March 1989. Acer died of AIDS-related cancer in September 1990.

Bergalis was not part of any high-risk group. Genetic tests concluded it was a 99.4 percent certainty that Acer had given her the virus.

The Bergalis family won a $999,999 settlement against Acer's insuror, CNA Insurance Co., and an undisclosed amount from CIGNA Dental Health of Florida, which had referred Bergalis to Acer.

In her last public act, 70-pound Kimberly took a 20-hour train ride to Washington to urge lawmakers to pass an AIDS testing bill named after her. It never made it out of committee, but Kimberly changed medicine.

"No one will forget this case," said Dr. Harold Jaffe of the Centers for Disease Control and Prevention's AIDS division. "We are going to practice medicine differently because of this case."

— PAUL LOMARTIRE

This painting, which hangs at Boca Raton Community Hospital, shows Debbie Drummond (left) and her brother Randy (third from left), who died when they drank poison. Also pictured are brother Bobby and sister Robin.

DEBBIE AND RANDY DRUMMOND

Born Dec. 25, 1952 and Aug 17, 1958
Died April 21, 1962

From tragedy, 'a miracle'

The people who made Boca Raton Community Hospital "the Miracle on Meadows Road" created a monument to two little children. If the hospital has a second name, it's Debbie-Rand, the name of the foundation that started it a generation ago and the league that has raised more than $16 million to support it.

But who were Debbie and Rand? Debra Ann Drummond, 9, and James Randall Drummond, 3, children of developer Robert Drummond, were victims of one of Palm Beach County's most disturbing crimes: They drank poison that their 11-year-old neighbor later confessed to disguising as milk and sneaking into their refrigerator.

In Boca Raton, then a town of 10,000, the nearest hospital was Bethesda Memorial in Boynton Beach. A closer hospital may not have made a difference, but the community rallied. One of every three city residents gave money to open Boca Raton Community Hospital. Robert Drummond died at 58 in 1989, in the hospital his family's tragedy inspired. Mother Gloria Drummond is still active in the hospital's foundation.

— ELIOT KLEINBERG

TIMER POWERS

Aug. 9, 1936 — May 21, 1992

'The very best of what it is to be human'

People loved Timer Powers.

The easy-going Indiantown resident, who gets the credit for rules limiting Martin County building heights to four stories, was a lifelong defender of the environment. As a Martin County commissioner and water management board member, he helped settle the Everglades pollution lawsuit and helped the Seminoles secure water rights in the Everglades.

But government service wasn't why people loved Powers, who died of cancer at 55.

Powers made people feel good about themselves and each other. His own simple, humble kindness brought out those qualities in others.

"He was the very best of what it is to be human," former Martin County Commissioner Maggy Hurchalla said when Powers died in 1992. "He was our hero. He was our friend. And it will always be a kinder place because he was here."

Other friends called Powers an extraordinary Christian and a man who worked behind the scenes to bring people together. Beloved by the Seminoles and Miccosukees, he also had credibility with farmers and ranchers and easily made friends with new residents. He sparked a spirit of cooperation among the most diverse groups.

He had deep feelings for South Florida's natural wonders, particularly the waters and the wildlife.

"The little creeks and the rivers and the waterways have no voice. I think of myself as their voice. I speak for the waters," he said.

"There's not that many people representing the critters, and if we fail to represent those who can't represent themselves, either nature or people, then we have failed."

— SALLY D. SWARTZ

MAGGY HURCHALLA

Born Dec. 11, 1940

Earth Mother

Martin County commissioner, 1974 to 1994

Because she took politicians and reporters skinny-dipping the night voters approved a bond issue to save Martin County's ocean beaches.

Because she's a grandmother extraordinaire, a mom who still brags about her grown children, a supportive sister to U.S. Attorney General Janet Reno and their brothers.

Because she shaped Martin County's "good nature" in 20 years as a county commissioner, keeping the beaches public, creating a program to buy lands for conservation and writing the county's comprehensive growth management plan.

Because her face still lights up when she talks about Jim, her husband of 38 years, or Jane Wood Reno, her charismatic, colorful mother, a journalist who died in 1992.

Because she revels in exotic travel experiences: riding solo on trains around Switzerland, hopping off to explore strange cities; meeting New Guinea's naked natives, climbing a mountain in Hawaii by herself, scuba diving on Australia's Great Barrier Reef.

Because she organizes spur-of-the-moment St. Lucie River Canoe trips on nights the moon is full.

Because she'll swap comfort for adventure, accepting wet sleeping bags, monster mosquitoes and getting lost on an adventure in the Everglades wilderness waters.

Because she seldom complains about the strength-sapping illness that invaded her lungs while she worked in a "sick" building and won't let it zap her zest for life.

Because she is 6-feet-1 in her bare feet and doesn't slouch.

Because she's a fighter, serving on the Rivers Coalition, an "odd bedfellows" group of businessmen and environmentalists united to clean up area rivers.

Because she is very, very bright but doesn't talk down to anyone.

Because she tells wonderful stories, some of which are true.

— SALLY D. SWARTZ

*Hurchalla's qualifications for being a politician:
"You should like people. You should be able to take stands. And you need to like what you see when you look in the mirror in the morning." Her mother instilled in her a love of nature (she's pictured here on Hutchinson Island) and decency. "My mother disliked respectability," she said, "but she absolutely demanded you do the right thing."*

Rosa Durando outside the South Florida Water Management District office in West Palm Beach, where she spends much of her time.

ROSA DURANDO
Born July 1, 1926

A crusader in tennis shoes

Those who mistake Rosa Durando for just another retiree in tennis shoes do so at their peril.

For two decades, she has been the agitator at the microphone before local governments and, of course, the South Florida Water Management District, which controls no less than the drinking water and flood control for more than 6 million people.

Her platform: Control growth.

The Brooklyn native, a former horse trainer, "retired" with her late husband to a training farm west of Boynton Beach after she flew off a horse and broke her back in the late 1950s.

When she spotted trucks that didn't belong in her neck of the Boynton woods, she became an environmental gadfly.

"We followed them, (and) there was a big drag line raising huge piles of shell rock," Durando said. She and neighbors went to the county, which criminally charged the company for carving the landscape without a permit.

"We won the case," she said, "believe it or not."

Since then, Durando has filed 18 other legal challenges to growth in Palm Beach County and run twice — unsuccessfully — for the Palm Beach County Commission, in 1988 and 1990. This year, some former water management board members urged her to apply for an appointment to the board, but she failed to get the appointment. Her response: "I'm not going anywhere."

Florida, she said, "has some of the best state (environmental) law in the country. It's just that nobody enforces them."

Durando believes the environmental forces are losing: "We have less land to play with, less natural resources, less species to protect."

So Durando keeps fighting.

Her car bumper sports this sticker: "Leaving Florida? Take a Developer."

— ELIOT KLEINBERG

ARTHUR RAYMOND MARSHALL
March 2, 1919 — Feb. 18, 1985

Voice of the Everglades

Biologist, naturalist, lecturer, writer and philosopher Arthur R. Marshall is hailed as the father of Florida's environmental movement. The Loxahatchee National Wildlife Refuge is named for him.

"He predicted the horrible things that were going to happen to us, and time after time, he was proved right," Hobe Sound environmentalist Nat Reed said when Marshall died of cancer at 65 in 1985 at his retirement home near Palatka.

Marshall's love of nature sprang from his boyhood. In 1925, when he was 6, his family moved to West Palm Beach, where he lived until he was 12 and spent many hours fishing in Lake Worth.

The biologist was a voice in the wilderness as far back as 1955, when he began 15 years with the U.S. Fish and Wildlife Service before becoming a University of Miami professor. He even had his own "Marshall Plan" — a blueprint for repairing the Kissimmee River-Lake Okeechobee-Everglades system that evolved into the Save Our Everglades program.

His belief: Overdevelopment is killing Florida.

Marshall suggested measures some called Draconian, others visionary. One water agency memo called him "a fanatic."

"Growth should be stopped rather than managed or controlled," Marshall once said. "In the same way a lake can have too much nutrients in it . . . and a farm can have too much fertilizer on it, a city can have too many people in it."

He helped establish Biscayne National Park and expand Indian River County's Pelican Island National Wildlife Refuge, first in the nation, from 3 to 750 acres. He helped stop the Cross-Florida Barge Canal. He wrote the 1969 report that helped kill a jetport planned for the heart of the Everglades and an expressway to serve it. That move led to establishment of the Big Cypress National Preserve.

"Art and Marjory Stoneman Douglas were the people who were way ahead of most of us in appreciating the values of the Everglades," then-Gov. Bob Graham said in 1984. "Marshall and Douglas saw the Everglades as the heart of South Florida. They realized we were pinching off the arteries and valves that made the heart function."

— ELIOT KLEINBERG

Bean Backus got his nickname from a friend, who called him Beanpot. Others called him "Beanie," but he preferred "Bean." At right, his oil painting Florida Landscape, *which was done in 1970.*

The A.E. "Bean" Backus Gallery & Museum

Capturing Florida's magic

When people talk about A.E. "Bean" Backus today, it's clear that they loved the man and his self-effacing generosity as much as his images of Florida — natural scenes so seductively real you want to jump through the canvas and amble along a palm-lined river.

Backus, a Fort Pierce native, is revered nationwide as the best painter of Florida landscapes. His estimated 5,000 works inspired countless imitators.

River of Grass, a mural that hangs in the Metro-Dade Commission chambers and is one of his most prominent works, would sell for at least $100,000 now, longtime friend and manager Don Brown estimated.

Born on the west bank of the Indian River, the subject of many of his works, Backus analyzed his surroundings: the way light changed the hibiscus and poinciana; the ragged, wild, wind-stirred look of palm fronds atop bowed,

ALBERT ERNEST BACKUS

Jan. 3, 1906 — June 6, 1990

spindly trunks.

"He brings almost scientific accuracy to his creative product that I don't think I have ever seen," said Kathleen Frederick, director of the A.E. "Bean" Backus Gallery & Museum in Fort Pierce.

He used his earnings, which sagged before skyrocketing in the 1960s, to put kids through school and support a wide range of nonprofit groups. Meanwhile, Backus walked around in Kmart shoes, dime-store shirts and cheap, polyester pants. His credo on philanthropy: "You have to give away $10 for $1 to do any good."

His always-open studio lured a melting pot of people, often giddy at the promise of his bull sessions on everything — literature, politics, religion. Haitian immigrants showed up on shore and Bean let them stay at his place, sometimes for a month.

Longtime friend Alto "Bud" Adams said Backus "painted it just like it was," creating a still frame of native Florida.

But Backus wouldn't prefer fame, or even his paintings, as the brushstrokes of his legacy, Brown said.

"What he really wanted to go down for was his kindness."

— THOMAS R. COLLINS

130

A genius of the South

ZORA NEALE HURSTON
Jan. 7, 1891 — Jan. 28, 1960

"You jump at de sun," Miss Zora's mother told her, and she did, she surely did.

Zora Neale Hurston wrote with passion and poetry and humor about the joys and turmoils of blacks living and dying far beyond the main roads of Central Florida. She rose to prominence, was gradually ostracized by her own people and died destitute in Fort Pierce, only to be reborn in the only way an artist can be — through her work.

"I was born in a Negro town. I do not mean by that the black backside of an average town. Eatonville, Florida, is and was at the time of my birth, a pure Negro town — charter, mayor, town marshal and all."

The tiny town of Eatonville, about 10 miles north of Orlando, embodies the atmosphere of rural Central Florida: Spanish moss dripping off the oaks, untended orange trees, houses made of concrete block, a church every three blocks.

In 1921, she published her first short story. She was 30, but, like most storytellers, an innate fabulist; she chopped 10 years off her age, making herself out to be a veritable literary prodigy. In 1925, she moved to New York, landing smack in the middle of the Harlem Renaissance.

She won literary prizes but earned little money. The novelist Fannie Hurst hired her as a secretary. *Their Eyes Were Watching God,* published in 1937, is Zora's finest book, a portrait of Janie Crawford, her three marriages and her rocky path to independence. (It's obvious Alice Walker used it as a matrix for *The Color Purple.*)

Zora didn't portray the characters as victims of life. Rather, she celebrated them, creating a world of rural blacks who, despite their marginal social position, acted freely, enjoyed their lives and their heritage.

But Zora's books never sold very well. In 1950, a *Miami Herald* writer tracked her down and found she was working as a maid. She told him that she was temporarily written out and was only working as a domestic to "shift gears."

In October 1959, Zora had a stroke. She died the following January, in a segregated Fort Pierce nursing home. There was no money, none at all. A collection was taken up among her friends and the few people in publishing who remembered her to pay for a funeral. There wasn't enough left for a headstone.

It had all seemed to come to dust for Miss Zora. Her four novels were out of print, as were the rest of her books. Then, with time, things changed. A black writer, a black female writer who could really write? Miss Zora's time had finally come.

In 1973, Alice Walker paid for a marker for Zora's grave. It reads:

"Zora Neale Hurston
A Genius of the South
1901-1960
Novelist, Folklorist, Anthropologist"

Correct in every detail — except for the birthdate.

Zora Neale Hurston is now a cultural icon. And that would be fine with Miss Zora, for she took the long view: "When the consciousness we know as life ceases, I know that I shall still be part and parcel of the world. I was part before the sun rolled into shape and burst forth in the glory of change. I was, when the earth was hurled out from its fiery rim. I shall return to the earth to Father Sun, and still exist in substance when the sun has lost its fire, and disintegrated in infinity to perhaps become a part of the whirling rubble in space. Why fear? The stuff of my being is matter, ever changing, ever moving, but never lost. ..."

— SCOTT EYMAN

OUR GOOD SAMARITAN:
In 1914, the only hospital for patients in the West Palm Beach area was a five-room cottage on Third Street near the FEC tracks. The original Good Samaritan Hospital building was completed in 1920, and the Delphine Dodge Memorial Hall (above) was added as an isolation ward in 1921. This is how Good Sam looked in 1940 (right) when it had a bed capacity of 122.

MILLIE GILDERSLEEVE
1858 — Feb. 16, 1950

Midwife to generations

Millie Gildersleeve, a freed slave from Georgia, may have been the first permanent black resident of what is now Palm Beach County. She was midwife to many of its pioneers.

Millie came to the "Lake Worth region" in 1876 with the Dimick family. She married M.J. "Jake" Gildersleeve (1857-1931) on the lawn of Cap Dimick's Palm Beach home, and in 1890, Dimick deeded her waterfront property for her home in what is now Riviera Beach.

Around 1886, she became a midwife to Richard Potter, the area's first doctor. When it was time for a pioneer baby to be born, Richard Potter would sail up to Millie's wharf, toot his whistle, and Millie would scurry out with her instruments.

Millie raised five children of her own and later worked for Russell Hopkins, grandfather of current West Palm Beach lawyer Randolph Hopkins. She died of cancer at 92 in February 1950. Many of her descendants — and the descendants of the babies she delivered — still live in West Palm Beach.

— ELIOT KLEINBERG

Millie Gildersleeve's waterfront property is now the site of Perry Oceanographics. Her great-granddaughter, Pansy L. Hobbs Harper, raised 12 children in West Palm Beach. She died in February 2000.

CLEM C. BENTON
Aug. 24, 1898 — May 3, 1982

House calls and caring

Dr. Clem C. Benton dispensed medicine and wisdom to black families along the Treasure Coast for half a century. He made house calls from Indian River County to Martin County and as far west as Okeechobee, sometimes accepting fruit, vegetables or ice cream as payment.

"He was just a man who had love and compassion for the people," said Helen Barr, who worked as his nurse for 42 years.

Benton grew up in Sanford, earned his medical degree from Nashville's Meharry Medical College in 1929 and opened his practice in Fort Pierce later that year.

He married Arlena Howard, a young history teacher from Alabama, and the couple had three children. After his wife died in 1942, he reared his children alone, taking time to have lunch at home with them every day.

"He was a good family man," said his daughter Margaret Benton, a Fort Pierce attorney.

Benton kept his office open late so patients could stop by after work. Early in his career, he would walk from his Eighth Street office, black medical bag in hand, to make house calls. He later made his rounds by car. He vaccinated hundreds of schoolchildren for free and waited on the sidelines of Lincoln Park Academy football games to treat the injured Greyhounds. In the 1930s, he helped found the Fort Pierce Memorial Hospital.

— LADY HEREFORD

"He was just a man who had love and compassion for the people," said Helen Barr, a nurse for Dr. Clem Benton for 42 years.

133

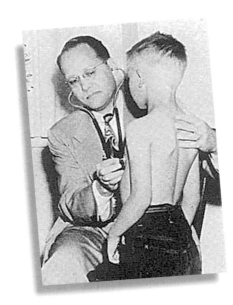

Brumback has spent 50 years improving public health.

C. L. BRUMBACK

Born April 19, 1914

The people's doctor

To measure Dr. C. L. "Carl" Brumback's influence, look at these numbers:

One decade ago, only 40 percent of the county's 7-month-old infants were immunized; today, 98 percent are. Ten years ago, 20 percent of Palm Beach County's pregnant women received no prenatal care; today, only 3 percent don't.

In the past three decades, the life expectancy here has risen by 10 years.

Brumback, Palm Beach County's first public health doctor, has spent nearly 50 years improving life for a diverse and growing population. In 1950, the young doctor tooled down the slick muck roads to the Glades in his Nash station wagon, determined to care for some 55,000 migrant workers.

By 1951, Brumback had identified 56 health hazards in Palm Beach County. Pollution was No. 1. "Raw sewage was being dumped into Lake Worth. The gas coming off Lake Okeechobee would tarnish silverware," he said in 1998. He photographed the horrendous conditions to sway public sympathy.

At 85, he still goes to the office on Evernia Street every day to run the public health residency program that has been copied around the country.

"He was a true innovator," said Dr. Jean Malecki, the health department's director, who was hired by Brumback 15 years ago. "He was ahead of his time with many of his ideas."

Brumback was among the first to enlist nutritionists and social workers to create a total wellness plan for migrant workers. His philosophy: Every dollar spent in prevention can save thousands in treatment.

"I would often be asked who it is I work for. Is it the state, the county or the federal government?" he said. "I tell them I work for the people. The people."

— DAN MOFFETT

Because the former pediatric intern and the nursing student — who met in the pediatric ward at Duke University in 1958 and got married the next year — didn't think raising three daughters was demanding enough. They opened their West Palm Beach home and their hearts to a dozen foster children, nearly all with serious health problems, and never failed to give those children all the love and attention they gave their own.

Because they set such an example of care and selflessness that they were named the region's child advocates of the year by the Children's Home Society in 1983. Because they still make time to chaperone safety patrol trips to Washington, D.C.

Because he stayed with the patients and community that depended on him for more than 30 years in the same office in Lake Worth, and made all parents believe their children were his favorites. "He always made plenty of time to talk to you," recalls Gladys Van Otteren, a childhood patient who, like many, came back with her own children. "He was always very gentle, always treating your problem like it was the most important thing on his mind."

Because he was never too busy tinkering with his Model T to change a diaper, or diagnose an illness.

Because she loved helping children so much during her years as head pediatric nurse at JFK Medical Center and later as director of services at The Children's Place that she leaped at the chance to start Connor's Nursery for kids with HIV in 1990. Because she ached when more than 40 of those kids died in the next 10 years but never quit helping the rest find as much joy as possible for as long as they lived.

Because she stayed as volunteer and board member after retiring as director of services in 1993 and nurse in 1997 to find her own joy in the development of drugs that are giving these children longer, healthier lives. "People think Connor's Nursery is a sad place to work," she said. "It isn't. It's a very happy place. Our mission is to give children the very best life possible while they're with us. I don't know why, but these children seem to be especially affectionate children."

— DOUGLAS KALAJIAN

'Florida is supposed to be a place where no one stays put, but we had patients who grew up, got married and came back with their own children. I think that says something.' — *Isaac Marcadis*

Album of the Late 20th Century

Gentle hearts

DR. ISAAC MARCADIS

Born Nov. 9, 1931

Pediatrician at The Children's Clinic
in Lake Worth, 1964 to 1996

BETH MARCADIS

Born Feb. 3, 1936

Pediatric nurse, retired

Dr. Isaac Marcadis and his wife, Beth, with some of the children he's cared for over the years. From left: Gladys Van Otteren and her kids Thomas and Bridget, Mrs. Marcadis, Dr. Marcadis, Alexander Van Otteren, Morgan Farrell, Andrew and John Van Otteren, Jake Farrell and Sherry Farrell (mom of Morgan and Jake).

ALEXANDER W. DREYFOOS JR.
Born March 22, 1932

The creative scientist

Because he's a self-made man. A New York native, Dreyfoos grew up under the most middle-class of circumstances — his father was a theatrical photographer — and struggled to pay his way through Massachusetts Institute of Technology, where he attended college. "I started my business in the basement of my home in 1963," he says of Photo Electronics, the company he founded with his late partner, George Mergens, and later moved to Palm Beach County.

Because he's a bit of a geek — and he's not ashamed to admit it. "If you had known me in the 1970s, I was much more comfortable in front of my oscilloscope with a soldering iron in my hand."

Because he's a visionary in more ways than one. As an engineer, he was the brains behind the Video Color Negative Analyzer, a machine that brought clarity and control to color photography. As an arts patron, he led the 14-year, $67 million campaign to build the 2,200-seat Kravis Center, which opened debt-free in 1992. And as an aspiring media mogul, he bought WEAT-Channel 12, a station once run out of a trailer, and turned it into a powerful and profitable CBS affiliate, WPEC. As he likes to say, he didn't want to be seen as a one-trick pony. "Singer never did more than a sewing machine, and Hoover never did more than a vacuum. What were the chances of my doing something else?" Pretty good, it turns out.

Because, unlike Burt Reynolds, he has an Oscar. He won it in 1971 for technical achievement.

Because he's a believer in a community for all. At WPEC, he was the first local TV executive to hire a black reporter. "Boy, did I catch a lot of grief from a lot of people," he recalls. At the Kravis Center, he pushed for programs for minorities, schoolchildren and senior citizens.

Because he's generous. When Photo Electronics was barely making money, he contributed $1 million to launch the Kravis campaign. Since selling WPEC for $164 million in 1996, he's made a series of $1 million-and-up gifts to MIT, Kravis and Palm Beach County School of the Arts (now the Dreyfoos School).

Because he knows how to have a good time. He flies his own plane and helicopter, races sailboats and scuba dives. He designed the home theater in his Palm Beach mansion — his "toy room," as he calls it. And enter the office of his West Palm Beach-based private capital management firm, the Dreyfoos Group, and you'll see poster-size versions of the breathtaking pictures he's taken in his travels, proving that his love of photography extends beyond the technical.

Because, in the end, even scientists just want to have fun.

— CHARLES PASSY

Chairman of the Kravis Center
for the Performing Arts, 1982 to present

Co-founder of Photo Electronics Corp.

Former owner of WPEC TV-Channel 12
(which he bought from John D. MacArthur
in 1973 for $3.5 million and sold
in 1996 for $164 million)

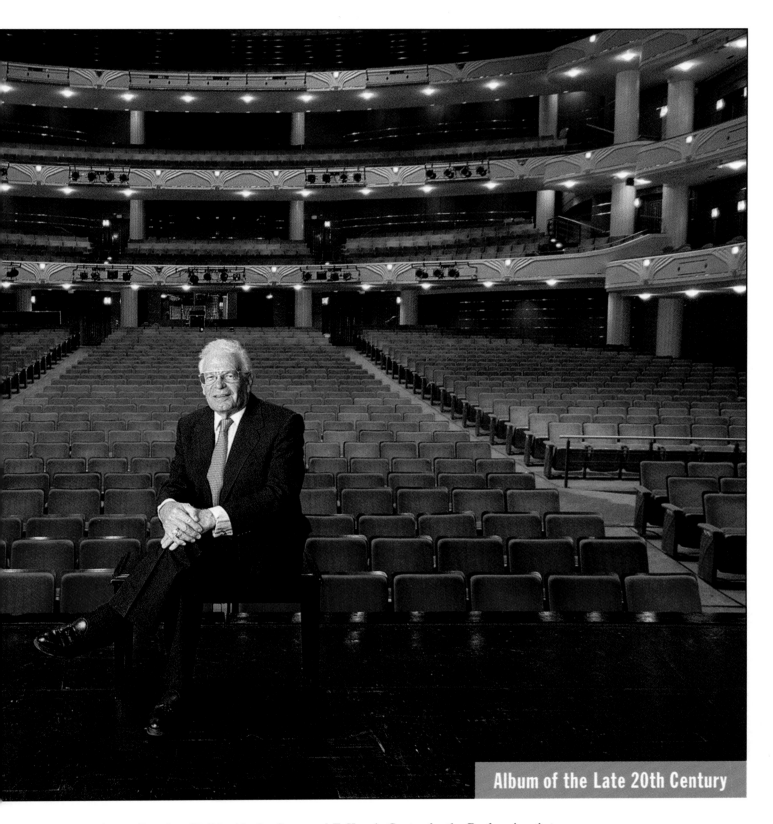

*Alex Dreyfoos at Dreyfoos Hall inside the Raymond F. Kravis Center for the Performing Arts.
The $55 million venue opened in September 1992. Dreyfoos Hall boasts 2,193 seats,
a 100-foot-high dome and dramatic red interior, plus a stage fit for the finest productions,
from ballet to Broadway. Dreyfoos and his wife, Carolyn, gave the largest single donation
to the Kravis Center: $5 million in 1998.*

Album of the Late 20th Century

Founder of Perry Oceanographics, which designs submarines and propulsion systems made from liquid hydrogen, and Energy Fartners, which is developing energy cells and power packs for cars and homes.

Former owner of more than two dozen newspapers (including *The Palm Beach Post*), radio stations and cable TV networks. He still owns two newspapers in the Bahamas.

Perry was inspired to build submarines while on a fishing trip in the Bahamas in the 1950s, and he launched Perry Ocean-ographics to build subs in 1960. In this 1989 photograph, Perry pilots his company's open submersible sub off the island he owns in the Bahamas, Lee Stocking Island.

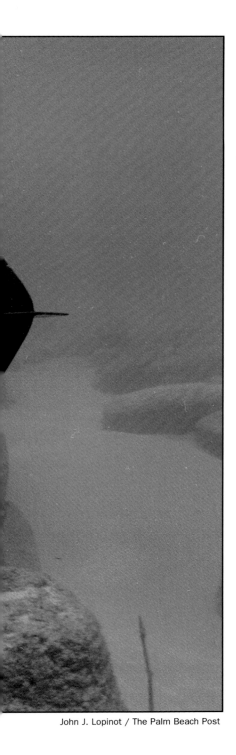

John J. Lopinot / The Palm Beach Post

Perry at Energy Partners, where scientists build power packs to fuel electric cars. "These are not batteries. They create energy from outside sources; batteries make energy from within."

The entrepreneur

JOHN H. PERRY JR.

Born Jan. 2, 1917

Because he was the son of influential and wealthy parents, but he never coasted. In fact, he became a man of many titles — engineer, pilot, businessman, publisher, inventor — and used his gifts and his wits to create for himself an even richer life.

Because in his 20s, after piloting B-17 and B-25 bombers in World War II, he went into the family newspaper business. When his father died in 1953 he took charge and expanded the business into radio and TV.

Because at age 82 he's still in business — his sixth enterprise. His interests range from newspaper publishing to marine biology to energy efficiency.

Because he and his companies have held more than two dozen patents.

Because his three-decade-long fight for a national dividend moved powerful members of both political parties to look upon deficit spending with new perspective.

Because his outlook sets an example for all: "I'm so busy having fun doing my work I don't need to take time off to have fun."

Because he never stopped trying to turn new ideas into reality. In the 1950s and '60s he introduced computer typeset-

ting to his 28 family-owned newspapers, including *The Palm Beach Post.* He saw the power of TV and bought his first station in 1953, in Jacksonville. He moved into cable TV on the ground floor.

Because his interest in undersea exploration led him to design a deep-diving submarine for marine research and salvage. And his love of the undersea ecology led him to open the Caribbean Marine Research Center on Lee Stocking Island in the Bahamas.

Because at the start of the new century he can be found at his latest enterprise, Energy Partners, designing power packs for electric cars.

Because it's been a long journey from the 2,600-acre Perry family farm in Kentucky, where Perry's father once plowed hillsides with mules and planted corn, to Palm Beach. "I was a little boy looking out the window of a train as it crossed over into Palm Beach in 1925. The Breakers hotel was still smoldering after burning down. That was a long time ago, wasn't it?" asks Perry. "And we've come a long way, Florida and America."

Because the prospects of a long journey did not deter John Perry. "I'd leave you with this thought," he said. "Study everything. History. The Western tradition of thought. Explore. Think. Add something to your community, to your life. And have fun."

— PAUL REID

CLEMATIS STREET: *At right, Anthony's in West Palm Beach during the boom-era 1920s.*

IN PALM BEACH: *Below, The Royal Poinciana Hotel boasted many fine shops, including Anthony's and Greenleaf & Crosby Jewelers, which also had a store at the Palm Beach Inn (the future Breakers hotel) and is still doing business on Worth Avenue.*

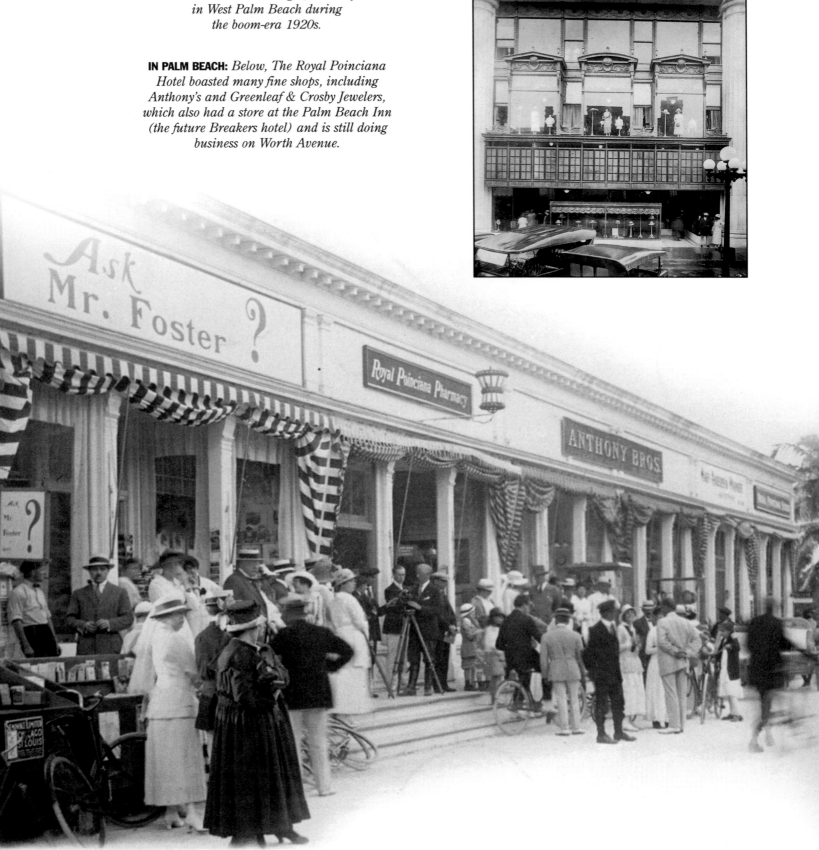

Emile D. Anthony   *A.P. 'Gus' Anthony*

THE ANTHONY BROTHERS

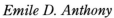

Changing with the fashions

The height of high-society fashion for men 100 years ago was the "Poinciana Uniform" — a navy sport coat, white pants, white shoes and a straw boater.

The outfit, still in style, was popularized by the Anthony brothers, who opened their first store in West Palm Beach in 1895 and also had a store in Henry Flagler's Royal Poinciana Hotel.

A.P. "Gus" Anthony was a born merchant, his daughter, Roslyn Anthony Anderson, recalled in 1994. "When his mother sent him to the store for black thread and the store didn't have any, he came back with brown thread. He knew how to solve a problem."

When his first West Palm Beach store — a jewelry business — went belly up after the 1895 freeze, Gus decided he'd never sell frivolous things again, just life's necessities, such as clothing. He started Anthony's department store with his older brother, J. Rembert, later that year. Younger brother Emile D. took over in 1914, and he ran 12 stores during the boom years.

He passed the business on to his sons. One of them, Carl, also started Anthony's Groves. Anthony's president now is Pope Anthony, son of M. Pope ("Ham") Anthony and grandson of Emile. They have 10 stores from Vero Beach to Boynton Beach and west to Naples.

Today's customer: The over-50 woman who's more interested in practicality than high society.

— JAN TUCKWOOD

WILLIAM BURDINE, FOUNDER OF THE FLORIDA STORE:

When William S. Burdine's Polk County citrus crop was wiped out by the 1895 freeze, he and a partner opened a dry goods store in Bartow. In 1896, Burdine bought out his partner and sent his son, John, to the tiny fishing village of Miami. (He skipped West Palm Beach because the Anthony family had the retail market cornered there.) The Burdines moved their operations to Miami in 1898, and the first Burdines opened on Clematis Street in West Palm Beach in 1925. That store closed during the Depression, but in 1941, Burdines bought out the Hatch's store at Olive and Clematis streets. In 1979, Burdines left downtown West Palm Beach and moved to the Palm Beach Mall. Today, Burdines boasts 50 department stores and more than $1 billion in annual sales — but no members of the Burdines family. The chain is owned by Federated.

Historical Society of St. Lucie County

RAULERSON STORE: *Most of the groceries and retail stores in the early days were family affairs, such as the Raulerson store on Second Street in Fort Pierce. Other long-time family businesses: Lainhart & Potter lumber company and Tylander's lumber company, Cater's Furniture, Sewell's Hardware and the J.C. Harris Co. in West Palm Beach. Family department stores that lasted for years included Rubin's in Fort Pierce, Fountain's in Lake Worth, Raulerson's in Okeechobee and Greene's in Stuart.*

STUART LANDMARK: *On May 15, 1901, George W. Parks purchased property in downtown Stuart and built the landmark Feed Store, originally the George W. Parks Sr. Grocery and General Merchandise Store. From this store, Parks introduced Gulf Oil products to the locals. The Stuart Feed Store is one of the few false-front store buildings in the wood frame vernacular style remaining in South Florida. It now houses the Stuart Heritage Museum, 161 S.W. Flagler Ave. in Stuart.*

STUART DEPARTMENT STORE:
Max and Florence Auerbach and their family ran the Stuart Department Store for nearly 50 years. Florence came to Stuart in 1938 with her father, Oscar Kanarek, to run the store (then called Kitching and Eckess). She married Max in 1946, and with Oscar and Florence's brother, Irving, they ran the store at St. Lucie and Flagler streets until 1984. The building is now an engineering firm.

143

DELRAY BEACH'S MAIN STREET, 1940s: *Atlantic Avenue's hip again after losing several long-time businesses by the 1980s. Among those leaving: Ocean City Lumber (1921), replaced by a blues bar and shopping area. J.H. Cousins Dress Shop, now a sportswear chain outlet. Ken's & Hazel's diner moved to Pineapple Grove after four decades, then closed after a fire. A. George & Sons, which sold men's clothing on East Atlantic Avenue since 1911. Ken's Barber Shop moved off the avenue after 46 years to make way for a sandwich shop but reopened on Federal Highway just south of Atlantic. The Masons left town after 90 years, their offices replaced by an advertising agency and Japanese restaurant. Not leaving: Hand's Office Supply, founded by pioneer Lauren C. Hand in 1934, and the Colony Hotel, Hubers Drug Store, Mercer-Wenzel department store, Ernie's restaurant and bar and J.B. Smith and Sons jewelers.*

Museum of the City of Lake Worth

GROCERIES AND GOLF: *Drink half-and-half in your coffee? You can thank the same man who brought a municipal golf course to Lake Worth: W. A. Boutwell Sr. (pictured in knickers at golf course dedication in 1926). He opened a grocery store and masonry supply when he came to Lake Worth in 1920, but in 1927, "I bought a herd, 5 acres of land and built a barn." When Boutwell Dairies was sold in 1965, his herd had reached 1,100 Guernseys and was the 10th largest in the U.S. Boutwell was the first to produce a half-milk, half-cream mixture.*

When George Greenberg's father, Max (above), arrived in Lake Worth in 1912, many residents still lived in tents, hence the name "Pioneer."

Pioneer and survivor

Looking for the best-dressed man on Clematis Street? It's got to be George Greenberg, who could be the street's most patient man, too.

His Pioneer Linens store, started in 1912 by his father, Max, has survived war, Depression, hurricanes — even the fickle fortunes of West Palm's downtown.

He did it, he said in 1992, "by becoming something of a destination."

"Through word of mouth, we get people from all over coming in. I'm filling orders from Germany, Australia and a rancher in Wyoming. The rancher wants towels with horse heads."

Once, a Saudi prince ordered 36 toilet lid covers. And where else would Donald Trump get his blanket covers?

GEORGE GREENBERG

Born May 29, 1915

Owner of Pioneer Linens, West Palm Beach

Max Greenberg moved his store from Lake Worth to West Palm Beach after the 1928 hurricane. It's been on Clematis ever since, and his son bills it as "America's only fine linens department store."

"If you build a better mousetrap, people will come," Greenberg said.

— JAN TUCKWOOD

THE KENNEDYS

'All the happy times...'

They didn't do much in Palm Beach but relax — cruising around in convertibles, eating at Greene's Drug-store, swimming at the beach — but the Kennedys will forever be linked with the island.

Rose Fitzgerald Kennedy first visited with her parents in 1911, and in 1933, she and her husband, Joseph Kennedy Sr., bought the Rodman Wanamaker home at 1095 N. Ocean Boulevard. The Mizner-designed manse was modest by Palm Beach standards, but fine for the ever-practical Rose.

She maintained the same routine for 50 years — arriving in Palm Beach after Thanksgiving and leaving after Easter. She went to Mass (usually at St. Edward's Church) each morning, then she'd swim or play a round of golf at Palm Beach Country Club.

Family tragedies couldn't be avoided, even in Palm Beach. In 1961, Joe Sr. suffered a stroke while playing golf. In 1983, David Kennedy, son of Robert and Ethel, died of a drug overdose at a Palm Beach hotel. And in 1991, William Kennedy Smith was charged and acquitted of raping a woman on the beach at the Kennedy compound, which was sold in 1995.

But Massachusetts Sen. Edward Kennedy's memories of the town are good ones:

"My most vivid memories of Palm Beach are still all the happy times around the pool with my brothers when I was growing up. It was a wonderful time to relax and catch up with family news. It was where my brother Jack chose to go to recover from his back injury when he was a senator. I remember Jackie had got him interested in painting, and he challenged me to try my hand at it during one of my visits.

"He decided we should both paint the same scene and then in the evening have our family and friends critique them — without telling who had painted which one. He had a real talent and bested me in the contest, but he started me on a lifelong hobby. Of course, after he became president, Palm Beach was where he liked to relax over the Christmas holidays. He loved the extra time he could spend with Caroline and John there. You could hear their laughter echoing all throughout the house. The first Christmas of his presidency was one of the most wonderful family gatherings we had."

— PAUL REID

Rose Kennedy and her son Edward at The Breakers hotel in 1972.

Distinguished men of the law

Phil O'Connell in 1969 (left) and his brother Stephen, the first alumnus of the University of Florida to become its president.

The $686 prize purse was too tempting to pass up, even though Phil O'Connell was due to graduate from law school in just three months. Besides, he had won his last 59 fights. This bout, in Madison Square Garden in 1931, was to be his 60th.

His opponent broke O'Connell's jaw in the first round. O'Connell gamely struggled through 10 rounds, and the $686 he collected helped him pay off his law school expenses.

His later fights would play out in West Palm Beach court-rooms.

O'Connell was born in Macon, Ga., in 1907 but grew up in West Palm Beach and opened a law practice. He was elected municipal judge in 1931, before he reached 25 — so young, in fact, city commissioners had to lower the legal age limit. Four years later, he was elected state attorney, a job he held until 1961, with four years off to serve in the Army in World War II, where he won a Bronze Star and a Croix de Guerre.

O'Connell's most famous case involved Palm Beach County's most shocking murder: the kidnapping and drowning of Judge C.E. Chillingworth and his wife, Marjorie, by two thugs, Bobby Lincoln and Floyd Holzapfel. The two had been hired by a municipal judge, Joe Peel Jr., who hated Chillingworth and feared that his own habit of taking bribes would come to light.

The murders convulsed the state. It took five years to crack the case, and O'Connell reluctantly had to offer Lincoln a plea bargain in exchange for his testimony against Holzapfel and Peel.

"The ghost of Judge Chillingworth will not rest until his killers are shoveling coal in the fires of hell and damnation," O'Connell told the jury.

O'Connell regarded the Chillingworth case as the capstone of his career. He retired as state attorney in 1961 and went into private practice. He helped found the Palm Beach County Blood Bank, was a founding director of Flagler National Bank and worked with the Salvation Army and the Boy Scouts of America. He died on Sept. 20, 1987.

Stephen O'Connell, his brother, had an equally distinguished career, becoming the state's 57th Supreme Court justice in 1955 and the first alumnus president of the University of Florida (1967-73). Both jobs involved massive pay cuts, but O'Connell didn't let that stop him.

"To serve there (at the University of Florida), to me, was a very personal privilege, because . . . being a student there had opened for me the windows and doors to a whole new world and made possible everything that came from that point on," Stephen O'Connell said. He is retired and now lives in Tallahassee.

— MICHAEL BROWNING

Phil O'Connell in his youthful boxing days.

What Permelia wanted

On Jupiter Island, it never has been just about money. Anybody can be rich. Some earn it. Members of the "Lucky Sperm Club," islanders joke, inherit it.

But not just anybody could pass muster with Permelia Pryor Reed to become a member of the exclusive Jupiter Island Club.

For 63 years, Permelia, her husband, Joseph, and later, their son Nathaniel, brought friends to this island and sold them its land.

They cultivated a tranquil life far different than the glitzy world of Palm Beach.

Joseph, born in France, reared in Denver and educated at Yale, was wealthy from his family's Denver business interests. He produced several New York plays and later founded the American Shakespeare Theater. One of his three books, *The Curtain Falls*, was a 1935 bestseller. He and Permelia, an heiress to the Remington Arms Co. fortune, lived in Greenwich, Conn., when they first visited Jupiter Island in 1931.

"We immediately fell in love with the island and within 10 days purchased a glorious piece of jungle," she wrote in *Kaleidoscope of Jupiter Island,* her book of island memories. The Reeds hired architect Maurice Fatio to build their home, Artemis.

They bought most of the land on the island, including the rundown Olympia Beach Hotel, built in 1916, a few cottages, tennis courts and a scraggly, nine-hole golf course. They bought the water company and large tracts of land in

THE REEDS

Joseph and Permelia Reed

Hobe Sound, and created the Hobe Sound Co. to manage it all.

Joseph's dream: to make the island a place where his family and his friends could live in comfort and privacy. He built houses, sold land to his friends, and within five years more than 40 homes went up on the island.

The Reeds made gifts of land and persuaded islanders to buy more, so that Jupiter Island is bounded by a wildlife refuge on the north, the Atlantic Ocean to the east, Blowing Rocks preserve to the south and the Indian River, backed by more wildlife refuge, to the west. In the 1930s, Reed donated the wilderness beach he loved to walk to save it forever as Hobe Sound National Wildlife Refuge. Permelia Reed persuaded legislators to make 14,000 acres of wilderness into Jonathan Dickinson State Park.

In 1937, Joseph renamed the old hotel the Jupiter Island Club. In 1996, Nathaniel Reed sold it to its members.

— SALLY D. SWARTZ

Florida's conservation conscience

NATHANIEL REED

Born July 22, 1933

Because his family's wealth would have allowed him to live a life of leisure, but instead he chose to serve: Five years in Washington as assistant secretary of the Interior for two presidents (Nixon and Ford); the state under two governors and as the creator of 1,000 Friends of Florida; the region as a hard-working member of the South Florida Water Management District board.

Because he could have sailed his own boat on peaceful waters but decided he'd rather rock boats in government and the environmental establishment.

Because he speaks out strongly and often against any assault on the environment, from ugly power poles along U.S. 1 in Hobe Sound to the state's failure to make farmers keep fertilizers out of Lake Okeechobee.

Because his command of the language lights the lives of those who hear him speak or read his letters.

Because his enthusiasm for life's simple pleasures — a "perfect orange" in a picnic lunch — sparks appreciation in others.

Because he cultivates a lifetime hobby that still excites, delights and challenges him: Fishing — for permit in Florida's Keys, for salmon in Russia, Norway and Iceland — and he releases his catches.

Because he recounts his piscatorial adventures in an annual "fishing diary" friends around the globe await with anticipation.

Because he shares his 66-year-

old memories of growing up on Jupiter Island with those who did not have that privilege, painting word pictures of a tropical paradise where the skies were filled with wild birds and the rivers with great sea trout.

Because while he can be quite elegant and proper, Florida's No. 1 environmentalist lets Hobie, his Brittany spaniel, sleep on the couch in his office.

— SALLY D. SWARTZ

At home on Jupiter Island with Hobie, Reed reflects on his legacy: "Nixon banning 1080, which was used to kill coyotes all over the West. The banning of DDT. The government helping buy 90 million acres in Alaska as part of a permanent refuge system. In Florida, making the environment such an issue every governor has had a Preservation 2000 chairman. As a legacy, I hope the Republican Party of Florida develops a strong environmental ethic. . . . Speaking to teenagers, I see a real awareness across the country and the world of the possibilities and problems they will face. There is the feeling this is one world, one Earth — and we all have to share the responsibility of whether we are going to make it."

Alfonso "Alfy" (right) and Jose "Pepe" Fanjul built their business with their father, Alfonso Sr. By the '80s, younger brothers Alexander and Andres had joined the business.

THE MCHARDY FAMILY, ACTIVE IN STUART SINCE THE '20s:
Richard 'Victor' McHardy is in front. Second row, from left: Alvin, Samuel and Quilly McHardy Sr. Third row: Quilly McHardy Jr., Ann McHardy Hazelton and Alvin R. McHardy Jr. with daughter Jordan, 3. Back row: Arlene McHardy, Margaret McHardy (looking to the right), Gloria McHardy and Gene McHardy. They're standing in front of George McHardy's 1925 home. "I cherish that house," said Victor, who worked as a pressman at The Stuart News *for 36 years.*

COSTELLA WILLIAMS, MATRIARCH OF NEW MONROVIA:
Williams began teaching in Port Salerno in 1929 in a one-room school-house. She retired from Martin County schools in 1975 and continued a life of service, even opening her garage door all day so the less fortunate can come by for clothes or shoes. "Anytime anyone needs anything, you can just call on Costella Williams," Gloria McHardy said.

THE FANJULS

First family of Florida sugar

Late in 1959, 21-year-old Alfonso Fanjul, the last member of his family still in Cuba, stood facing a group of men sent by Fidel Castro.

Resting their machine guns on an office conference table, they told Fanjul what he already knew: They had come to take his family's land.

So it happened that the Fanjuls' 400,000 acres of sugar cane and sugar mills became property of the Castro government, and the Fanjul family became exiles.

Over the next 40 years, the Fanjuls became the first family of Florida sugar, building an empire that began with 4,000 acres of farmland in western Palm Beach County.

That parcel, bought for $160 an acre in 1960, has grown into a giant with more than 180,000 acres, 3,000 employees and three sugar mills. Sales are in the hundreds of millions.

In 1984, the family bought the sugar interests of Gulf & Western Industries in Florida and the Dominican Republic. The deal also included the 7,000-acre Dominican Republic resort of Casa de Campo — a hotel, golf courses and about 900 private residences, including Casa Grande, the Fanjuls' private compound.

While the Fanjuls guard their privacy, they've actively raised money for some very public politicians. Alfonso "Alfy" Fanjul was one of Bill Clinton's key money-raisers in Florida in 1992, and Pepe Fanjul served as vice chairman of presidential candidate Bob Dole's finance committee in 1996.

Perhaps the most well-publicized example of the family's political influence was the disclosure in Kenneth Starr's report that President Clinton took a phone call from Alfy Fanjul while trying to end his relationship with Monica Lewinsky.

The brothers' influence and wealth have rankled some — particularly because, for years, they benefited from government sugar price supports without being U.S. citizens.

That changed in 1999, when Alexander, Andres and Pepe became U.S. citizens. Alfy has applied for citizenship and is still waiting to be called to take the oath.

Meanwhile, the family continues to fight a series of lawsuits from former cane cutters who allege the Fanjul sugar companies underpaid them for years.

But in Palm Beach society circles, the Fanjuls "rule the roost," according to a spread on the family's opulent lifestyle in *W* magazine about a year ago. They spend leisure time at the Dominican Republic estate golfing, sailing, fishing and riding. Pepe travels the world on annual shooting trips.

And they give generously to charities. Lillian Fanjul de Azqueta, sister of the four Fanjul brothers, started New Hope Charities for poor children in Pahokee more than a decade ago. Florida Crystals Corp., the umbrella company for Flo-Sun's Florida holdings, gives away about $1 million a year to New Hope, the United Way and other groups.

Helping others is something the brothers say they have done since their earliest days in Florida, when other Cuban exiles came to them for jobs.

Recalls Alfy Fanjul: "They turned into the nucleus that built the new sugar industry in Florida."

— JULIE WARESH

THE McHARDYS

East Stuart pioneers

George McHardy arrived in Stuart from the Bahamas in the early 1900s and became a stone mason. He built a stately white-washed brick house in East Stuart in 1925, and his extended family built a legacy of service in Martin County.

One by one, George's brothers came to join him in Stuart. First Richard, then Dan, then Charles.

Today, many McHardys are teachers, coaches, speech therapists and other professionals in Florida.

Outside his Uncle George's brick house, hardly a car goes by without a friendly toot to Victor McHardy, 83, George's nephew and one of the family patriarchs, along with his brothers Sam McHardy of Stuart and Quilly McHardy of Port Salerno ("My other brother Earl lives in heaven"). "I know everybody, I've been in that church over there for 70 years," Victor says.

The church is the St. Paul African-Methodist-Episcopal Church across the street. When Victor was a boy, Uncle George had a store on the first floor of his house and all the children would come over after church for ice cream.

Gloria McHardy has been married to Victor's son, Alvin, a retired teacher and dean, for 37 years. A former first-grade teacher, she's now the guidance counselor at Parker Elementary School and an active volunteer in the New Monrovia neighborhood of Port Salerno. In July 1999, she cut the ribbon on the 3,000-square-foot Costella Williams Learning Center at New Monrovia Park for after-school care and summer programs. "We want them to take pride in themselves and the community," said Gloria.

— JERI BUTLER

Generous man of the land

GEORGE MORIKAMI

Nov. 5, 1886 — Feb. 29, 1976

Photos from Florida State Archives

The year before he died, George Sukeji Morikami planted 53 Japanese persimmon trees by hand, hauling water by the bucketful to the seedlings. "I'm planting trees for future generations," he said.

What he planted, and what he gave, grew into so much more than he could have imagined.

Morikami was one of two dozen Japanese bachelor farmers who developed the Yamato Colony between Boca Raton and Delray Beach soon after the turn of the century. Frontier Florida welcomed anyone willing to work the scrub and swamp that could be cleared only by hand. Soon the population was up to 50, and the colony had a post office, railroad station and acres of pineapples, peppers and tomatoes.

Morikami came as an indentured laborer, paying $150 to a Japanese silk merchant in Miami. He had to work three years to pay it back and earn a bonus. But his sponsor died, and Morikami never returned to Japan. He kept planting, long after the Yamato Colony had disbanded.

By 1925, he had $250,000 in five banks, but he lost it all in the Florida bust. He started over again.

His philosophy: "Whenever you see good land, if it's cheap enough, buy it. Expect to turn it over to a little profit. That's what I did."

He amassed 200 acres of land, which he could have sold for millions, but he gave it to Palm Beach County for a park "because America has been so good to me."

Morikami died alone in his four-room trailer west of Delray Beach, his Japanese philosophy books at his bedside and his American citizenship dear to his heart.

"I came with nothing and now I'm leaving without anything," Morikami said a few weeks before his death. "This is a wonderful country."

On his land, the county built the Morikami Museum, which expanded in 1993 to 10 times its original size. Here, exhibits keep the Japanese culture of the Yamato Colony alive. And George Morikami's trees live on and on.

— ELIOT KLEINBERG

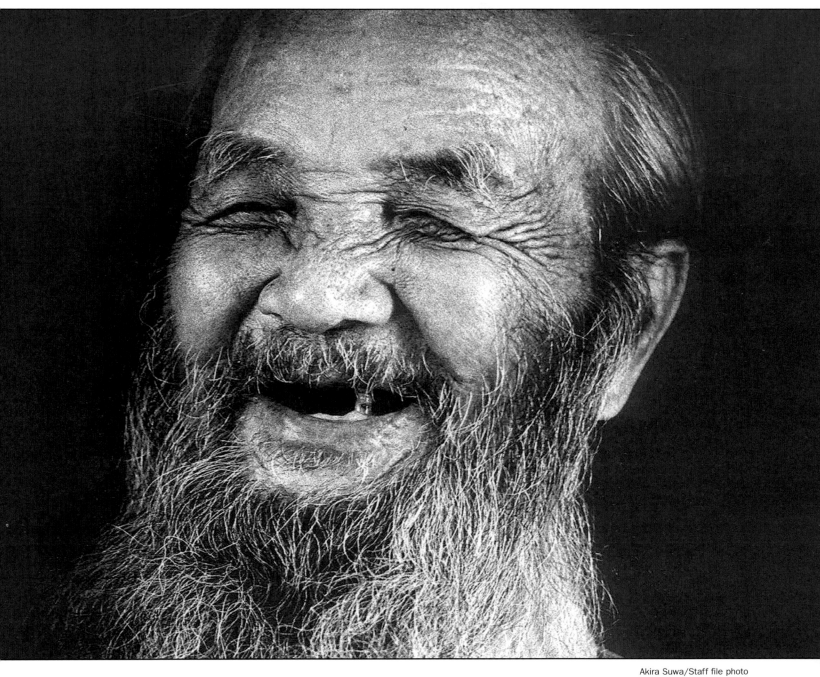

Morikami came to the U.S. in 1906 (facing page), worked hard labor his first three years without getting paid and was taunted during the Japanese scare of World War II. Still, he loved America. "Here's a good example of a man whose whole heart was involved with doing good for others," former county commissioner Bill Medlen said.

153

The farmer's best friend

Red Mounts at the South Florida Fair in the '30s, when Palm Beach County grew more sweet corn and green beans than anywhere else in the United States. In the early days, travel to Glades farms "wasn't a one-day trip," he once said. "We took a barge from 20-Mile Bend to Okeechobee. ... The only road to Belle Glade was a rock strip almost too narrow for two cars to pass."

MARVIN 'RED' U. MOUNTS

Aug. 9, 1899 — Oct. 28, 1969

When Marvin "Red" U. Mounts came to Palm Beach County in 1925, folks thought he was crazy for wanting to work the land instead of sell it.

"It was right in the middle of the Florida boom," Mounts once said, "and everybody kept telling me I should get into the real-estate business."

But Mounts became the county's top agriculture agent — and the farmers' best friend.

By the time he retired in 1965 after 40 years, more than 100,000 acres of vegetables were being farmed. That was 10 times more beans, squash, potatoes, celery, corn — basically, America's winter vegetable basket — than when he started.

Marvin Mounts Jr.

Agriculture grew from a $2 million to a $120 million annual industry, and at one point, Palm Beach County led the country in production of corn and green beans. Mounts also encouraged sugar cane as a major crop and introduced a carpet grass that thrives in wet soils for cattle grazing.

These days, Mounts' link to plants survives at the botanical garden on Military Trail that bears his name.

"He had this great love for the farmer," said his son, Circuit Judge Marvin Mounts Jr., who has spent nearly 30 years on the bench. "Something about raising crops, it has something to do with the very essence of life."

His father made a difference "doing the little things" — starting a 4-H chapter to encourage future farmers, searching out the best fertilizers and pesticides and helping farmers learn about marketing.

Red Mounts was raised in a sod house on Oklahoma's Cherokee Strip before heading to the University of Florida, then south to Palm Beach County.

"My father knew this county enjoyed a great future in agriculture and in tourism," Judge Mounts said.

"He felt a little nostalgic about the disappearance of the small farms, but he saw that as an inevitable part of growth."

— JOHN PACENTI

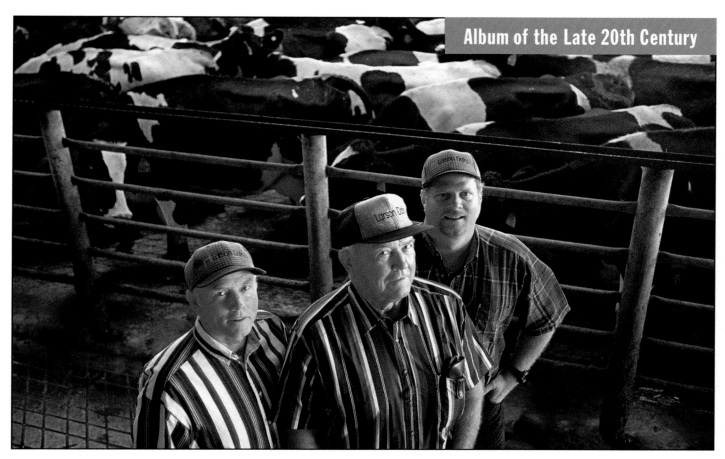

Red Larson with sons Woody (left) and John. Before the day ends, 9,000 Larson Dairy cows will be milked twice, filling the silver tanker trucks that proudly proclaim "Drink REAL Florida Fresh Milk." Every so often, Red keeps his hand in by showing a worker how to 'strip' a cow, pulling the last squirts from the udders when the milking machines are finished.

Dairy men

LOUIS 'RED' LARSON

Born March 9, 1924

LOUIS 'WOODY' LARSON JR.

Born March 21, 1951

JOHN LARSON

Born Oct. 27, 1958

Because the Larson name has been synonymous with dairying in Florida since the middle of the past century, ever since Louis "Red" Larson started with a small herd in Dade County in 1947. Red and Rita Larson kept moving themselves, their four children and their cows — 8,000 to 9,000 now — northward to escape the pressures of development, seeking a re-fuge where kids and cows could flourish.

Because in Okeechobee County, where grain silos loom over prairies and cows outnumber people, Larson Dairy is an industry giant that leads with a benevolent hand and an eye to the future. It has long been the largest dairy in Florida and one of the top 10 in the nation.

Because when government passed laws forcing dairy farmers to clean up their waste for environmental reasons, the Larsons took the lead and spent millions revamping barns, testing and instal-ling new waste containment systems.

Because when scientists wanted to study a widespread cow virus that resembles HIV but doesn't cause AIDS, the Larsons offered their herds as a living lab-oratory for study.

Because the Larsons, father and sons, have served at the highest organizational levels of their industry, yet never lost sight of the reality of their lives. As expressed by Louis "Woody" Larson Jr. in listing the dairy's officers, "Dad is chairman, I'm president, and John is vice president — all that means is that we have a title, and we still get to work seven days a week."

Because Red Larson made sure he, his family and everyone who enters the Larson Dairy headquarters gets a gentle reminder of how the empire was built — a wall-mounted glass case displaying a tat-tered old jean jacket, worn straw hat, red bandanna and holey-fingered gloves, the uniform of a man who spent years of 18-hour days in barnyards long before he moved to the boardroom.

— MARY MCLACHLIN

Florida State Archives

U.S. Sugar, formed in 1931 by Mott (right), gave more than $1 million to Clewiston schools and youth groups in 1996 alone.

CHARLES MOTT

June 2, 1875 — Feb. 18, 1973

Clewiston's benefactor

C harles Stewart Mott started at the top and went up from there. He founded South Florida's modern sugar industry and set up one of the nation's largest foundations.

Mott was born into the applesauce family in 1875 but opted for an engineering career. He got the family wheel company involved in making axles for a new product called the automobile, selling the firm in 1913 for stock in a company called General Motors. By 1960, he was GM's largest individual shareholder.

In 1931, Mott formed U.S. Sugar Corp., the state's first sugar giant. It remains the nation's largest producer of raw sugar. It also grows rice and corn on about 165,000 acres in Palm Beach, Hendry and Glades counties, and citrus on 29,000 acres in Hendry County.

What's more, nearly everything in the company's town — Clewiston — bears the stamp of U.S. Sugar. The company gave more than $1 million to schools and youth groups in 1996 alone.

"Every man is in partnership with the rest of the human race in the eternal conquest which we call civilization," Mott once explained.

Mott was a craggy-faced six-footer who cared more about results than theories. Through his foundation, he put up $1.3 million for an economics building at the University of Chicago because he wanted economists who would figure out how to cure inflation rather than debating whether it was the cause or the result of lower buying power.

The foundation, which he set up in 1935, became a giant in 1963 when he gave it $128 million worth of GM stock. Today it is worth more than $1.9 billion.

— ELIOT KLEINBERG

Florida cowboy

ALTO 'BUD' ADAMS

Born April 4, 1926

Because he loves the Florida grasslands and chose a trail different from his father's, a chief justice of the Florida Supreme Court.

Because he has spent 50 years planting and protecting the pastures and has opened his ranch for tours so the public can experience back-country Florida.

Because he has left his stamp on the United States beef industry with a new breed of cattle, the gentle, strong, heat-tolerant Braford.

Because he's had one job, (ranching) one wife (Dot) and one house (a 1949 cypress home with no central air conditioning).

Because his three sons also like cattle ranching, wildlife, Sunday family dinners and the big sky.

Because he's sure beef is the best source of protein for the American diet, though he admits occasionally eating chicken ("But I don't brag about it").

Because he's a lanky, soft-spoken but hard-driving cowboy and at 73 has taken on the challenge of developing leaner cattle called ARbeef.

Because he'd rather work in his garden and experiment with fruit trees than talk about himself.

Because he knows raising cattle can be tough, so he also grows citrus, figuring with two crops, there will always be something to sell.

Because he has 65,000 acres of pasture, ponds, orange groves and oak hammocks in three Florida counties and has preserved habitats, resisted development and kept ranching alive.

— JERI BUTLER

*Bud Adams on his ranch west of Fort Pierce. "If I've contributed anything,
it's we've fed a lot of people and we've left the land in very good condition."*

These lush trees were among thousands at Menninger's Stuart home. He treasured each plant, particularly a fishtail palm given to him by horticulturist Ed Hosford.

EDWIN MENNINGER
March 18, 1896 — Feb. 17, 1995

The Flowering Tree Man

Mention Ed Menninger's name around Stuart, and the reaction would be, "Oh, you mean 'The Flowering Tree Man.'"

Menninger, a Kansan whose father founded the Menninger psychiatric clinic in Topeka, studied chemistry and journalism. He came to West Palm Beach in 1922 to recover from the flu and stayed to take over a floundering weekly newspaper and move it to Stuart. He would play a leading role in the creation of Martin County three years later.

The Stuart of 1922 had only six phones and electricity was available only from 5:30 p.m. to midnight. It also was far too drab for Menninger's taste.

"Florida has no native flowering trees," he would declare, though when pressed would admit there were a few.

"Rush home and plant trees," he would tell anyone who would listen.

He followed his advice, corresponding with horticulturists all over the world to obtain seeds and wisdom. He once said he had 15,000 trees in pots in his yard and claimed to have introduced more than 2,000 species to Florida. His avocation became his career in 1958, when he sold the paper that had become *The Stuart News*. His books included *Flowering Trees of the World*, *Seaside Plants of the World*, *Fantastic Trees* and *Edible Nuts of the World*.

He remained opinionated and determined into his 10th decade. When asked how it felt to turn 90 in 1986, he said, "Terrible," then smiled.

He died in February 1995, just weeks before his 99th birthday. Thousands of his trees live on.

— BILL McGOUN

158

RUTH WEDGWORTH

May 10, 1903 — Dec. 9, 1995

First lady of the Glades

The word legend is overused. But it truly fits some people, such as Ruth Springer Wedgworth. Wedgworth was a leader in the Glades for 65 years. She built an agricultural empire in a time when women were expected only to cook the food. She established a day-care center for the children of migrant workers when many whites thought this was no concern of theirs. Until a year before she died, she still went to the family office every day, even though she had officially retired in 1986.

The Glades was still reeling from the hurricane of 1928 when Herman and Ruth Wedgworth arrived in Belle Glade in 1930. Eight years later, they had a 320-acre vegetable farm, a packing plant and a fertilizer plant. They were building an ice plant when Herman Wedgworth was crushed under the frame of an ice machine in 1938.

Under Ruth's leadership, Wedgworth Farms grew into 7,300 acres of sugar cane and 10,500 acres of pasture.

"I decided to carry on," she once said of her resolve when left a widow with three children. "I had a family to raise. There was nothing to do but go ahead."

A half-century ago, when Jim Crow still was the law, Wedgworth led efforts to set up a 24-hour day-care for children of migrant workers. She served on the city's first biracial committee. And as a Palm Beach County school board member (1947-52), she pushed for migrant education.

"We stopped the labor buses and took the children off so they could go to school," she said.

She was well into her 80s before her son George, head of the Sugar Cane Growers Cooperative of Florida, could persuade her to stop driving to West Palm Beach on the then two-lane State Road 80. "I've seen people rust out," she said in 1987, "I want to wear out."

In 1975, she was the first woman to be the Belle Glade Chamber of Commerce's "man of the year." In 1987, the Florida Department of Agriculture designated her as Woman of the Year in Agriculture. She was the first woman elected president of the Florida Horticultural Society, and she was inducted into the Florida Ag Hall of Fame in 1988.

Her greatest legacy, however, is a Belle Glade that is a better place for her efforts.

— BILL McGOUN

Ruth Wedgworth raised three children: Helen Wedgworth Boynton, George Herman Wedgworth and Barbara Wedgworth Oetzman. George Wedgworth, pictured here with his mother, is founder and president of the Sugar Cane Growers Cooperative of Florida, a group of medium-sized sugar growers near Lake Okeechobee. Wedgworth has been an outspoken advocate for sugar farmers, and his belief that agriculture and good environment practices can coexist in the Glades. "Farmer-bashers and other detractors have their own agenda," he told the South Florida Water Management District board in 1988. "They have found it in their own interest to point fingers and try to make agriculture a scapegoat (for pollution in the Everglades)." In 1990, Wedgworth and his sisters donated $1 million to the University of Florida's Everglades Research and Education Center in Belle Glade. Their father, Herman, was the Education Center's first plant pathologist in 1930.

HOWARD B. SWYERS

Dec. 9, 1911 — Sept. 22, 1997

"He was what I would call a benevolent dictator," said former student Ray Bender. "He had the guts to be forceful, yet the compassion to make the whole system work."

LEANDER KIRKSEY

March 16, 1909 — Jan. 15, 1995

"If things had been a little different, he would have been one of the greatest classical violin players in this country," former student, drummer David "Panama" Francis, said of The Chief.

The Boss and The Chief

Howard B. Swyers and Leander Kirksey. They were called "The Boss" and "The Chief." Between them they taught music to Palm Beach County students for almost a century.

Kirksey was the son of a slave. He studied chemistry at Florida A&M, but chose the concert hall over the laboratory after graduation. After beginning his career as band director at Florida A&M — and helping launch the careers of greats like Julian "Cannonball" Adderley — Kirksey came to West Palm Beach in the mid '40s to start the first band at Industrial High School and its successor, Roosevelt.

He was the first black inducted into the Florida Music Education Association's Hall of Fame. His career spanned 40 years, until 1970, when he retired to enjoy music on his terms.

"Music is a universal language," he said in 1987 before a reunion in his honor. "It's a disciplinary virtue."

Swyers also added music to young lives, and he did so with absolute confidence and absolute authority. A sign posted in Palm Beach High, where he was band director from 1944 to 1959, captured his philosophy: He may not always be right, but he's the boss. Later, he took over band programs at Central Junior High School and Jupiter High, before finishing his career as principal at Palm Beach High.

Swyers and Kirksey made more than music and musicians. They created citizens. And lifelong friends.

Rosanne Kalil Bush, a student of Swyers in the early 1950s, speaks for hundreds of Kirksey's and Swyers' students when she says: "We thank him for his dedication and love of working with young people and for passing on to us his love of music. We will never forget him."

— PAUL REID

Sonja Lutz particularly enjoys teaching her senior English honors class, pictured with her here, 'because they are responsible and rise to my expectations, which are very high.' On the day this photograph was taken, the class traveled around the campus of Glades Central portraying different pilgrims from Chaucer's The Canterbury Tales. They've read Macbeth and Hamlet and recently put on a show celebrating Shakespeare. 'Two of my boys did a Hamlet rap that was really great,' Lutz said. 'My kids love Shakespeare. Hamlet is their kind of guy.'

Album of the Late 20th Century

Teacher extraordinaire

SONJA LUTZ
Born July 8, 1937

Teacher, Glades Central High School, 1970-present

Because she has spent 30 years teaching English and French at Glades Central High School, a place where the students need her more than most.

Because she gave up her life as a Delta flight attendant and moved to Belle Glade — a town that resembles her hometown of Mason City, Ill., with its black soil but with sugar cane instead of corn — and stayed when others moved on.

Because she is a quiet, unassuming 62-year-old woman who is something no one else in the county is — a two-time teacher of the year (and a William T. Dwyer Excellence in Education Award winner, too).

Because her mind is rarely off those kids, as she tries to come up with fun new ways to teach the same ol' things.

Because she is still known for the year she taught writing though "trashology" — her students penned notes to famous people, asking for an item from their garbage cans, receiving a torn Christmas card from Bette Davis, a parking ticket from Burt Reynolds, part of a novel from Sidney Sheldon.

Because she has inspired many to dream a little bigger — the Harvard student, the epidemiologist, the lawyers — and, of course, one of her sons, who last year joined her on the faculty of Glades Central High.

Because in between coming up with innovative ways to teach, she's raised five children of her own.

Because she intends to stick with it until her planned retirement in 2004, unless her husband agrees to take her on a cruise around the world before then.

Because she truly acts like it's not so tough to teach high schoolers the finer points of *Hamlet*. "I like the kids and they like me, and that's half the battle," she says.

— STEPHANIE DESMON

161

Album of the Late 20th Century

S. Bruce McDonald at Boca Raton Middle School. His philosophy, according to his daughter, Silvia: 'Your purpose in life must be to help people reach beyond their immediate grasp.'

Teacher at Roosevelt High School in West Palm Beach, administrator at Central Junior High School and assistant principal at Roosevelt, 1956-70

Principal, Boca Raton Junior High School (now Boca Raton Middle), 1970-75

Area superintendent of schools and other administrative jobs, 1975-84

Principal influence

S. BRUCE McDONALD
Born May 3, 1928

Because McDonald had many reasons to be angry — his father was shot by a white policeman in a West Palm Beach park when he was 3, and McDonald himself was arrested once after trying to help a white person — but he channeled his ire into action.

Because he worked his way up through a segregated school system and became the first black principal of a mostly white school — Boca Raton Junior High School — in 1970.

Because in the testiest moments of integration in Palm Beach County, McDonald decided to *negotiate* rather than demand — and that made the crucial difference. In life, he said, "there are times when you have to decide if you would have authority or influence."

Because he used his background as a sociology student to cool the hotter heads around him, particularly when the school district began busing black children from Delray Beach to Boca Raton.

Because he worked with local business and religious leaders and parents, white and black, to help those new students from Delray Beach, who often were poorer than their peers. "The community of Boca," he said, "was probably the best ally a person could ask for."

Because he relied on this advice from his mother: "You can do anything anyone else can do. You are a man amongst men, and you happen to be black."

Because he is 71 years old but still embraces a challenge. In September 1999, he agreed to serve as interim administrator of the troubled Urban League of Palm Beach County.

Because when he returned to Boca Raton Middle School to have this portrait taken, the brand-new principal, Butch Mondy, recognized him immediately. Why? There's a 4-by-5-foot photograph of McDonald, his staff and his students from Boca Junior High School's first year hanging outside Mondy's office — and a collage commemorating each of the school's 30 years. McDonald started that tradition, and even today, he wants to share the spotlight with his school.

"The first thing he said to me was that he wanted to make sure the school got the proper credit," Mondy said. "Right away, I could tell he was a true, quality person as well as a wonderful educator."

— ELIOT KLEINBERG

CHARLES STEBBINS JR.
Oct. 22, 1910 — July 1991

Standing up for equal pay

Charles H. Stebbins Jr. wanted to be paid the same as a white teacher. In his quest, he became the Rosa Parks of Palm Beach County's public teachers.

Stebbins never benefited from the battle for which he agreed to be the poster boy; the day it ended in victory, he was waiting tables in New York. But a federal judge's decision that the county's black teachers must be paid the same as whites set a stunning precedent in 1941. And it was a step toward the landmark 1954 Brown vs. Board of Education decision that outlawed school segregation.

Palm Beach County's white teachers with five years of experience had received a $25 raise in 1941 to $140 a month. Furious black teachers, who got no raise, founded the Palm Beach County Teachers Association, and about 85 percent of the county's 115 black teachers joined.

The next step was a federal lawsuit. The group brought in NAACP attorney Thurgood Marshall, later the U.S. Supreme Court's first black justice. The group needed a name to put atop the suit: Stebbins.

"He was not afraid. He had the guts," recalls Delray Beach educator C. Spencer Pompey Jr.

Stebbins taught social studies at West Palm Beach's black Industrial High School — until his moment with history. Stebbins was fired. A school board official offered him $500 and his job back if he'd drop the case. His wife was ill with tuberculosis — she would die a year and a half later — but he declined. The black union reneged on a promise to pay him a year's salary if he lost his job.

"He was blackballed throughout the state," said Stebbins Jefferson, his niece and a *Palm Beach Post* columnist. "He was the troublemaker."

He never returned to education, and he died in 1991.

— ELIOT KLEINBERG

'You've got to build a dream'

C. SPENCER POMPEY

Born July 31, 1915

As a boy, Charles Spencer Pompey was afraid of cows. Growing up in Live Oak, in rural Suwannee County, cows were a fact of life, something you encountered every day.

One day, his mother, Mary Louise Wright Pompey, the daughter of a freed slave, decided to cure him of his cow-phobia.

"Let's go up close to them and see what they do," she said.

Mother and son walked into a pasture filled with looming cows.

"And we got up close to them," Pompey, 84, remembers. "And they didn't do anything. They just kept on grazing. That day I learned a lesson. You've got to get close to something to know it, whether it's a cow or a person. Don't judge from afar."

Today, Pompey is the grand old man of the civil rights movement in Palm Beach County. He got close to whites and won them over. By quiet, steadfast, civil insistence on his rights, he accomplished more for his people than a host of rabble-rousers and firebrands. By emphasizing education, by teaching, by coaching, by serving as principal, by launching what may have been the first class-action suit in U.S. history, Pompey quietly, firmly advanced equality and justice for blacks in a state haunted by lynchings and the sinister glow of burning crosses.

He did it by sheer dint of decency. Even today, sitting in his Delray Beach home across the street from a park named after him, Pompey conveys a peaceful air of kindness backed up by calm authority.

"He's always been like that," said his wife of 51 years, Hattie Ruth Pompey. "When I'd yell at the children to behave, all he would have to say is, 'Now, Cheryl ...' and they would listen to him and behave."

Education is the key to Pompey's life, and his mother is the key to his education. "At a time when black children were going to school for three months out of the year, she sent us to Florida Memorial College in Live Oak, and we were in school eight months each year. She worked as a laundress to pay our tuition.

"I graduated valedictorian of my high school class, but it took me seven years to get my college degree. Study a year, work a year, that's what I did. I hitchhiked to Daytona to Bethune-Cookman and met Mrs. Mary McLeod Bethune. I had no money, but I wanted to go to school. She took a look at me and said, 'Go on in.'"

"Depart To Serve" was the motto of Bethune-Cookman. Pompey came to Palm Beach County in 1939 and built a home "in the woods" on an oyster-shell road just east of what is now Interstate 95 in Delray Beach. He and fellow teacher Charles H. Stebbins helped found the Palm Beach County Teachers Association. In 1941, when black teachers with five years' experience were earning $100 a month, and white teachers with the same background were making $140 a month, the black Teachers' Association filed a class-action suit in federal court.

A promising NAACP lawyer named Thurgood Marshall argued the suit and won. Pompey went on to become president of the local NAACP, president of the Teachers' Association, a member of the board of directors of the Delray Beach Historical Society and honorary director of the Palm Beach Junior College Black History Archives, at a school where a scholarship is named after him. He retired as principal of Carver Middle School in 1979.

In 1947, under Pompey's leadership, Carver High became the first black high school in the state to host a track meet. In 1950, thanks again to Pompey, Delray Beach became the first city to set up a recreational program for blacks.

"I'm a Depression kid," Pompey says. "My father died in 1920 and left my mother with five children to raise. I didn't have anything, but I didn't know I was poor. When we went to school, the state didn't provide books, so we bought our own and handed them down in the family, brother to brother to sister. But my mother always said we had to go to school."

He has never lost hope. He professes his faith every Sunday at the St. Paul African Methodist Episcopal church in Delray Beach.

"You can't accept the present as permanent. That's the one piece of advice I have for young people. You've got to build a dream. Go to school. Get something in your head.

"Things are going to be better."

Pompey's mother died in 1984 at the age of 104, the oldest living resident of Suwannee County. She once visited her son in Delray Beach and looked at the vacant 10-acre lot across the street from his house.

"Who owns that? Why don't you buy it?" she asked.

"To me, having land just meant farming," Pompey laughs. "I had enough of farming, picking cotton, dipping (pine) gum, handling tobacco. I didn't want any more land, but she couldn't understand that."

The city of Delray Beach bought the land and turned it into a recreational park named after Pompey himself in 1978.

What is it like to live across the street from a big park named after you?

"It doesn't make me proud. Quite the opposite. It makes me humble."

— MICHAEL BROWNING

C. Spencer Pompey at the Delray Beach park named for him.

Provided by Spencer Pompey

1947, DURING THE DRIVE TO REGISTER BLACK VOTERS:
*Pompey with George McKay, president
of the Delray Beach Voters' League, and
the Rev. Nathaniel Jenkins, pastor of Greater
Mount Olive Baptist Church (founded in 1896).
Jenkins spearheaded the drive.*

**1950, COACH POMPEY WITH CAPTAINS
OF HIS STATE CHAMPIONSHIP TEAM:**
*Jack Adderley (left) is now a retired teacher.
Herman Pride is a professor at Southern
University, the largest black college in the
United States, in Louisiana.*

"Duncan (above) had the ability to transform the most commonplace into beauty and splendor and sweetness and grace," former PBCC president Edward M. Eissey (left) said. One of Duncan's great thrills was the Watson B. Duncan III Theatre, dedicated in 1986.

HOW ONE COLLEGE GREW: *Palm Beach Junior College, the state's oldest, opened on the campus of Palm Beach High School in October 1933. It moved to Morrison Field, then to the Lake Park Town Hall in the '50s before moving to its current campus in 1956. Edward M. Eissey — left, at the Eissey campus of PBCC in Palm Beach Gardens — a PBJC student in the late '40s, was the college's president from 1978 to 1997, when enrollment grew from 8,600 to 53,000. In 1988, the college changed its named to Palm Beach Community College.*

'Gladly would he learn, and gladly teach'

WATSON B. DUNCAN III

Feb. 16, 1915 — Feb. 21, 1991

When asked about his role model, Burt Reynolds looks not to Hollywood but to Lake Worth: to Watson B. Duncan III, a pied piper of literature for generations of Palm Beach Community College students.

With ruffled hair and an impish laugh, Duncan was an overgrown Puck who brought literature to life.

"He was the only man who could make me weep reading the great letters of Shakespeare, all the while dressed as an Easter egg," said actor Monte Markham, one of Duncan's students.

He didn't just teach, he *performed.*

He pranced. He skipped. He bellowed. He whispered. He loved the sound of certain words: *Xanadu, Istanbul, ecstasy.*

And, of course, anything by William Shakespeare.

"He loved Shakespeare. He breathed Shakepeare. He lived Shakespeare," said his nephew, the Rev. Montford Duncan Jr. And his devotion came early.

The Charleston, S.C., native — son and grandson of Methodist ministers — was told by an eighth-grade teacher that he would someday teach Shakespeare. He studied at the University of South Carolina and the Shakespeare Institute at the bard's hometown of Stratford-on-Avon. He taught high school for eight years, then came to what was then Palm Beach Junior College in 1948.

Students waited up to a year to get into one of his classes, which overflowed with at least 100 students. His reputation grew nationwide, but he never wanted to leave the state's oldest junior college.

"Palm Beach Junior College has given me everything I wanted," said Duncan — professionally and personally. He met his wife, Honey, in 1949 when she sat in his front row as a freshman.

Reynolds, who started at PBJC in 1956, credits Duncan with nothing less than his career. Duncan had started the school's drama program in the early 1950s and cast young Buddy Reynolds in the role of the alcoholic in *Outward Bound.*

"He was a 6-foot-4 curmudgeon elf," Reynolds said. "His laughter was so engaging ... when you heard it, you just started giggling yourself."

Duncan came to work on a Wednesday in 1991 and got the class laughing uproariously over Chaucer's *The Miller's Tale.* He died the next day of a heart attack at 76.

In his office in the PBCC theater named for him, a quote from Chaucer is framed in needlepoint. It was Duncan's choice for his epitaph: "Gladly would he learn, And gladly teach."

— ELIOT KLEINBERG

Burt Reynolds on Watson B. Duncan III

"It's that large leprechaun's fault that I'm an actor.

"I was going to Florida State University, and I lost a wheel playing football. I came back (to West Palm Beach) to pick up a few credits and have an operation ...

Reynolds in 1954

I went to the junior college, which at that time was in Lake Park. We had one building and a church. In the church, English literature was taught by the leprechaun, Watson B. Duncan. I went into the class not really caring about Byron, Shelley and/or Keats ... in fact, I thought they were the starting team for the Boston Celtics.

"After about three or four classes, I moved forward, down to the front of the class, because he is and was and will always be, I think, the finest teacher in the United States. I can't tell you the pleasure it was to finally realize that there was something more in my life besides athletics, to become fascinated with the arts.

"Then, he said to me, 'You're going to be in a play.' And I said, 'I don't want to be in a play,' because people that are in the theater are all crazy and fairies and all that stupid stuff ... and he said, 'Readings are at 3 o'clock.'

"At two minutes of 3, at what we laughingly called the student center, which is where they parked the fire engines, I looked at the clock. For some reason — I don't know why, I've never known why — I walked upstairs to this room and sat down, and he handed me this script, and I said a couple of words, very badly, I'm sure, and he said, 'You got the part.'

"I think we ran three nights. The first night, just before my big speech, a fire broke out — which may have been set by the critics. The fire engines were right below the auditorium, and a lot of the audience, I guess, were volunteer firemen. Anyway, everybody seemed to leave. I, of course, went right on acting.

"It was a magical time for me. It was a time when I felt at home on the stage. I felt this is the place I want to be."

167

H. IRWIN LEVY

Born June 23, 1926

Retirees' pied piper

H. Irwin Levy created Century Village and changed the face of Florida. In 1968, he looked at 680 acres of ranch and swamp land in suburban West Palm Beach and saw a retirement haven.

He and his partners marketed heavily in the Northeast. Memories of summers in the Catskills became endless summers in Florida. Lethargy was replaced by leisure and recreation.

The people bit. Levy sold nearly 8,000 one- and two-bedroom condominiums in about four years. A Century Village opened in suburban Boca Raton and two in Broward County.

Copycats followed. Florida began to gray in a big way. In October 1997, Levy formally sold the villages' holding company and name. By then, Century Village had become a metaphor.

LEVY: *He hired comedian Red Buttons to sell Century Village.*

168

To sell his company's new development, Perini built a star-shaped building to serve as hub of its "Million Dollar Homes Exhibit." A brochure touted the Palm Beach Lakes development as "Tomorrowness in action." The building, at Okeechobee and Florida Mango roads, was gone by the mid-1960s.

Father of the Westward Expansion

In the mid 1950s, West Palm Beach was only a mile wide. But a single land deal set off a westward land rush now limited only by the Everglades.

The man behind it: Massachusetts developer Louis R. Perini Sr., then the owner of the Milwaukee Braves.

The West Palm Beach Water Co., owned by Flagler interests, still controlled the water supply, and the sewer system was so primitive that raw waste flowed into the Intracoastal Waterway. A polio outbreak spurred the city into action.

In 1955, the city bought the water company and nearly 27 square miles of land west of the city limits. About 21.75 square miles became the water catchment area. In 1957, the city sold off the remaining 5,500 acres to five investors, including Perini, for $4.35 million.

The "Westward Expansion" became one of the state's first planned communities. About 30 million cubic yards of fill was moved, converting swamp into dry land and deepening the lakes. No one worried about wetlands protection then.

It was a boon for blacks, many of whom had moved to Riviera Beach after their segregated neighborhoods ran out of room. In fact, the first development was Roosevelt Estates, a moderate-income neighborhood for black families.

Financial troubles forced the other partners out, but Perini hung on, and eventually the development grew. Interstate 95 cut through, then came the Palm Beach Mall, the city auditorium and stadium, the Forum offices, the Land of the Presidents golf course, the Villages of Palm Beach Lakes and other developments.

Eventually, Perini's development would account for a third of the city's area.

"West Palm Beach would be just a non-entity today if not for that development," former city attorney Grover Herring recalled in 1994. "There is no developer that could have done what Perini did. Had this not been done at that particular time, it would have been impossible to do it later because of all the environmental laws."

— ELIOT KLEINBERG

169

John D. MacArthur at his regular hangout, the Colonnades Hotel coffee shop, in 1977. The eighth-grade dropout made his fortune selling $1-a-month insurance policies during the Depression, and he never stopped counting his pennies. "He was as tight as the bark on a tree," said attorney Joe Farish. Others say MacArthur was so cheap that he didn't run the air conditioner at the Colonnades in the summer and never accepted a cocktail napkin because that was a waste of paper.

The eccentric Mr. Mac

JOHN D. MACARTHUR

March 6, 1897 — Jan. 6, 1978

Next to Henry Flagler, no developer has influenced Palm Beach County as much as John D. MacArthur. Both were self-made millionaires who grew up poor, and both were sons of preachers.

But MacArthur stood as Flagler's unrefined opposite. Ornery, cheap and profane, MacArthur reviled blue bloods. He had more patience for those in blue collars.

He turned against the teachings of his father, William Telfer MacArthur, the traveling preacher. Instead, he lived by the lore of his brother, Charles, the playwright and hard-boiled newspaperman.

Once, when asked why he dressed like a bum, MacArthur explained: "Sometimes, it's better to feel like a bum than a millionaire."

He awoke at 4:45 every morning, smoked three to four packs of cigarettes a day, drank 20 cups of coffee and swilled Scotch. He lived to be 80, and in the process, he built north-

ern Palm Beach County.

MacArthur sold mail-order insurance in Chicago before coming to Palm Beach County in 1955 to collect on a loan. He took control of 80 percent of Lake Park and all of what he would name North Palm Beach. He kept buying, adding thousands of acres. He founded Palm Beach Gardens in 1959 and decided to stay and watch it grow.

When he died in 1978, he was the second wealthiest man in America. He gave his fortune to a foundation named for him and his second wife, Catherine, the bookkeeper whose fierce Scottish isolationism, perserverance and direct nature made her quite possibly the only person he feared.

He didn't set up the MacArthur Foundation to do good. "I'll do what I know best and make (money)," he told his lawyers.

"You fellows will have to learn how to spend it."

But the foundation has done good. It's given away more than $2 billion and continues giving at about $150 million a year. Its last major act in Palm Beach County came in 1999: It sold 15,000 developable acres to Watermark Communities and another 15,000 acres of environmentally sensitive land to the government.

— JOEL ENGELHARDT

Photos by JOHN J. LOPINOT/Staff Photographer

*MacArthur helps replant a 60-foot Norfolk pine that
he moved to the Colonnades Hotel on Singer Island.
He had nearly 200 trees moved and replanted,
including huge banyan trees, because he hated
seeing trees destroyed.*

John D. MacArthur, in his own words:

"THERE ARE SOME BEARDED JERKS
and little old ladies who call me a despoiler
of the environment. But I believe I have
more concern than the average person.
For example, I built Palm Beach Gardens
without knocking one tree down. I moved
the biggest tree ever moved in Florida —
they said it weighed 80 tons, although
I doubt it ... Many environmentalists today
are obstructionists and just throw rocks
in your path. They are trying to keep people
out of Florida. To me, that is un-Christian.
The poor slobs in New York and New Jersey
saved their money and bought a little piece
of land down here, and now the obstructionists say they can't use it."

"EVERY TIME I give somebody something,
I am besieged by a thousand others with their
hands out. Frankly, I don't believe you can buy
your way into heaven and prefer not to be
known as charitable."

"SCOTSMEN ARE SUPPOSED to be very tight.
Cheap is a better word for it. I've never denied it.
I inherited it. My father was a Scotsman even
if he was born in New York City three days
after the boat landed."

"I AM NO GENIUS, and at least a dozen times
in my life, if I had gone east instead of west, the
show would have been stranded in Podunkville."

"THE ONLY REASON I own 100 percent
of the stock of my 'empire' is that no one
with $100 would invest in an impossible
undertaking. My own brother spent hundreds
of hours giving me valid reasons why I had
attempted an impossibility. By all the rules
of the game, Bankers Life & Casualty Co.
should have gone down the drain 40 years ago.
The only explanation I can offer is luck."

171

GENERAL DEVELOPMENT CORPORATION

They put the Port in St. Lucie

ATTENTION, SNOWBIRDS: *The General Development Corp. came to Florida in 1958 with such a deal — a lot for $995 in fabulous Port St. Lucie. Before GDC was done, it left a legacy of places with nautical names: Port St. Lucie, Port Charlotte, North Port, Port Malabar, Palm Bay, Sebastian Highlands, Vero Beach Highlands, Port LaBelle and Port St. John.*

General Development Corp. swept into Florida in 1958, bought up acres of wilderness and quickly made northern residents a deal: Plop down $10 for a lot and $10 per month for 10 years, and you, too, can have a dream Florida retirement home for less than $20,000.

Swept up by the sleek marketing pitch and free weekend in Florida, thousands came and bought.

To build Port St. Lucie, GDC subdivided 80 square miles of swamp and pine forest into 80,000 home lots. Today, Port St. Lucie has 83,254 residents and is the largest city between Broward and Orlando. It's expected to grow to 132,000 residents by 2020.

Port St. Lucie features no downtown and just a few main roads — but residents don't seem to mind.

"Planned communities did not exist in 1961," said Ralph "Cap" Cain, a longtime GDC employee and Port St. Lucie resident. "It didn't make sense to designate a downtown when there was no one here yet. You have to have people before the commercial and industrial."

Born of a partnership between Chemical Research, Gardner Cowles of *Look* magazine and the home-building Mackle Co. of Miami, GDC used a blueprint to carve out nine eerily similar communities with nautical names: Port St. Lucie, Port Charlotte, North Port, Port Malabar, Palm Bay, Sebastian Highlands, Vero Beach Highlands, Port LaBelle and Port St. John.

Despite the company's success for 32 years, it never overcame early accusations that it had duped people into paying too much for homes and went bankrupt in 1990, a year before pleading guilty to fraud charges. Reorganized as Atlantic Gulf Communities in 1992, GDC maintains a powerful legacy: It's called sprawl.

— TERESA LANE

THOMAS J. WHITE SR., FOUNDER OF ST. LUCIE WEST: *White built the New York Mets spring training stadium that bears his name. He also built the first privately financed interstate exchange. He donated 90 acres for Barry University and Indian River Community College to build adjoining campuses. He bought the 4,600-acre Peacock Ranch in 1984, and Port St. Lucie annexed his St. Lucie West in 1985. In addition to high-end golf course homes, St. Lucie West accounts for much of the city's commercial and industrial tax base. White died at 73 in 1989. His son, Thomas Jr., runs Thomas J. White Development Co. "Port St. Lucie's a sprawl. We're a master-planned community," St. Lucie West spokesman Danny Miller says of the difference between his development and the rest of the city.*

C. OLIVER WELLINGTON
Oct. 1, 1886 — Feb. 6, 1959

A.W. 'BINK' GLISSON
Aug. 1, 1914 — March 14, 2000

SAMUEL FRIEDLAND
Nov. 23, 1896 — April 9, 1985

Good old boys, a flying cow and acres of Acreage

A New England accountant and a couple of good old Florida boys created the sprawling suburb with the elegant name: Wellington.

"I'm the third generation of Floridians," A.W. "Bink" Glisson, born in 1914 in North Florida, likes to say. "My great-great-grandfather was a Seminole Indian, and my great-great-grandmother was an alligator."

During World War II, Glisson met C. Oliver Wellington, a wealthy Boston-area accountant who wintered in South Florida. During a drive in the country, they spotted a tract of land south of State Road 80 and west of U.S. 441. Wellington had Glisson buy the 18,000 acres of swamp and named it the Flying C.O.W. Ranch — C.O.W. for his initials, flying because he was a pilot.

"He told me to buy anything that I thought would double in value in 10 years," Glisson said. "Some of the farmers out here said, 'Hey, Bink, you got a crazy Yankee buying swamp land. See if you can sell him some of mine.'"

The Wellington family sold Glisson about 1,200 acres, giving him 10 years to pay $300 an acre. Glisson sold it later the same year for $1,000 an acre.

Fort Lauderdale developer Jim Nall then bought 7,400 acres from the Wellington estate, platted the property, and the community was off and running. Wellington incorporated in 1996 and is scheduled to get a big mall by December 2001.

Wellington died in February 1959. Roy Glisson, Bink's brother and partner in many of the land deals, died in July 1999.

What Wellington was to the town that bears his name, Samuel Nathan Friedland was to the Acreage.

The Russian immigrant founded the Food Fair supermarket chain, built two hotels in Miami Beach and the famed Diplomat Resort in Hollywood and gave away millions for hospitals and scholarships. He also invested heavily in land, including 64,000 acres in central Palm Beach County in 1956.

This land included parts of what later became Royal Palm Beach, the J.W. Corbett National Wildlife Refuge and Pratt & Whitney.

"The opportunity will never happen again," he told his lawyer at the time. "There's an ocean on one side, so you can't grow that way. Miami can't grow anywhere but north. Palm Beach is going to grow west, and this is it."

Despite his business acumen and philanthropy, Friedland was criticized for his drain-and-build philosophy. Son Jack took over Food Fair in 1971 but it went bankrupt seven years later, and Sam Friedland agreed to pay $2.5 million amid charges he misled stockholders. Friedland died April 9, 1985, at 88, in Hollywood. Family members and partners retain a 7,000 acre citrus grove and other land.

— ELIOT KLEINBERG

PETER CUMMINGS OF MARTIN DOWNS: *On Aug. 8, 1980, Martin County commissioners placed the future of the county in Peter Cummings' hands. That's the day they approved his plan to build Martin Downs, a 4,000-home golf course community spread across 2,500 acres in Palm City. Besides leading the charge of newcomers into Martin County — its population jumped from 60,600 in 1979 to more than 115,000 today — Cummings changed the face of the county. He lured commercial centers, chain stores, movie theaters. He helped found the Council for the Arts and showed groups such as the United Way the way to big-time fund-raising. He gave money to the county library system, and the Palm City branch is named for him and wife Julie. With son Casey in the family business, 52-year-old Cummings is poised to extend his influence well into the 21st century.*

Album of the Late 20th Century

Otto "Buz" DiVosta has built nearly 20,000 houses and townhouses in Palm Beach, Martin and St. Lucie counties during the past 40 years. That number is expected to skyrocket in the next several years because DiVosta has bought 610 acres of former MacArthur Foundation land in Palm Beach Gardens and Jupiter. He also is building most of the houses in the 2,055-acre Abacoa development in Jupiter, where this photo was taken.

Mr. Construction

Because practically everyone has lived or known someone who lives in a DiVosta house or townhouse. People wait in line overnight for a chance to buy one.

Because he rose to prominence in the 1980s using an innovative construction method in which parts of the house are assembled in advance and trucked to the site to be installed. He brought suppliers and contractors in-house and asked each carpenter, plumber and electrician to focus on one part of an "assembly line" process.

Because that method lets him build a house in 47 days — about half the time it takes his competitors. Despite that break-neck pace, the homes are well-built — and affordable, too.

Because he managed to stay success-ful even after his partner, Clifford Burg, left the company in 1989.

Because he's obsessed with the details — such as finding the right kind of wood for doors or removing and disposing of

OTTO 'BUZ' DiVOSTA

Born June 11, 1934

loose nails on his construction sites.

Because he never went to college and instead designed his first home when he was 20.

Because he can't explain why his par-ents nicknamed him "Buz" — with only one "Z."

Because his own garage is 9,000 square feet — as big as his house — and stores 25 classic cars.

Because at the traditional retirement age of 65, he has no plans to step down, even after selling his DiVosta and Co. to Pulte Corp. in 1998. Aside from the cars, few things hold his interest the way build-ing a house does.

— PAUL OWERS

ARTHUR VINING DAVIS

May 30, 1867 — Nov. 17, 1962

Arvida's dynamo

A t 91, the silver-haired Arthur Vining Davis founded the company that would develop much of Boca Raton and Palm Beach County's southwestern suburbs: Arvida.

A short man — 5-foot-4 — with a booming voice, the energetic Davis established a vision for his more than 100,000 acres in South Florida. The Arvida name would become synonymous with planned, upscale developments, including Broken Sound, Boca West and Weston.

The son of a minister, Davis graduated Phi Beta Kappa from Amherst College in 1888 and worked his way up from an entry-level job at an aluminum producer, Pittsburgh Reduction Co., to chairman of Alcoa.

But it was land that made Davis a rich man. He began buying South Florida land after World War II. In 1956, he bought the Boca Resort and Club and surrounding land from J. Meyer Schine for $22.5 million — at the time, Florida's largest real-estate deal. Land south of the resort originally was used as polo fields, but Davis, realizing the development potential of the Intracoastal Waterway property, moved polo west on Glades Road and carved out the Royal Palm Yacht and Country Club. Today, houses at Royal Palm have sold for as much as $6 million.

John Temple presided over Arvida during its Boca boom period of the 1980s. He started with the company in 1975 as it began to develop 100,000 Florida acres. In seven years, he became president. In 1984, Disney spent $214 million to take over Arvida. Temple left three years later, when Disney sold the company for $400 million. He now operates his own development company.

— AVA VAN DE WATER

GEORGE ELMORE

Born Dec. 8, 1929

The road builder

P erhaps no man knows Palm Beach County better than George Thomas Elmore.

For decades, his sensible counsel made him one of the county's most influential business leaders, just as his dominance in his field — road paving — made him instrumental in forging the county's sprawling shape.

Elmore and his company, Hardrives of Delray, did more than pave roads, including some of the earliest sections of Interstate 95. He dug holes to get raw materials for building roads. And where he dug, subdivisions sprang up — usually on wide-open rural lots, with the homes built around the holes that fill with rainwater and offer prime waterfront living.

"I like space. Planners want to stack everybody into a cube and tell them to use Tri-Rail. Excuse me. I'm sorry. I want to walk out my door at night. I don't want to get on an elevator and go into a parking garage," he once said. "I like the sprawl because of the openness."

Elmore co-chaired the south county campaign to build the Kravis Center for the Performing Arts, although he opposed a downtown West Palm Beach location. He is known for his sound advice on the Economic Countil of Palm Beach County, a group representing the county's business elite, and he is a backer of the Florida Atlantic University Foundation.

— JOEL ENGELHARDT

E. LLWYD ECCLESTONE
Born March 8, 1936

The Power Hitter

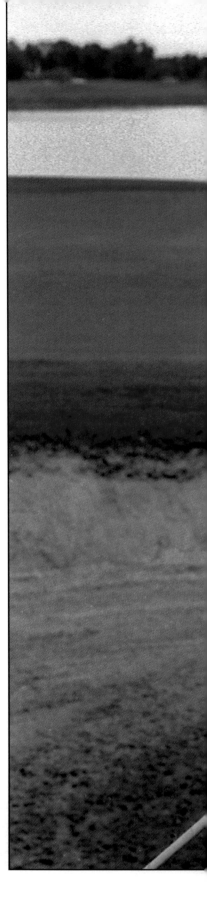

Because he estimates he has developed $1.3 billion of assessed property in Palm Beach County since he arrived in 1965, back when "there wasn't even a traffic light at U.S. 1 and PGA Boulevard."

Because he has given thousands to political campaigns during that time, becoming the most politically powerful developer in 20 years. "If it helps the county, it will help me," he says. "Palm Beach County is better off today than 35 years ago."

Because he admits he's too blunt sometimes, but defends himself with a characteristic straight answer: "Everything I've done is out there where everyone can see it, feel it and touch it."

Because these are some of the things you can see: PGA National, The Forum office buildings on Palm Beach Lakes Boulevard, Old Port Cove in North Palm Beach and Lost Tree Village near North Palm Beach. His Ecclestone Organization employs about 1,200 people.

Because the PGA of America was threatening to bolt for Dunedin in the late 1970s when he bought 2,000 acres and called it PGA National. The residential and resort development now is home to as many as 18,000 people during the season.

Because he led the 1988 expansion of Palm Beach International Airport, insisting on a parking garage and a snazzy inside design that didn't look like "a plastic airport interior."

Because he chipped in $500,000 in 1992 to help the Kravis Center open debt-free.

Because he spent a weekend with Marshall Benjamin in the Bahamas in the early 1970s talking about how the county needed a good, private prep school — and those conversations and large checks from Ecclestone and others helped start the Benjamin School in North Palm

Beach. He was whisked off to boarding school when he was a kid, and he wanted his four children to have a first-class private school at home.

Because he's known as a straight shooter, by friends and enemies alike. "He's the ultimate opposition," says Andre Fladell, a Delray Beach chiropractor and political operator who faced off against Ecclestone many times during the early 1980s. "Nothing is done in the dark. He warns you first that he's going to kill you, then he points the gun at your head and takes you out. You've got to love someone who comes right at you."

Because one of his critics — County Commissioner Karen Marcus — put their differences aside for at least a day and attended his third wedding in 1997.

Because Edwin Llwyd Ecclestone was a "Jr." for most of his life, but he dropped the "Jr." from his name after his father's death in 1981 and can't understand why people and the press don't honor that. "He did his thing, and I did mine," he said of his father.

Because he's a staunch Republican who enjoys fighting for causes he believes in. In 1989, he spearheaded the effort to change the Palm Beach County Commission from an at-large election of five members to single-district voting for seven members. He won — reducing the power of the anti-growth condo voters in southern Palm Beach County.

Because he puts out voter registration cards in his office lobby. "I think it's important for everybody to vote — for better or for worse," he said.

Because he owns seven golf courses and doesn't play golf.

Because *Sports Illustrated* called him "baby-faced but tough" when he sailed his boat to victory in the Canada Cup in 1972. And he still is.

— PAUL OWERS

*E. Llwyd Ecclestone, pictured here at his PGA National Resort, was featured in a 1982 newspaper
article titled 'Palm Beach County's Power Hitters.' Of the 10 men in that article, he's the only one
who's still active. 'That's because he doesn't lie,' said one of his frequent political foes, Andre Fladell.
'And he doesn't run out of money.'*

Patrons of the arts

BOB MONTGOMERY
Born June 9, 1930

MARY MONTGOMERY
Born July 9, 1930

Because he came from a family that understood and respected the judicial system — his father was a prominent criminal defense attorney in Alabama — and that love of law guided him throughout his life. His dad, of course, wanted him to be a doctor.

Because she opened his eyes to art when they married 46 years ago — and they, in turn, passed that joy to others. "You talk about the woman behind (the man)... She'd be the (abstract painter) Helen Frankenthaler of the day but for the fact she married me," he says.

Because he loves a good fight — and the battles he's won have been big indeed. As a young attorney in Jacksonville, he successfully challenged the "blue laws" that prevented stores from opening on Sunday. As a malpractice lawyer based in West Palm Beach, he's won more than 50 $1 million-plus verdicts against hospitals, doctors, insurance companies, airlines and car manufacturers. But the victories are never sweet when it comes to malpractice. "I'm a tragedy lawyer," he says. "I deal in children's deaths. I deal in airplanes going down."

Because he admits when he's wrong. In his early career, he represented what he now calls the bad guys — corporate America. When he won a decision 27 years ago against a little girl injured in an accident, it occurred to him that he was on the wrong side of the courtroom. "From that moment on, I just couldn't do it anymore," he says.

Because he helped win the biggest battle of them all: Florida's $11.3 billion settlement with the tobacco industry.

Because her current goal is to make contemporary art understandable and accessible at the Museum of Contemporary Art in Lake Worth, which the Montgomerys bought in July 1999. "Now the students at the Armory Arts Center will be able to go across town and see what the young, cutting-edge artists are doing, and we'll have people there who will answer questions and train them in the visual arts," she says.

Because there's practically not a single cultural organization in Palm Beach County that hasn't benefited from their leadership and generosity: The Kravis Center, Palm Beach County Cultural Council, Armory School and Visual Arts Center. Why does a power couple care so much about

culture? He recites a favorite quote — "You have to be a fist of steel and a glove of silk" — and then adds, "The arts, that's (my) silk part."

Because, as chairman of the Palm Beach Opera, he's made the organization into one of the crown jewels of the local arts scene — with an annual budget of $4 million and a growing international reputation. And that's without the opera house he plans to build in downtown West Palm Beach.

Because they live the lifestyle of the rich and famous,

Attorney Bob Montgomery and his wife, Mary, have given money and time to nearly every cultural organization in Palm Beach County. He's chairman of Palm Beach Opera, they founded the Armory School & Visual Arts Center (now Robert and Mary Montgomery Armory Art Center), they're involved with The Children's Place at Home Safe, the Palm Beach County Cultural Council and the Kravis Center. What's more, their own Palm Beach mansion is filled with art. "I've got a museum in my house," he says.

Album of the Late 20th Century

and their own art collection includes works by Picasso and Paul Klee.

Because they open up their mansion for parties — sometimes three a week — to help their charities. "If somebody needs something, we try to figure out how we can help," Mary says.

Because all that money aside, he's a liberal Democrat. "I get great glee from being around my heartless captains-of-industry friends," he jokes.

Because he speaks like a Southern gentleman — except when he's in the midst of a trial. Then he becomes, in the words of one law professor, "a terror in the courtroom." Even his wife admits that being married to Bob Montgomery "isn't for the thin-skinned."

Because he's a journalist's best friend: Ask him for a quote and he'll deliver an earful of sound bites. It all goes back to a little advice his dad once gave him: "If you want to change things in the world, keep your name in the newspaper, be the news good or bad."

— CHARLES PASSY

HALEY MICKENS
1873 — 1950

ALICE FREDERICK MICKENS
April 14, 1888 — Jan. 19, 1988

God and school

Haley Mickens helped start Palm Beach County's first black church. His wife, Alice Mickens, turned the humiliation of separate and unequal schooling into a calling.

Haley Mickens

Mickens made a living running the wheelchair concession for E.R. Bradley's Beach Club casino. The "wheelchairs" were three-wheeled rickshaw-type vehicles also called "Afromobiles" because they were usually pedaled by blacks. One day in 1893, while meeting with friends in the Styx, the black section of Palm Beach, Mickens said, "Fellows, we could at least have a prayer meeting." That led to Payne Chapel A.M.E. Church.

Alice Mickens helped lead the civil rights fight in West Palm Beach. She helped open theaters to blacks and boost standards at schools. She was on the board of Bethune-Cookman College in Daytona Beach for more than 30 years and a longtime friend of Mary McLeod Bethune. She often lobbied with Bethune in Tallahassee.

She dined with Eleanor Roosevelt, opened her home to Nobel Peace Prize winner Ralph Bunche and helped persuade the state to open a home for wayward black adolescent girls.

Alice Micken's foster daughter, Alice Moore, was often alongside her. Moore, who taught at Roosevelt Elementary School for 30 years, has worked to keep the memory of her foster parents alive.

— ELIOT KLEINBERG

Mickens family

The 1917 Mickens house at 801 Fourth St. is on the National Register of Historic Places.

Elaine and Ronald Alvarez with honor students at Bear Lakes Middle School.

Album of the Late 20th Century

Guardians of the young

RONALD VINCENT ALVAREZ

Born Oct. 9, 1944

Circuit Court judge, Palm Beach County, since 1993; assigned to juvenile division, 1996-1999; transferred to family court in 2000

ELAINE WEBB ALVAREZ

Born Feb. 9, 1947

Child advocate; leading force behind creation of Children's Services Council of Palm Beach County in 1987

Because through the death of his father when he was a child and the death of her brother Mark in Vietnam, they both gained a sensitivity to the burdens others carry through life and resolve to help ease them. Because they've leaned on, learned from and helped each other through 30 years of marriage.

Because she was horrified to learn in the mid-1980s that Palm Beach County locked up teens who ran away from home and kept them locked up longer than kids who committed crimes. And she refused to believe the experts who told her there was no point trying to get state money to build those runaways a shelter.

Because she didn't believe the same experts when they said it was impossible to get the legislature's OK to create a local board to oversee and pay for children's services, much less get voters to give it taxing power.

Because she learned the art of political persuasion and gave up so many family dinners with their two now-grown sons so she could bend ears and twist arms until she finally showed all those experts just how wrong they were. (The shelter, now called Safe

Harbor, and the Children's Services Council both became reality in 1987.)

Because, "This is a person who not only feels deeply but thinks comprehensively about not just a few children but all the children," says Jack Levine, president of the Center for Florida's Children, a statewide advocacy alliance.

Because in 20 years as a lawyer specializing in injuries and wrongful deaths, he made a reputation for putting people before money. (And because of that, he was honored with the Florida Bar's Pro Bono Service Award for the 15th judicial circuit in 1986.) Because he also made time to coach Little League.

Because in his three years as a juvenile court judge, he has been consistent in demanding that foster children be treated with dignity and that troubled teens get treatment instead of just getting locked away.

Because he has remained insistent on both in the face of pleas and protests that there is simply no money for such things. "In providing for the safety of the child and the safety of the public, finances are really irrelevant," he says.

— DOUGLAS KALAJIAN

HARRIETTE GLASNER

Born Dec. 30, 1905

Convictions and courage

When Harriette Glasner was 19, she found out she was pregnant. Her husband had left town one step ahead of the law and fraud charges. She was poor, with a 3-year-old son, and virtually alone.

She wanted an abortion. But it was Chicago in 1925.

"I managed to find $75 and I went to this back room, and I had an abortion without anesthetic," she said.

Glasner nearly died, and the ordeal steeled her for a life as a women's rights crusader.

"I have never been concerned about the reactions of anybody if I was doing something I believed in," Glasner said. "It's not easy sometimes when you were working for something that's not popular. But if you believe in it, you keep doing it. After all, you'd feel like a coward if you didn't stand up for what you believed in."

She remarried in her mid-20s, to Rudolph Glasner, who made his fortune when he got the contract to press metal for virtually every U.S. tank in World War II. She ran the Chicago chapter of the American Red Cross, outfitting hospital ships. They had a daughter in 1946.

The couple retired to Palm Beach in the 1950s, and Glasner founded the region's first chapter of Planned Parenthood — she calls that her greatest accomplishment — and helped launch the Unitarian Church and the Urban League. She's been a part of the American Civil Liberties Union since the 1920s, and the local chapter met in her living room for three decades.

"My dear," she says knowingly. "You can do anything if you just get started. You've just got to know who to ask. And I know who to ask."

— ELIOT KLEINBERG

DR. WALTER STOKES

May 23, 1898 — June 9, 1996

Martin County's straight shooter

Growing up in rural Florida, Walter Stokes was an avid fisherman and hunter who learned early that the most precious resources must be protected. He left Florida to fight in two world wars, win an Olympic gold medal, graduate from medical school and law school and stand alongside Margaret Sanger in the fight for women's rights. But he never forgot those early lessons.

Stokes brought his crusade against overdevelopment to Martin County in 1963. A beach was named for him because he fought to ensure public access to beaches. He led a successful drive to designate the Savannas wetlands a state preserve. And he helped create and run the Environmental Studies Center.

Stokes also was a psychologist and author of three books, most notably, *45 Levels to Sexual Understanding and Enjoyment.*

And he was an accomplished rifleman who won seven world championships in marksmanship and the Olympic gold medal in 1924. In 1993, he was inducted into the U.S. International Schooting Hall of Fame.

Many say that he did his life's most important work in Florida, helping to keep Martin County unspoiled.

"My top ambition was to be a hunting and fishing guide in the fields of Florida," Stokes said in 1993. "Everything else was frittering away my time."

— STEPHEN KIEHL

This Olympic gold medalist also was a champion of nature.

Quote in portrait: " I think that's what I have been, a person of hope. I believe in people enough that they also believe and then they own it themselves."

NOVEMBER 20, 1992
CAROL PUTNAM RSCJ
4/26/21 – 4/16/93

Director Sister Marie Celeste Gatti with a portrait of Hope Rural School's co-founder, Sister Carol Putnam, a Society of the Sacred Heart nun who died in 1993.

'We're always reaching for something better'

THE NUNS OF HOPE RURAL SCHOOL

It's a little school on the edge of a one-stoplight town, where the kids come and go and learn many things. Especially about the persistence of nuns.

Hope Rural School in Indiantown turns 20 in April 2000. That's 20 years of giving migrant children breakfast, lunch and an after-school snack. Of celebrating the kids' native culture — most of them are Guatemalan — but insisting they learn English and speak it at school. Of watching 60 percent of Hope's students graduate from high school and seeing many of them go on to four-year colleges.

Hope Rural School has blossomed from a day-care center to a nationally recognized grammar school that goes up to sixth grade. It survives on donations.

"We're always reaching for something better," said director Sister Marie Celeste Gatti, a Sinsinawa Dominican nun from the teaching order based in Wisconsin.

She's been teaching here for 14 years. Before her there was Sister Carol Putnam, who founded the school with Father Frank O'Loughlin in 1980. She died in 1993, and her portrait hangs over the entrance to the cafetorium with these words: "I think that's what I have been, a person of hope."

Here's what gives Sister Marie Celeste hope today: At a school conference in October, the parents of all 125 children attended. "That's how much these parents care," she said. "They're very interested that their children do what they couldn't do."

And many have. There's Vincent Carrasco, son of Mexican migrant workers who graduated from Notre Dame University. And Consuelo Vivas, who's now a student teacher at South Fork High School. And Dan Whitton, a successful artist.

There are heart-breaking stories, too, said Sister Marie Celeste, and she loses track of about 10 percent of her students.

But she never loses hope.

— JAN TUCKWOOD

THE BUTTS FAMILY: NOW
IT'S SOLD BY THE INCH:

*When Jeannette Butts
DeWitt died at 86 in
1993, her sister mused
about the bean fields the
Butts family once owned,
now replaced by big-tick-
et developments and a
sprawling shopping cen-
ter. "We sold it by the
acre," Myrtle Butts
Fleming said. "It's sold
by the inch now." The
parents of Jeannette and
Myrtle moved to Boca
Raton from Central
Florida after devastating
freezes in the 1890s and
operated a 3,500-acre
bean field. The property
once owned by the family
sprawls on each side of
Glades Road between
Florida's Turnpike and
Interstate 95, property
that now includes the
Town Center at Boca
Raton mall and the Boca
West community. They
sold most of the land to
the Arvida development
giant, selling the last of it
in the early '60s.*

THOMAS J. FLEMING JR.

Sept. 21, 1916 — March 15, 1976

Father of FAU

*'Education is our responsibility,'
said Thomas Fleming (left), with
Lyndon Johnson at the opening of FAU.
'We can't just sit and gripe about it.'*

Tom Fleming was a big man — 6-feet-4, 200 pounds and full of what his friends called "command presence."

The banker's direct and flamboyant personality persuaded the state to bring Florida Atlantic University to Boca Raton, an amazing achievement in the late 1950s, when North Florida politicians called the shots (they even dared to call the Tampa college "University of South Florida").

"Tom was the spark plug," Adelaide Snyder, FAU's director of university relations, said in 1978.

Fleming, who founded two banks in Boca Raton and was a city councilman and mayor, helped push politically and financially for the college, pouring in both his own money and raising it by using slogans such as "Boca U in '62; open the doors in '64."

After Fleming got his wish — FAU opened in September 1964 — he continued to chair its foundation, helping raise even more money.

"Education is our responsibility," he said in 1961, when his bank, First Bank & Trust, became the first in the nation to set aside 1 percent of its profits for higher education. "We can't just sit and gripe about it."

He attacked all of his passions with similar drive, including his devotion for his alma mater, the University of Florida (he also had a master's from Harvard). "Shoot, I didn't know there was any color combination but orange and blue until I was 25," he once said.

The Georgia native grew up in Fort Lauderdale and was known for his one-liners and warm heart. He had a personal greeting for every employee who passed him in the hall, and scheduled parties and pranks around full moons.

Fleming and his first wife, Myrtle, of the pioneer Butts family, also were active in the Butts family bean farm.

He died of cancer at 59 in 1976, leaving an estate of $5 million, a large collection of Florida landscapes painted by famed Fort Pierce artist Beanie Backus (see page 130) and a lasting legacy of higher education in South Florida.

— ELIOT KLEINBERG

MARSHALL E. 'DOC' RINKER

Dec. 8, 1904 — April 11, 1996

*Doc Rinker
epitomized the
rags-to-riches
dream of the
industrial age.*

Hard work, soft heart

Marshall E. "Doc" Rinker built a one-man, one-truck rock and sand-hauling venture into a half-billion-dollar building materials business, then poured his energy into supporting the things he believed in most — education, religion and the arts.

Rinker arrived in Palm Beach County from Indiana in 1925 driving a Model T Ford. He bought a dump truck with borrowed money and started a hauling and concrete company that barely managed to stay afloat during the Depression.

His reputation for hard work, integrity and willingness to take risks made

When he considers the growth of Palm Beach Atlantic College, which was established in 1968 and now has more than 2,000 students, Dr. Don Warren says, "It's clear to me that human beings could not have done this. It has to be the hand of God. We've been greatly blessed." One of his favorite sayings: "Do your giving while you're living, so you'll be knowing where it's going!"

DR. DONALD WARREN

Born May 18, 1927

Cardiologist and backer of Palm Beach Atlantic College

Big man on campus

Because he tended the hearts of Palm Beach County's richest and poorest for more than 40 years as one of the area's first cardiologists.

Because he's the founding-and-still chairman of the board of Palm Beach Atlantic College, a hands-on civic service job he's toiled at for 35 years through good and bad times.

Because he's been the very backbone of the little Baptist school that he helped nurture into a thriving, four-year, liberal arts institution on the cusp of becoming a university.

Because he seized the opportunity of circumstance and persuaded his wealthy patients to contribute to good causes, especially a college that emphasizes work and worship as well as learning, and hospitals that need the charity of the rich to treat the needs of the poor.

Because tough-minded tycoons such as John D. MacArthur, Marshall "Doc"

Rinker and Theodore Johnson trusted him with their hearts and their money so fully that they gave tens of millions of dollars to those causes.

Because you won't find a "Donald Eugene Warren" building or bridge or fountain — not even a charity golf tournament — proclaiming his works.

Because he says there's something better than having his name spread around: "I know what I've done — I can see it."

Because he lists his home phone number in the book and always has.

Because he says the best inscription for his tombstone would be this: He kept at it.

— MARY McLACHLIN

---

him a legend in the building industry and one of the nation's wealthiest men. Rinker Materials Corp. was the state's biggest concrete producer when he sold it for $515 million in 1988.

He became a full-time philanthropist, bestowing millions on schools, hospitals, church and cultural organizations. He gave nearly $15 million to Palm Beach Atlantic College, which named its business school for him and made him a life trustee.

The University of Florida's M.E. Rinker School of Building Construction is named for him in honor of the $7 million he gave and millions more that his gifts attracted. Stetson University's Rinker Auditorium, Rinker Field and the Rinker Institute of Tax and Accountancy honor nearly $4.5 million he gave to the DeLand institution, which he served as a trustee for 30 years. He also gave $1.5 million to Good Samaritan Medical Center and $1 million to the Kravis Center for the Performing Arts, site of the Rinker Playhouse.

When Doc Rinker died in 1996 at age 91, his friend George Elmore said of him:

"He demanded quality, from his people and his product."

— MARY McLACHLIN

"He has tremendous energy and savvy. His best trait
is his ability to perceive how something can be put together
for future investment. He sees the big picture."
— *Rick Rochon, president of Huizenga Holdings*

H. WAYNE HUIZENGA
Born Dec. 29, 1939

The sports fan

H. Wayne Huizenga at his Floridian golf resort, which officially has two members: himself and wife Marti. There are about 200 honorary members, from golfer Tiger Woods to singer Celine Dion. The 300-acre resort's mailing address is Martin County's Palm City, though it is actually in St. Lucie County: 'In the winter, I like to come here at 7 p.m. or 7:30 on Fridays after work for dinner. I play golf on Saturday. On Sunday I like to go to a little Presbyterian church near here.' The Huizengas built the lavish resort in 1997 as an extension of their home, a place for guests to relax and have fun. Prominently displayed inside: The 1997 World Series trophy and the home plate from the winning game.

Because he brought professional baseball and hockey to South Florida, helping define it as a big-league market: "It was a coup we were able to get a baseball team at the time. We were not the favorite to get a team. . . . When we stepped up and bought the hockey team, that really wasn't our primary goal, but we wanted to do it for South Florida."

Because the Marlins won the 1997 World Series, though Huizenga was criticized for trading away highly paid stars before selling the team in 1999: "The purists would like to believe it is not a business today. But when free agency came in and ran all the salaries up, it meant the days of sports just being for the community are long gone. Don't get me wrong. That still is important. There is just more to it than that."

Because he made his fortune on his own after he dropped out of college. He bought one garbage truck and turned it into the world's largest waste disposal company. Then he bought eight video stores and turned them into the world's largest video chain. He rated 88th on the 1999 Forbes list of richest Americans.

Because he could have lived in luxurious anonymity if he wanted, but he chose to spend millions of dollars on philanthropy in Florida. In January 1999, he and wife, Marti, donated $1 million to be shared by the United Way in St. Lucie and Martin counties, since their resort, The Floridian, straddles both. Earlier, they gave large gifts to charities in Broward County, where Huizenga Holdings is based and where they also have a home.

Because he took the Panthers to the 1996 Stanley Cup finals in their third season, an unexpected and electric moment: "It was fantastic. It pulled the community together. It helped cement the future of hockey in South Florida." The team is for sale but has a long-term contract to play in South Florida.

Because he knows how quickly a team owner can go from public hero to public villain, yet he has remained a committed owner of the NFL's Miami Dolphins: "I see myself being a Dolphins owner as long as I'm alive."

— CHARLES ELMORE

Chairman and co-CEO of AutoNation Inc., 1997-present
Owner, Miami Dolphins football team, 1994-present
Largest shareholder, Florida Panthers hockey team, 1992-present
Original owner, Florida Marlins baseball team, 1991-99
Chairman, CEO, Blockbuster Entertainment Corp.; company sold to Viacom in 1994
Co-founder, president, Waste Management Inc., 1971-84

187

The local 'Boys of Summer'

CONNIE MACK

Dec. 22, 1862 — Feb. 8, 1956

Manager of the Philadelphia Athletics, 1901-1950, who brought spring training to West Palm Beach in 1924

Connie Mack (left) greets Palm Beach High School coach Red Whittington in the '50s.

Howser   *Score*   *Ankiel*

This area's fascination with baseball started when Connie Mack was a kid.

In the early 1900s, every town had a baseball team. There was no better way to spend a Sunday afternoon than playing a double-header.

Mack, who managed the Philadelphia Athletics, brought the A's to West Palm Beach for spring training at Wright Field, which later would be renamed Connie Mack Field.

Ned Harris, who grew up in West Palm Beach, was the first area product to make it to the big leagues — as an outfielder with the Detroit Tigers in 1941. **Whitey Platt**, a West Palm Beach native, and former Lake Worth High School pitcher **Andy "Swede" Hansen** were close behind.

Soon there were many major-leaguers from the Palm Beaches.

"One of the big things was the climate," said Palm Beach County Sports Hall of Famer Bobby Riggs, a retired coach and principal who was born in West Palm Beach and was the clubhouse boy at Wright Field in the 1930s and early '40s. "Kids could play baseball year-round."

From Palm Beach High came pitchers **John Gray** and **Ken Johnson,** the first major-leaguer to pitch a no-hitter and lose; **Dick Howser,** the 1961 American League Rookie of the Year, who would achieve his greatest fame by managing the Kansas City Royals to the 1985 World Series championship; left-hander **Herb Score,** one of the early "bonus babies," who seemed destined to be one of the best of all time until his career was cut short by a line drive to the eye; the **Brown brothers,** catcher **Dick** and infielder **Larry;** and outfielder **Paul Dicken.**

Rick Rhoden of Boynton Beach, a two-sport star at Seacrest and Atlantic high schools, was a first-round draft choice of the Los Angeles Dodgers; pitched in the All-Star Game; became one of baseball's best-hitting pitchers; and, after retiring, has established himself as one of the top players on the Celebrity Golf Tour.

Joe Grahe of Palm Beach Gardens and **Rusty Meacham** of Stuart both made it to the majors after pitching a Jensen Beach/Jupiter team to the 1986 American Legion World Series championship. That club was managed by **Bob Shaw,** who defeated Sandy Koufax 1-0 in the third game of the 1959 World Series.

And now there's that young left-hander from Port St. Lucie who could become the greatest of them all: **Rick Ankiel.**

The road from Wright Field to the majors might have been bumpy, but it was well-traveled, fueled by tradition that started in the 19th century — when Connie Mack was catching pitches on the bounce.

— CHUCK OTTERSON

Bob Balfe (left) interviews Babe Ruth at Connie Mack Field, shortly before Ruth's death in 1948.

The Balfe family

He wrote about the game of life

BOB BALFE

May 26, 1909 — Dec. 22, 1987

Bob Balfe covered sports for *The Palm Beach Post* and *Evening Times* for more than half a century. He worked 14-hour days and seven-day weeks, developing a style and philosophy that caused people to describe him as "the conscience of the community."

"He had a humanistic approach to sportswriting," said retired Forest Hill High Principal Bobby Riggs, who was born in West Palm Beach and knew Balfe as an athlete, coach and administrator. "He didn't write about who won or lost but how they played the game."

Balfe's name was synonymous with sports in Palm Beach County from the 1930s until his death in 1987. With golfer Jack Nicklaus and baseball manager Mayo Smith, he was a member of the Palm Beach County Sports Hall of Fame's first induction class in 1977.

His funeral was attended by hundreds of civic leaders, educators, athletes and coaches, many of whom he had profiled in his columns, "Time Exposure" and "It's Post-Time."

Riggs once asked him, "As great a writer as you are, why do you stay here instead of going to a big metropolitan newspaper?"

Balfe's reply: "Why leave? Sooner or later, every great sports person is going to come through here."

"He believed that," Riggs said, "and he was right."

Cardinal Newman's Sam Budnyk, the winningest football coach in the county's history, remembers Balfe for his "impeccable character and total integrity."

"I had complete trust in him," Budnyk said. "He never broke your trust. He was a man of such honor — an inspiration and an example. He lived the values that made this country great."

— CHUCK OTTERSON

189

THE COACHES

Wallen   *Coffey*   *McCoy*   *Ceravolo*

Shaping young competitors

Coaches in the Palm Beach County Sports Hall of Fame:

Sam Marshall, Hank Martin, Red Whittington, Bill Adeimy, Ed Boell, Bobby Riggs, Ben York, Harry Winkler, Bucky McGann, Sam Budnyk, Gus Broberg, Randy Cooper, Dick Melear, Floyd Andrews, Buddy Baarcke, George McCampbell, Brad Mitchell, Carney Wilder, Joe Ceravolo, Lincoln Knowles, Whitey Platt, Bob Shaw, Donna Horton White, Marty Gold, Willie Irvin, Al Reitz, Dusty Rhodes, Len Brown, Henry Holmes, Ben McCoy, John McDonald, Mac McKinnon, Howard Reynolds, Abner Bigbie, Jack Marcum, Eddie Rhodes, Felipe Alou, Dan Calloway, Jim Heaton, Barry Hill, Johnny O'Brien, John Anderson, Andy Botney, Antoine Russell, Al Sutton, Roger Coffey, Jack Eassa, Mel Obradovich, Jim Maynor, Jack Boise, Ed Eissey, Jerry Jacobs, Jay Seider, Sam Agresti, Willie Gibson, Harry Howell, Mickey Neal, Ed Harris.

Coaches in the St. Lucie County Sports Hall of Fame:

Charles King, Robert Jefferson, Vernon Floyd, Rick Dixon, Larry "Hunk" Slay, Charles Hines, Havert Fenn, Mike Easom, Horace Hunter, Ben Bryan, Rock Harrison, Reginald Gordon, Adella Grove, Norton Eans Hellstrom, Mike Leatherwood, Alvin Chavis, Bob Bottger, Tina Hart, Clyde Russell, Jon Toler, William Nixon, William McNeely Jr., Chris Shay Jr., Charles Henderson, Dick Wells.

It would be impossible to pick out one or two area coaches — or even a half-dozen — as the most influential of the 20th century.

How does one measure their influence? The thousands of athletes they have sent on to college and pro careers? The innumerable men and women who have become better citizens because of a coach's discipline?

"You're hoping in some small way you're molding young people," said Cardinal Newman football coach and Athletic Director **Sam Budnyk.** "If I can make them just a little bit better in one thing, whether it's work ethic or unselfishness or perseverance, I've contributed something to their lives."

Budnyk, who is in his 40th season as a head coach at Newman and its predecessor, St. Ann's, is the winningest football coach in Palm Beach County, with more than 245 victories.

Others with similar influence include the late **Don Wallen,** who turned a lackluster Martin County High School basketball program into a state champion and became the winningest basketball coach in Florida history; **Randy Cooper,** who performed a similar turnaround with the football program at Seacrest (later Atlantic) and was *The Palm Beach Post* Football Coach of the Decade; **Floyd Andrews,** who won state titles at Roosevelt and North Shore and, with Wallen, was co-

coach of *The Post* Basketball Team of the Decade; **Roger Coffey,** who won two state football titles at Delray Carver in 1968 and '69, the first in the county's history; St. Lucie County Sports Hall of Famer **Mike Easom,** who has won more than 800 games and four state baseball championships at Indian River Community College (three in four years); Clewiston's **Al Morrell,** one of only three football coaches in state history to win 100 games in one decade; **Joe Ceravolo,** the only area basketball coach to win state titles in high school (Twin Lakes, 1970) and college (PBCC, 1978), who also won a professional championship (USBL Southern Division); **Ben McCoy,** who won more than 200 football games at seven area high schools and one in Minnesota; **Al Sutton,** for whom Suncoast's football field was named after he retired in 1998; **Mike Leatherwood,** who has won more than 500 games and one state title as basketball coach at IRCC; and IRCC swimming coach **Chris Ip,** who literal-

Sam Budnyk of Cardinal Newman is the winningest football coach in Palm Beach County. "Anyone can teach them how to block and tackle," Budnyk said. "You try to teach them to be prepared, be committed, give it everything they've got."

ly is in a class by himself.

He has led the men's and women's teams to 10 national championships, extending the men's streak to 25 consecutive national titles — the longest streak by any college team in any sport. The IRCC women have won 21 national titles.

"To me, of all the coaches in Palm Beach County, two stand out because of longevity," said Sports Hall of Famer **Bobby Riggs,** who coached at Palm Beach High and Forest Hill. **"Red Whittington** coached for over 25 years at Palm Beach High. The other would be Sam Budnyk."

Riggs said that "the greatest satisfaction I've ever had in my life" was having players he had coached tell him he had made a difference.

"Some had stepfathers who beat them and worked them like dogs," he said. "Some of them were hoods and kept getting into trouble until they discovered something they could do — like playing football — besides chase girls.

"When guys like **Red** and **John McDonald** and **Clyde Crabtree** were coaching, there wasn't a great deal of turnover. We perceived it as a career. There was a lot of sentiment and tradition. Now, it's like a free agency in sports; coaches are moving every year."

Among the coaches who stayed at one school for many years and achieved success on and off the field were the late **Jim Heaton**, for whom Forest Hill's baseball field is named; Lake Worth Athletic Director **Jack Marcum,** whose friendly rivalry with Heaton produced many exciting games and future big-leaguers; retired track coach **Dick Melear** and fellow Palm Beach County Sports and Florida Athletic Coaches Association hall of famers **Jay Seider, Mickey Neal, Harry Howell,** Budnyk and Ceravolo; FACA Hall of Famer **Willie McDonald;** Pahokee legend **Web Pell; Spencer Pompey, Brad Mitchell, Havert Fenn, Willie Irvin** and **Sam Marshall,** men who not only were successful coaches but

also were pioneers in civil rights; and the late **Hank Martin,** whose Conniston Junior High football team once won 50 consecutive games.

More than 175 of Budnyk's former players have received scholarships to 51 NCAA Division I schools and 31 Division II and III colleges. Kicker John Carney, quarterback Craig Erickson and wide receiver Chris T. Jones went on to the NFL. Others became civic leaders.

"Anyone can teach them how to block and tackle," Budnyk said. "You try to teach them to be prepared, be committed, give it everything they've got.

"It's amazing. I get them in the ninth grade, 14 years old. By their junior or senior year, I've seen the transition from boys to young men — from the fear in their eyes to confidence that they can handle whatever they have to face. That's my greatest satisfaction."

— CHUCK OTTERSON

Jack and Barbara Nicklaus have lived in Palm Beach County for 35 years.

JACK NICKLAUS
Born Jan. 21, 1940

Golfer of the century

Golf magazine called Jack Nicklaus the Golfer of the Century in 1988. Ten years later, the PGA of America gave his wife, Barbara, the inaugural PGA First Lady of Golf Award.

But in Palm Beach County, their influence spreads far beyond golf. The Nicklauses embody the best of life in Palm Beach County: good sportsmanship, good business and good works.

They moved to North Palm Beach in 1965 and have lived in the same Lost Tree Village home since 1970. Nicklaus also based his business, Golden Bear International Inc., in North Palm Beach. He is so identified with this area that the Convention and Visitors Bureau gave him an award for his "contribution to the international image of Palm Beach County tourism."

Nicklaus has won 100 professional tournaments highlighted by 18 major championships — six Masters, four U.S. Opens, three British Opens, five PGA Championships. He has designed, co-designed or redesigned golf courses around the world, including 18 in Florida. Of those, six are in Palm Beach County. A seventh course — The Bear's Club in Jupiter, where Nicklaus is founder, designer and president — was scheduled to open this spring.

This private club is expected to reflect the best of Nicklaus' design work and his love of the land. He has a passion for plants (particularly palm trees) and keeps a staff of six to tend his own 3.5-acre spread at home and the landscaping at The Bear's Club.

Barbara has helped raise more than $10 million for charities locally and in Ohio, their home state. One major beneficiary: The Benjamin School, which their five children attended and where Jack serves on the foundation board.

"When Jack decides to do something — anything — he does it 100 percent," says Barbara, who married Jack in 1960 after their junior year at Ohio State.

He's focused his work in Florida, he said in 1989, "where more and more people can come down here to earn a living ... not just to live the life that's here, but to work and try to build something."

— GREG STODA

Nicklaus, in his own words:

On his success: "The success I've had in my career, I give Barbara at least 50 percent credit. The success we've had with our five children, I give her 99 percent of that."

On The Bear's Club, his new high-end golf-course community off Donald Ross Road: It represents a "lifelong dream" to build a course that not only carries his name but also shows "my love, my passion and my respect for the game."

On designing golf courses: "I get a big kick out of doing something that's going to be here long beyond my golf game and my lifetime. It's a legacy that I leave."

Chris Evert plays the net with a youngster during a 1988 youth tennis clinic in Philadelphia. Evert is well-known for her work with children, including her Chris Evert Charities, which raises money to help abused children and fight drug abuse.

CHRIS EVERT

Born Dec. 21, 1954

She showed us how to play the game

Christine Marie Evert learned to play the game on the courts of Holiday Park in Fort Lauderdale, where her father, Jimmy, coached tennis for most of her life — and his.

The pigtailed "Chrissie" marched into the semifinals of her first U.S. Open at 16, missing the start of her junior year at St. Thomas Aquinas High School. With her trademark two-handed backhand and booming groundstrokes, Evert never fell below fourth in the world from 1972 until 1989, the year she retired, and she was No. 1 from 1975 to '81.

Along the way, she won 18 Grand Slam championships, $9 million and accumulated a .8996 winning average, the highest in professional tennis history. Many called her game and her winning monotonous, but her "ice maiden" persona warmed as she matured. Evert's rivalry — and deep friendship — with Martina Navratilova remains one of the most poignant in sports history.

Rounding out her life: marriage to Olympic skier Andy Mill, and their three sons: Alexander, Nicholas and Colton. At home in Boca Raton, she's a typical car-pool mom, conducting business on her cell phone.

Her Chris Evert Charities has raised more than $5.2 million to fight drug abuse and help abused children, and she's been known to pick up a racket at the Evert Tennis Academy, a family-run venture also in Boca Raton.

— ELIZABETH CLARKE

Evert, in her own words:

On her life since retirement: "My first instinct is to tell you I'm a lot different. The first half of my life was all about me. The second half of my life is all about everybody else but me. I like myself better in this role. The vanity goes out the window, and I feel much more grounded. But I'm the same person. I'm still competitive. I still get moody."

On the most important thing she's done since retirement: "Raise children. It's the biggest responsibility people will have in their lifetime. People always ask me what was better — winning Wimbledon or having a child? I think, winning Wimbledon is great for a week but then you're off to your next tournament. Kids, they're a 24-hour reminder. They're life. The other thing is a feeling, a memory. But I feel very lucky to have had both."

On why she gives back to the community: "I don't give back so much. When I look at what schoolteachers have to deal with or policemen, they're the ones who give back. I don't consider myself extraordinary. I should do something. I think everyone should do something. But I don't consider taking a meal to a poor family any different from me putting on a celebrity pro-am and raising money."

On her relationship with Martina Navratilova today: "Martina and I have pretty much gone different directions. She spends about five months a year in Africa. She's finding herself and what she wants to do with her life. I've found that. We have a strong bond when we see one another, but we don't see one another that often. Yet there's that special feeling that's always going to be there."

193

Derek Harper became a local legend during his years at Northshore High School (right). The basketball star, who retired from playing in 1999, returns to West Palm Beach every summer to work with kids.

DEREK HARPER
Born Oct. 13, 1961

North Shore's favorite son

D erek Harper has played in the NBA Finals and is one of the basketball league's all-time leaders in three-point field goals and steals.

Yet, when asked for some of the most satisfying moments of his career, Harper cites the number of kids from Palm Beach County he has influenced during his 16 seasons in the NBA.

"That is my sole purpose in life right now," Harper said from his second home in Dallas, where he played for the Mavericks. "I have always wanted to make a difference."

Harper became a local legend during his years at North Shore High School in West Palm Beach. Harper returns every summer to give back to his hometown.

"I give back because somebody gave to me," Harper said.

"I remember being sick in elementary school and (former Twin Lakes High School coach) John Cartwright coming to my house to get me well to get me to Daytona to play in a tournament."

Harper's contributions go beyond the financial commitments he makes every year to the Derek Harper's Holiday Basketball Classic and Derek Harper Basketball Camp. He meets young men every summer who approach him just to say they attended his camp during their high school years. Some, he says, would never have had the opportunity to attend a basketball camp.

"I'm proud to be from that area," Harper said. "Some of my greatest memories are from Palm Beach County."

— TOM D'ANGELO

Roland Martin (right) and his son Scott fish on Lake Okeechobee near his Clewiston marina.

ROLAND MARTIN

Born March 13, 1940

The angler

Because he's won more Bass Anglers Sportsman Society (B.A.S.S.) fishing tournaments — 19 — than any other angler. He's been B.A.S.S. Angler of the Year nine times and qualified for the year-end Classic 22 times. Some have called him the Babe Ruth of bass fishing. He's perhaps the most famous of Florida's 2.9 million adult anglers.

Because he's an instinctive angler who can sense changes on the water, what those changes mean to the fish below the surface and the probability of a bite. Some people call it luck. He calls it struggling to find opportunity — then adjusting his technique to catch the fish. "Only the better fishermen can capitalize on this," he said.

Because at age 59 he looks 10 years younger than he is and doesn't plan to retire anytime soon.

Because his TV show, *Fishing with Roland Martin*, which airs on TNN, has promoted fishing as a family sport and made Martin and Lake Okeechobee famous across America during its 25 years on the air. Martin moved to Clewiston from Tulsa, Okla., in 1980 after spending several winters

there making TV shows. He started his marina in a water-front shack leased from U.S. Sugar Corp.

Because Martin, who has a degree in biology from the University of Maryland, promoted catch-and-release fishing back in 1971, when he and Jerry McKinnis released two 10-pound-plus Lake Okeechobee bass on television. The TV segment promoted a flurry of letters from viewers who thought releasing fish was insulting to the sport — and others who praised them for letting the fish swim free.

Because he followed his heart and became a bass fishing guide on the Santee and Cooper rivers near Charleston, S.C., — against his parents' wishes — after serving in the military and working as a school teacher in Brazil. Using his knowledge from guiding, Martin started fishing B.A.S.S. tournaments in 1970.

Because he loved fishing, even though his father didn't, and mowed lawns as a middle-school student in exchange for fishing trips with older, experienced anglers. By age 16, he was good enough to fish on his own. Martin built his own pontoon boat from old military fuel tanks and got a permit to fish the reservoirs near his home in Laurel, Md.

Because he's passed on the fishing gene to his son Scott, 24, who started fishing the Wal-Mart FLW Tour in January 1999 and won the co-angler division and $45,000 in his first season. The younger Martin plans to fish against his dad in the professional division starting in January at — where else? — Roland Martin's Marina.

— WILLIE HOWARD

195

Album of the Late 20th Century

Willie Gary delights in his success. His house on Sewall's Point in Stuart has 50 rooms. Lincolns and Rolls-Royces fill the garage. His gold Rolex is custom-made. "I like nice things because when I was young I had no things," he said. "But there's no value in a thing. There's only value in what it takes to earn that thing. My dad used to say, 'Make the money, but don't let the money make you.'"

The American Dream

Because Willie Edward Gary never met a roadblock in life he didn't plow through, because he never quit, never stopped dreaming. Because he wins.

Because he was born a sharecropper's son, and in 1965 he became one of the first two black students from Indiantown to attend college — the other student, Gloria Royal, became his wife. He returned to Martin County in 1969 with his law degree and less than $100 to his name. He hung his shingle in Stuart and won his first case. Now, his law firm has 30 associates, 120 employees and brings in hundreds of millions of dollars each year in settlements.

Because Willie Gary fights the big guys and wins. When the biggest Canadian funeral home company was putting small U.S. funeral homes out of business, Gary won a $400 million settlement against the company. He takes on utilities that put poor people at risk, airlines and insurance companies and incompetent doctors. But he'll side with the big guy if he thinks they're right — sugar companies that are accused of cheating migrant workers, doctors falsely accused of malpractice. "I don't care if you're black or white, rich or poor, big or small," said Gary. "But you gotta be in the right. The law is color-blind."

Because his law firm office is in the gorgeous building that used to be Stuart's Pelican Hotel. He washed dishes at the hotel as a college student; now he owns the building. "I've worked every day of my life since I was big enough to plant seedlings in groves. I tell students, I tell my own sons: 'Work. Work with a purpose. Nothing happens by accident. It

WILLIE GARY

Born July 12, 1947

happens by purpose.'"

Because he is a practicing Baptist, has never had a sip of beer, doesn't smoke, loves gospel music and watches *Hour of Power* faithfully.

Because he spends so much time each month in classrooms telling kids how to fight, how to win, how to live fair, live right, how to ask for nothing but a chance to prove yourself. "I want all children to have a level playing field, but don't come complaining to me that you're in such-and-such condition because you are poor or because you are black." If you want what I have, he tells kids, you better get working.

Because he gives back more than he takes — more than $12 million dollars in scholarships, grants to colleges, gifts to hospitals, free legal work.

Because he throws a helluva party, can sing well enough to sign with a recording company, can dance all night. And he can get President Clinton, Evander Holyfield, the Rev. Jesse Jackson and Don King all around the same dinner table at his home.

Because his three sons are in law school. His wife keeps a Bible in every room of their house, and Willie Gary reads them.

Because he's the best trial lawyer in America, according to F. Lee Bailey.

— PAUL REID

Trapper Nelson with an alligator. Kids who lived along the Loxahatchee River would collect gopher turtles and sell them for 25 cents to Nelson, who then chopped the meat into stew.

Florida State Archives

Wild man of the Loxahatchee

TRAPPER NELSON

1909 — July 1968

How did Victor Nostokovich of Trenton, N.J., become the legendary woodsman known as Trapper Nelson? It's a story of a man with a scandalous past who came to a mysterious end.

Nostokovich had served time in Mexico for gun-running, and he caught a freight train east when he got out of jail. He ended up in Jupiter with a new name.

A strapping man at 6-feet-2-inches and 240 pounds, "Trapper" built a private paradise in a wooded area along the Loxahatchee River. He planted trees and pineapples. He skinned raccoons and cooked the carcasses. Occasionally, he'd head to town to get supplies and pick up copies of *The Wall Street Journal*.

To pay the taxes on his land, Trapper built a miniature zoo and handmade cottages hewn from slash pine. He arranged for boat captains from West Palm Beach to bring tourists 7 miles up river by pontoon to have lunch in the wild and view his bobcats, raccoons, possums, alligators and snakes.

On some days, hundreds would come and buy a souvenir orchid or handmade trinket. Palm Beach socialites — the Kennedys included — would visit for a taste of wild Florida. Heavyweight boxing champion Gene Tunney once remarked that Nelson's burly hands made his own look feminine.

Trapper eventually accumulated 858 acres but had trouble paying his taxes after the state closed the zoo because of unsanitary conditions.

His health soon declined, and so did his mood. He cut trees to block river access to his camp and barricaded the road to his property. Visitors who didn't have his permission to stop by were turned away with shotgun blasts.

In 1968, Trapper was found dead after that same shotgun blew a hole in his belly.

A coroner declared it a suicide, but some who knew of his run-ins with townsfolk believe he was murdered. The mystery fueled his legend and sparked rumors that he'd hidden a treasure somewhere on his property.

Nelson's 658-acre home became part of Jonathan Dickinson State Park in 1970. Visitors can canoe along the Loxahatchee River to tour his two cabins, docks, chickee huts and a huge stack of wood he chopped that still remains.

Oh, and those rumors? Some were true. In 1984, park rangers pulled away mortar near his fireplace and found more than 5,000 coins worth about $1,800.

— JEFF HOUCK

A big heart and a juicy headline

GENEROSO POPE

Jan. 13, 1927 — Oct. 2, 1988

Generoso Pope Jr. never apologized for the tawdry supermarket tabloid that became a household word and put Lantana on the map. And he quietly shared many of the millions he made off JFK conspiracies, Elvis sightings and UFO kidnappings.

Pope lived for the tidbits of gossip that "inquiring minds want to know," the stuff that sent the *National Enquirer* flying off the racks. In shirtsleeves and necktie and puffing his Kents, he shared the six-day, 60-hour workweeks of his employees and signed off on every story. Pope essentially invented the genre and was the first with the idea of placing his tabloid at the spot where shoppers are most impulsive: the checkout line.

At its height, the *Enquirer* sold 5 million copies a week and boasted "the largest circulation of any paper in America."

"I believe that what goes in the publication can't be decided by a committee," he said . "It has to be one person because no two people think alike. It's just a gut feeling I've developed to try and keep track of what the public really wants."

To lure journalists, he paid outrageous salaries and topped them with big bonuses for scoops. And he got them: Liberace's AIDS, the gardener who found Grace Kelly in her dying moments, photos of Gary Hart and Donna Rice cavorting in Bimini.

He also raised money for hard-to-adopt orphans, burn victims and other disadvantaged people.

His largesse was local as well: He donated to Lantana, local hospitals, the Little League and JFK Medical Center in Atlantis, where he was chairman from 1987 to 1988 and is estimated to have given more than $3 million. *Forbes* magazine estimated his wealth at $150 million in 1985.

A son of Italian immigrants and a child of the Bronx and Manhattan, Pope learned the ropes from his father, who owned an Italian-language daily, *Il Progresso*.

"My father and I were very close," Pope once said. "I guess I got printer's ink in my blood." He ran the paper until his father died, turned it over to brothers, then heard the mainstream *New York Enquirer* was for sale. He borrowed $20,000 and bought the 17,000-circulation paper for $75,000 in 1952. It took six years to break even; by then he had already turned the paper into a tabloid specializing in crime stories featuring gruesome photos, what he called "gore." Circulation rose to 1 million a week. He moved it from New Jersey to Lantana in 1971.

Not everything was rosy; lawsuits kept Pope's lawyers in Italian suits. Carol Burnett, Frank Sinatra, Cary Grant, Cher and Shirley Jones all won court judgments or settlements. Pope always downplayed the lawsuits, saying he wasn't sued any more often than other publishers.

His greatest symbol was the towering Christmas tree, at times higher than 100 feet, erected every year on the *Enquirer* grounds along Federal Highway. The tree came down for good shortly after Pope died.

His widow, Lois, sold the *Enquirer* and *Weekly World News* for $412.5 million and started a charitable foundation.

The *Enquirer's* new owner, American Media, bought competitor Globe Communications in November 1999 and said that the *Enquirer* will move to Boca Raton.

— ELIOT KLEINBERG

One of Pope's biggest coups came in 1977 — the last photo of Elvis.

Last of the cowboy sheriffs

JAMES D. HOLT

Feb. 13, 1932 — Dec. 21, 1992

Burt Reynolds called his friend a "lawman's lawman. He was a true patriot, a gentleman and my friend." He gave Holt a small role in one of his fims.

He had his name hand-tooled on the back of his leather belt and occasionally remembered to pin his badge on his blue jeans, but he rarely had to identify himself in Martin County.

He was Sheriff James D. Holt, and he was the law in Martin County for 20 years — the only sheriff many residents and most law-enforcement officers had known until he died of bone cancer in late 1992.

A true cowboy who had his own ranch and horses and cattle to tend, Holt never had a computer on his desk — he had a gold-plated six-shooter.

He was a world-class tracker and was known for sticking with a manhunt until the suspect was caught. He loved leading a posse through the woods and the wetlands in search of bad guys, catching them and putting them in jail. Few escaped, and crooks feared Holt on their trail far more than a kennel full of tracking dogs.

"James D. was like a bulldog," recalled former sheriff's Maj. John Murphy. "James always felt if we looked one more time, we might find whoever we were looking for — and usually we did."

— JILL TAYLOR

'Most genial of lawbreakers'

BILL McCOY

Aug. 17, 1887 — Dec. 30, 1948

Bill McCoy put his picture on his whisky label — but he was a teetotaler himself.

When Bill McCoy broke the law, he did so with such honesty, good cheer and success that everyone called him "the real McCoy."

From 1921 to 1925, McCoy was a rumrunner, transporting 175,000 cases of liquor from the Bahamas to New Jersey and New York.

In a biography of McCoy published in 1931, Frederic Van de Water wrote, "The slippery, irreverent, swaggeringly resourceful McCoy was a scourge, a menacle, a continued threat against the peace and dignity of the United States ... (but) even his bitterest foes admitted, he was the most genial and endearingly candid of lawbreakers."

McCoy and his brother, Benjamin, moved to Central Florida in 1898 and started a boat-building and water-bus service. But when offered big money to captain a ship running alcohol from Nassau to Atlantic City, N.J., McCoy's real adventures began.

After his rumrunning days, McCoy and his brother purchased what is now Sailfish Point on Hutchinson Island. McCoy was also a painter whose works are still displayed in some Treasure Coast homes.

Today, Sailfish Point is an exclusive development and marina valued at $350 million.

— STEPHEN KIEHL

Cracker Johnson on Banyan Street, where he owned property. The king of black West Palm Beach earned his nickname because he could pass for white.

The Robin Hood of black West Palm Beach

CRACKER JOHNSON

Nov. 17, 1877 — July 2, 1946

Cracker Johnson has one foot on the running board of his roadster. He's all fedora and saddle shoes, so cool you'd swear this was a movie still.

But it's just James Jerome Johnson, king of black West Palm Beach. The blue-eyed Johnson earned his nickname because he could pass as white. He came through West Palm Beach in 1900 and bought up property: A rooming house on Banyan Street, a movie theater — the Dixie, later

called the Strand, on Rosemary and Third Street — and a nightclub called the Florida Bar, with waiters in tuxedos. He helped start a private club for "colored gentlemen." Blacks couldn't borrow money from white-owned banks, so they borrowed from Johnson.

He also is believed to have smuggled liquor during Prohibition, and he ran the bolita numbers game. Johnson, who couldn't read or write except to sign his name, was raking in up to $10,000 a week by the 1940s.

He died in a gunfight behind the Florida Bar after trying to help a friend. Hundreds of people, both black and white, came to the funeral of a king.

— ELIOT KLEINBERG

The masters of Mar-a-Lago

MARJORIE MERRIWEATHER POST

March 15, 1887 — Sept 12, 1973

Marjorie Merriweather Post got her cash from her dad, the Post of the breakfast cereal — and she got some of his quirks, too.

This combo made her the entertaining, extravagant belle of Palm Beach for half a century.

Her 1927 palace, Mar-a-Lago, featured 58 bedrooms, 33 bathrooms (with gold fixtures, of course), three bomb shelters, a theater, a ballroom, a nine-hole golf course and 17 ocean-to-lake acres.

Marjorie made some bad decisions in love — she married four times — but she rarely made a bad decision in business.

When cereal magnate Charles William Post killed himself in May 1914, his 27-year-old daughter inherited $11 million. At her death at age 86, that had grown to $117 million.

"I am not the richest woman in the world," she once said. "There are others better off than I am. The only difference is that I do more with mine. I put it to work."

She spent $2.5 million to build her "little cottage by the sea," and when the Florida boom went bust in 1926, she refused to lay off any of its 600 builders. "This would have added more unemployment," she reasoned. "Hence we went ahead."

She could be superficial — she made her servants measure dinner place settings with a ruler to ensure uniformity — but also generous.

She supported a World War I Red Cross hospital in Europe. She staged a benefit that raised $100,000 to build a new hospital: Good Samaritan Hospital. She threw parties for 1,100 Palm Beach mansion servants. She sponsored a soup kitchen in Manhattan's Hell's Kitchen. In World War II, she leased her yacht to the army; it sank a sub at Normandy.

Her marriage to E.F. Hutton produced daughter Nedenia (actress Dina Merrill). When Marjorie married her fourth husband, Herbert May, Alice Roosevelt Longworth commented: "Oh my, I can't possibly keep up with all the husbands' names. I just call her 'Miss Post Toasties' and let it go at that."

In 1964, Post offered Mar-a-Lago to the state, which balked at the quarter-million-dollar annual overhead. When she died in 1973, she willed it to the federal government as a winter White House; the feds gave it back seven years later.

— RON HAYES

Square dancing with Mrs. Post in the 1920s

An evening at Mar-a-Lago, described in 1983 by Betty McMahon of Palm Beach:

"It started promptly at 7. She was always in the receiving line. Maybe one cocktail would be served at the reception, and then we'd go in to this wonderful dinner. Beautiful roast beef, mashed potatoes — everything was very simple but done well. Jell-O and cakes for dessert — General Foods products, of course. After dinner, we would all go into the ballroom. Mrs. Post hired all these pros to push us around the floor, which was fun. She loved people who danced. At 10:30 or 11, they would play some good-night song. We all held hands and circled back and forth and then said good night to everyone."

Palm Beach in the 1920s was the epitome of glamour. Billie Burke and Flo Ziegfeld helped Marjorie stage plays and costume balls.

DONALD TRUMP

Born June 14, 1946

Marjorie Merriweather Post would no doubt have been swept away by this swanky Mar-a-Lago soiree, a $500-a-seat gala to benefit the Preservation Society of Palm Beach.

She did love a party. And everyone was there.

But it was March 1986 — 13 years after the cereal heiress' death — and Mar-a-Lago's new owner was property baron Donald Trump. It was his first season on the island after purchasing the furnished palace for $10 million. And what grander way to make a gracious impression than hosting those who value what Palm Beach prizes most — its heritage.

"Mrs. Post had a unique and elegant style," Trump said as local luminaries arrived at the South Ocean Boulevard estate built in 1927. "I think every bit of that aura should be preserved."

Trump not only preserved Mar-a-Lago, he resurrected the mansion, turning it into a private club in 1995.

It costs $100,000 to join, not counting annual dues. Celebrities are encouraged, blue blood not required.

Donald Trump — born to Mary MacLeod Trump and Fred Trump, a New York real estate tycoon — began amassing his fortune with middle-income property on Coney Island. Now, he owns skyscrapers galore in Manhattan, including Trump Tower, Trump Parc, Trump Palace and so on. His reach extends south to Atlantic City, N.J., where four sprawl-ing casinos bear his name.

And in West Palm Beach, the entrepreneur owns Trump Plaza, a 33-story condo complex on Flagler Drive, and Trump International Golf Club on Congress Avenue and Summit Boulevard.

Many would agree, though, that his most notable contribution to Palm Beach County has been the revitalization of the Mediterranean-style landmark where Post once held her legendary square dances and lavish charity balls.

— LORETTA GRANTHAM

CHRIS MATULA/The Palm Beach Post

Trump at Mar-a-Lago: $100,000 buys a membership.

Dolly and Homer Hand at the Glades Campus of PBCC.

Two Hands, none better

It's not much of an exaggeration to say that Belle Glade without Dolly and Homer Hand would be like Bedford Falls without George Bailey in the movie *It's a Wonderful Life* — a far lesser place.

Not only were they instrumental in getting a branch of Palm Beach Community College to the Glades in 1971, but Mrs. Hand was the guiding light for the Dolly Hand Cultural Arts Center on campus.

She didn't know that the center, with its 500-seat theater, was going to be named for her until she drove up to the 1982 opening with then-PBCC president Ed Eissey.

"We do what we do" to help, not for publicity, Mrs. Hand said.

Others are not so reticent. "The whole area is blessed to have them as part of us," said former Belle Glade Mayor Tom Altman in 1997, when Gov. Lawton Chiles and his wife, Rhea, visited Belle Glade to make the couple the first recipients of the Chileses' Heartland Award for "people who exemplify long-term commitment and service to communities."

Frances "Dolly" Rutledge, a Belle Glade native, graduated from what then was Palm Beach Junior College in 1945. She met Homer Hand, a native of LaBelle, at a Clewiston skating rink. The two married in 1954 and settled in Belle Glade. Mr. Hand is a real-estate investor and Mrs. Hand a

FRANCES 'DOLLY' HAND

Born Dec. 20, 1928

HOMER HAND

Born Jan. 15, 1928

non-practicing lawyer.

Together, they have helped the community in more ways than any single person knows.

"I've never seen anyone give to a gamut of needs like they have," Gov. Chiles said in 1997.

Beyond the donations to the PBCC Glades campus, the Hands have provided aid to perhaps 500 students over the years, ranging from full scholarships to clothing. The Hands have helped the Methodist Children's Home, the Living Christmas Tree project and various churches.

Mrs. Hand was a PBCC trustee from 1973 until 1989. Her successor: Mr. Hand, who was appointed to his third term in 1997.

Eissey once called Dolly Hand "the most exceptional individual I have ever met."

But her biggest reward comes not from compliments but from the kids she and her husband have helped: "To see those young people succeed is just a wonderful blessing."

— BILL MCGOUN

PALM BEACH HIGH SUPPORTERS:

Dr. Reginald Stambaugh (Class of '47) led the fight when it looked like the high school would be torn down and replaced with a modern school in 1992. Alumni lobbied the school board. "We found that many people have emotional attachments to Palm Beach High — memories, family, tradition, community," Stambaugh said. They won. Palm Beach High and the older buildings to the south, Central School and the old junior high, were restored. Now it's the campus of the Alexander W. Dreyfoos School of the Arts. And now, said Stambaugh, "It's a jewel."

FROM LEFT, FRONT ROW: Robert C. Davis (Class of '48), Marilyn Stone (Class of '43), Betty Jane Williams (Class of '47), Pearl Messer Callaway (Class of '38), Mary-Jo Hartwell Horton (Class of '47), Lois Garland Phillips (Class of '47). Back row, from left: Reginald Stambaugh, Bill Miller (Class of '47), Mary Anne Riggle Wandelt (Class of '57), Donald Ayers (Class of '47), Steve Newell (Class of '62), Bobby Riggs (Class of '43) and Julian M. Rowley (Class of '29).

LAKE WORTH HIGH SUPPORTERS:

In the early '90s, it looked like Lake Worth High might be closed and a new school built in the western suburbs. But Principal David Cantley and School Board member Jody Gleason got influential grad Dennis F. Dorsey and civic group Project Lake Worth involved, and they turned the tide. More than $30 million in renovations began in 1996. Four generations of Dorsey's family have gone to Lake Worth High.

FROM LEFT: Dennis F. Dorsey (Class of '53), founder and president of the Lake Worth High School Alumni Foundation; Mac McKinnon, longtime athletic director; Eldene Spriggs of the Alumni Foundation and Lake Worth Dollars for Scholars Foundation; Rock Tate (Class of '76); Arby Bankhead, long-time teacher; Virginia Sullivan Thomas (Class of '45); Charlane Finch Macon (Class of '48); Ann Hoffman Harvey (Class of '46); David D. Cantley, former principal; Al Elam (Class of '52); Gail Paglialungo (Class of '67); William C. Jenner of the Palm Beach Community College Foundation; School Board member Jody Gleason; Tom Vaughan (Class of '61).

THE ALUMNI WHO SAVED THEIR ALMA MATERS

True to their schools

Because when it looked like the old Palm Beach High, founded in 1908, and the old Lake Worth High, built in 1922, would meet the bull-dozer, a passionate group of their students rallied — to prove that memories can be as important as money.

Because their push for preservation has rubbed off on alumni of other schools, including the old Industrial High School, which got a last-minute reprieve from the wrecking ball in 1999.

Because they believed in the words of West Palm Beach architect Leslie Divoll, who said the historic buildings represent "one generation speaking to another."

— JAN TUCKWOOD

CHRISTINA ORR-CAHALL

Born June 12, 1947

The art lover

Director, Norton Museum of art, 1990 to present

Because she led the Norton through a $23-million expansion, creating a new, more professional museum for the 21st Century. The new Norton opened in January 1997 with 77,500 square feet and 19 galleries, more than double the size of the original museum.

Because she gives credit to "the team" — the staff, the diverse museum board and the donors who built a museum for the whole community. "This wouldn't have happened with just me."

Because as spacious and impressive as the new building is, it was the storage space for the Norton's vast collection, most of it purchased by museum founder Ralph Norton, that brought tears to her eyes. "One of my most poignant moments was when I walked into the new storage area by myself. It wasn't the glamorous part of the museum, but I thought, finally, we were doing right by the art."

Because she left the Corcoran Museum in Washington, D.C., in the late '80s after a complicated controversy over the exhibition of homoerotic photographs by Robert Mapplethorpe — and she never complained and never explained when she came "home" to head the Norton Museum of Art. The media firestorm surrounding her Corcoran departure taught her a lesson: "It made me less sensitive to outside criticism and more careful to execute self-criticism. I try to be honest with myself."

Because she has expanded the museum's educational programs from one part-time employee to seven full-time curators and instructors.

Because she wrote her doctoral thesis at Yale on Addison Mizner, the quintessential Palm Beach architect.

Because she keeps learning. She reads two books a week, always around a theme. One year it was the equator. Another year, Ireland. She read several histories of Ireland, Yeats' poetry, Irish art books, Frank McCourt's books, Frank O'Connor's new biography. "It's like taking a course." (And speaking of courses, she recently took one in koine Greek at Palm Beach Atlantic College just because she loves language.)

Because if she had to choose one favorite painting at the Norton, she might choose one that she didn't like much back in the '70s when she was the Norton's curator. "This (Robert) Motherwell painting, an elegy about the Spanish Civil War (*Personage*, painted in 1943). When I came back 10 years ago, I decided I really had to spend more time with that painting. So I spent 15 minutes a day, 12 weeks in a row just sitting in front of it. One day, I sat with it for an hour, and now the painting and I have a rapport. It's become one of my favorites. Every inch of it is in my head. It's very beautiful and truly elegiac, almost musical and poetic."

Because she's found her greatest professional satisfaction at the Norton — and it has benefited the community. "My dream always has been to make a difference in Florida. So to see the Norton today, to see how much the community cares, that's living out my dream."

— GARY SCHWAN

Album of the Late 20th Century

Christina Orr-Cahall blends into a painting, La Galleria *by David Hollowell. 'This museum is a place where everyone is welcome.' Her advice for enjoying the Norton's collection: 'Don't try to see everything in 45 minutes. Pick four postcards from the museum shop and go see those four paintings. Stand in front of each one for 10 minutes. Then come back the next week and pick four more postcards.'*

FOUNDERS OF THE NORTON: *Ralph Norton was a Chicago industrialist with a keen interest in art and a wife, Elizabeth, with a great eye. In 1939, the Nortons (at left) retired to West Palm Beach and built a museum for their collection. The Norton Gallery of Art opened in 1941. After Elizabeth's death, Norton married an art instructor at the Norton school, Ann Weaver. He died in 1953 at 77. The Ann Norton Sculpture Gardens opened in 1979.*

BIG PLANS: *City Planner Dan Cary (above) stands in the middle of Banyan Street in downtown West Palm Beach, where he hopes to locate the city's new city hall complex.*

ART DISTRICT: *Lawrence Corning (left) next to the old Ferndix building, part of his arts district on Dixie Highway in downtown West Palm Beach. Corning has converted several old buildings into artists' studios and galleries.*

They brought us back to Main Street

The idea was hardly original: Bring back downtown. Throughout the 1970s and '80s, it seemed almost impossible. But by the century's end, the old downtowns were getting new respect. Here are some of the people who made the difference ...

Dan Cary, executive director of the Treasure Coast Regional Planning Council in the early '90s, promoted the return to main street. He and wife Meriliz worked to save historic Stuart. Cary encouraged West Palm Beach Mayor Nancy Graham to bring in husband-wife architects **Andres Duany** and **Elizabeth Plater-Zyberk** to revitalize downtown. He's now the head planner in West Palm Beach with a big, new project: Finding the perfect place and style for a new city hall.

Ramon Trias, an architect whose childhood in Barcelona, Spain, filled him with a passion for beautiful cities, set his sights on transforming downtown Lake Worth in 1992.

"I was 24 years old and I didn't know any better," Trias said. "I said, 'Let's propose a plan that builds on the history of the town and preserves old buildings. Let's come up with a good pedestrian design for our streets and we'll figure out how to do it later.' To this day, Lake Worth is working on the ideas," said Trias, who then worked for the Regional Planning Council and is now Fort Pierce's development director.

Two years ago, Trias persuaded Fort Pierce commissioners to spend $150,000 to move and renovate the Seven Gables house, built in 1905 to mirror the mansion in Nathaniel Hawthorne's *The House of Seven Gables*. Today it is a visitors center. Nearby, Fort Pierce's landmark Sunrise Theatre, built in 1923, is getting a multi-million-dollar facelift. It will reopen in 2001.

In Fort Pierce, he's found signature styles that can be echoed in new construction, like the city's new waterfront library. And Trias is teaching the next generation about preservation. "I've created some coloring books," he said. "One is a fourth-grade text on Mediterranean Fort Pierce. I'm publishing three more by January, dealing with other periods."

Lawrence Corning's family has deep Palm Beach roots — his grandmother was society doyenne Sue Whitmore. But instead of coasting on the family fortune, he began buying and restoring old buildings in West Palm Beach. He reached a goal in 1998 when the stretch of Clematis from the Florida East Coast tracks to the police station was named a national historic district. "You can't lose the historic property that shows your roots," he said.

SEVEN GABLES: *Ramon Trias in front of the Seven Gables House in downtown Fort Pierce, which is now a welcome center. "This house will create a new brand symbol for the city of Fort Pierce," he said. Below, a sketch from Ramon Trias' coloring book on Mediterranean Fort Pierce.*

MIZNER PARK: *Developer Tom Crocker and community supporter Jamie Snyder stand on a balcony overlooking the center of Mizner Park in Boca Raton. As chairman of Boca's Community Redevelopment Agency in the mid-'80s, Snyder not only urged Crocker to develop Mizner Park, but she also came up with a plan for the revitalization of downtown and masterminded the rebuilding of Sanborn Square, Barry Plaza and other projects.*

STUART CHAMPIONS: *Peter and Joan Jefferson.*

Joan and Peter Jefferson didn't just champion downtown Stuart, they moved in at a time when just about everyone else had moved out. They bought the 13-store Post Office Arcade with partners Ann and David MacMillan in 1990.

As an architect, Peter had faith in the city's design. As mayor, Joan had faith in its future. The tumble-down Art Deco arcade was restored and converted into a mixture of apartments and shops. The Jeffersons moved to North Carolina in 1995.

The success of developer **Tom Crocker's** shopping plaza near Glades Road and I-95 in Boca Raton caught the interest of **Jamie Snyder**, then chairman of the city's Community Redevelopment Agency.

"She came up to me at a party and suggested that I should be interested in downtown," Crocker says. "I agreed to meet with her, mostly to be polite. She turned out to be a terrific salesman."

Snyder urged Crocker to find a way to turn the half-empty Boca Raton Mall into a downtown hub.

City voters approved the plan for Mizner Park in 1989, including $56.5 million in bond money to buy the property, build the fountains and make other improvements. The debt, which brought a citywide tax increase, still provokes critics. But Mizner has become a major downtown draw since it opened in 1990. It is about to become home to the Boca Raton Museum of Art, and a private group is raising money for a concert hall. Snyder was one of the concert group's founders.

"More than any other person, she deserves credit for

THE DOWNTOWNERS

causing downtown Boca to be redeveloped," Crocker says. "You can look at me and say I did it for the money. But Jamie did it because it was the right thing to do. She was being a good citizen."

Frances Bourque took on the task of saving the former Delray Beach Elementary and High Schools and transforming them into the Old School Square arts complex.

In 1986, she lobbied for state grants, and she lobbied just as hard to get everyday folks to contribute $5 or $10 toward the project's eventual $6 million-plus cost.

"Here was a blight at the crossroads of Delray Beach," she said. "And it really was a crossroads. It was where the black and white communities were split. Where the east and west were split. It was a time when it appeared that none of the community was pulling together."

Old School Square opened with a museum in 1990, a theater and gym in 1993, and a bandshell is still to come. It has become the anchor of the city's beachward revival — and it showed the unifying power of a good idea.

"When I started, I didn't know diddly," Bourque said. "But I know people, and I know people are good. My gift was inspiration. I could look beyond where we were to where we ought to be, and other people listened. I was just an instrument."

— DOUGLAS KALAJIAN

Palm Beach High School Museum

Burt Reynolds as a Palm Beach High football star, 1954.

Palm Beach High School Museum

Mary Alice Sullivan and Buddy Reynolds were named best all-around couple in the Palm Beach High School Class of 1954. We all know what happened to Buddy, but Mary Alice gained some fame of her own. She married tire company heir Russell Firestone and divorced him in a nationally publicized case.

Our Buddy

BURT REYNOLDS

Born Feb. 11, 1936

W hether playing the victor or the victim, actor Burt Reynolds has always had a safe harbor: his family and friends and Palm Beach County.

Reynolds has hit legendary highs — from being the world's No. 1 box-office draw in the '70s to an Academy Award nomination for *Boogie Nights* in 1997 and an Emmy win for *Evening Shade* in '91 — and legendary lows — his divorce from Loni Anderson and his bankruptcy.

But throughout his four-decade career on the world's stage, Reynolds has always returned home, to the place where his old pals call him "Buddy."

Reynolds moved to Palm Beach County as a fourth-grader. His father, Burt Sr., became police chief of Riviera Beach, and Buddy became a football star at Palm Beach High. When a shattered knee ended his football dreams at Florida State University, Reynolds came home again, to Palm Beach Junior College. There, a wonderful teacher — Watson B. Duncan III — introduced him to the stage and a new life.

At the 45th reunion of the Class of '54 this fall, Reynolds fell right back in with Mo Mustaine and his old gang. Sure, he's the most famous guy from Palm Beach County, they said, but he's still the same old Buddy.

Burt Reynolds on Palm Beach County, in his own words:

"THE FIRST TIME I ACTUALLY SAW THE OCEAN was on Highway A1A in Jupiter. It was so green and beautiful. Little did I know what a big part of my life the little town of Jupiter would become someday. In those days, it was a truck stop.

"As advertised, Riviera Beach was right on the water, too ... When we arrived, the small town had a few thousand residents and two trailer courts: The Sea Breeze and Star Camp. With few belongings, we bought an old trailer and moved into — you guessed it — Star Camp."

"Most people believed paradise was actually seven miles south and over the bridge — the exclusive island of Palm Beach ... None of that interested me as much as the swampy wilderness to the west. You could've offered me the largest mansion in Palm Beach, and I would've turned it down in favor of the mysterious woods that ran all along the northern shore of Riviera and the Everglades to the west ...

"It's never a picnic being the police chief's son. Yet, in my eyes, no man was greater than my dad. Nobody stood taller or stronger. He was my real-life John Wayne. He defined the rules of manhood. It was like trying to replace Babe Ruth — an impossible task. I suspect this is why I've spent my whole life thinking that no amount of success would make me as much of a man as my father.

"I've never lacked for confidence, but I still wrestle with the constant need to prove myself. I can still hear my dad say, 'Son, if you're gonna be in a fight, you hit first, and as hard as you can — and *always be the one standing when it's over.'*

"I was the first among my age to sneak into the drive-in. I dove off the big bridge when it was raised when none of my older friends would. I amazed them by accepting a dare to dive off an airboat onto the back of a deer in the Everglades, which could be dangerous and a stupid stunt. After leaping from the cruising boat, you grabbed hold of the deer's soft neck, prayed the animal didn't cut you to ribbons with the razor-sharp of its hooves, and then rode it for a few yards into the swamp and hoped you didn't land on a gator. By age 12, I didn't have a best friend, but, boy, I had a reputation."

■

"... I REMEMBER THAT SUMMER between my junior and senior years was when I finally entered the enormous estates in Palm Beach.

"... In the summer, the island was deserted. These titans of money and status took their backgammon sets, Geritol and martinis to Kennebunkport or Newport or wherever else they summered, and unknowingly left their boarded-up homes to us. During the day, we camped on their fabulous private beaches. Later, under the cover of darkness, we snuck inside and, behind the hurricane-shuttered windows, lit candles, played our little radios and danced up a storm."

■

"... I ENROLLED at Palm Beach Junior College. Most of the easy classes, to which I naturally gravitated, were already full. So I signed up for the unlikeliest of choices, art appreciation and English literature. On the first day, I arrived late — thank you, Dr. Freud — and only one seat was available: front row center, under the watchful eye of Professor Watson B. Duncan III, the best teacher I ever had."

"After being on stage, something clicked. As was the pattern in my life, I gravitated toward the challenge of participating in drama class. It was no different than football, which I played to prove myself worthy of recognition. Whether sports or drama, I wanted to be good, to try for the triple, not just swing back and forth.

"Yet no one was more shocked than I at the end of the year when my performance in *Outward Bound* won the 1956 Florida State Drama Award. I gladly accepted the first-prize scholarship to the Hyde Park Playhouse in upstate New York. Even though I didn't anticipate acting being anything more than an extracurricular activity, I wouldn't have to spend the summer chopping sugar cane or working on a fishing boat."

— FROM BURT REYNOLDS'
1994 AUTOBIOGRAPHY, *MY LIFE*

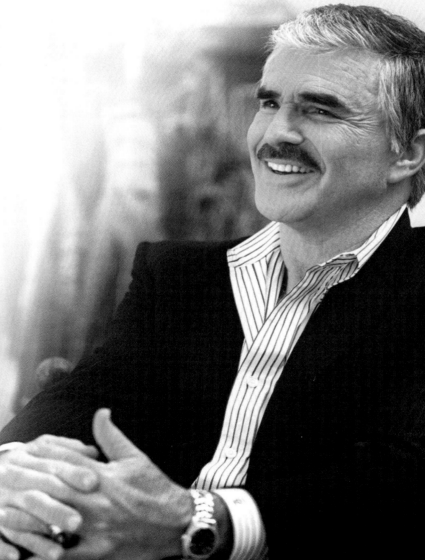

Reynolds' dinner theater and Institute for Theater Training in Jupiter helped launch careers.

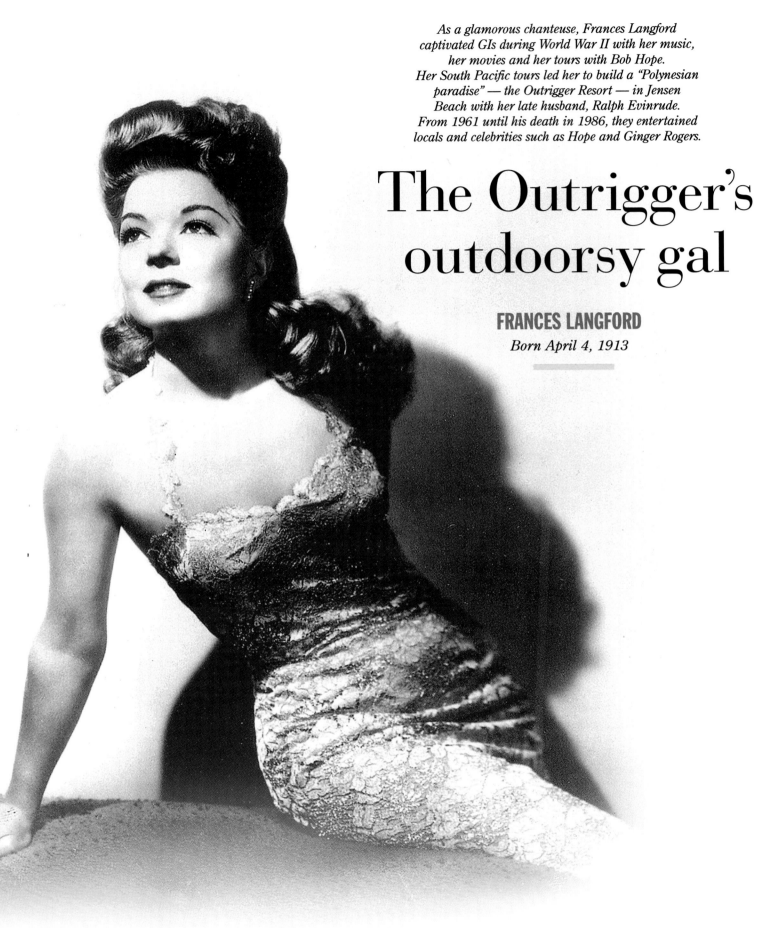

As a glamorous chanteuse, Frances Langford captivated GIs during World War II with her music, her movies and her tours with Bob Hope. Her South Pacific tours led her to build a "Polynesian paradise" — the Outrigger Resort — in Jensen Beach with her late husband, Ralph Evinrude. From 1961 until his death in 1986, they entertained locals and celebrities such as Hope and Ginger Rogers.

The Outrigger's outdoorsy gal

FRANCES LANGFORD
Born April 4, 1913

Today, Frances Langford spends much of her time aboard her yacht Chanticleer. She's always loved boating and fishing. Her collection of mounted ocean fish adorns the walls of the Florida Oceanographic Society's Frances Langford Visitor Center.

Frances Langford was singing, and Ralph Evinrude was falling in love.

In and of itself, Evinrude's attraction to Langford was not unusual. Millions of men had done the same thing during Langford's selfless USO tours with Bob Hope during the war, when the highlight of the act was her creamy rendition of *I'm in the Mood for Love,* written for her in a movie called *Every Night at Eight* in 1935. Langford personified the girls the boys had left behind.

But the war had been over for nearly 10 years, as was her marriage to actor Jon Hall. Now Langford was singing in a nightclub in Milwaukee. Evinrude, the son of the founder of the Evinrude Outboard Motor company, was enchanted by her music and her. He invited everyone in the show back to his house for bacon and eggs.

Ralph Evinrude

"He was so nice and shy, such a sweet man," remembers Langford. "I had the nerve to tell him I preferred Johnson outboard motors. Then he told me he made those, too."

After their marriage in 1955, Langford brought Evinrude to her 400 acres around Jensen Beach. Langford had begun amassing the land in 1936, when she bought a 100-acre parcel for $15,000.

"I always wanted someplace where people couldn't move in on me," she says.

Frances Langford has always been a Florida girl. Born in Lakeland in 1913 to a carpenter and his wife, she was drawn to the outdoors, especially when it came to fishing. (She once landed a 419-pound marlin.)

Evinrude fell in love with his wife's state just as he had fallen in love with her. After building a motor testing division on the north side of the St. Lucie River, where he could tinker with his engines to his heart's content, Evinrude adopted Martin County as his own base of operations.

Langford and Evinrude opened the Outrigger Marina, which berthed their stunning 118-foot yacht, Chanticleer. They also opened a small restaurant as a convenience for people who had just docked their boats.

"The first night, there was this long line outside the place, and we looked at each other and said, 'What is this?' People had decided that this was where they wanted to eat. So we started adding on rooms, then some guest houses."

The glorified lunch counter grew into the Outrigger Resort on the Indian River, the primary restaurant for the area in the late '50s and '60s.

Evinrude became a noted philanthropist, helping to fund hospitals and the Jensen Beach fishing pier, as well as a park named after his wife.

Ralph Evinrude died in 1986. Soon afterward, Frances closed the resort. She continued to maintain the marina and the Chanticleer. She's remarried, to Harold Stuart, the assistant secretary of the Air Force under Harry Truman. Summers are spent in a house on Georgian Island in Canada, and in September she begins the long trip home to Jensen Beach aboard her boat.

"The greatest thing in my life was entertaining the troops," she says. "And I have Bob Hope to thank for that. It was exhausting, but it didn't matter; I was raised camping.

"Looking back on it, I've had so many lives. New York, Hollywood, and Florida. Always Florida."

— SCOTT EYMAN

Album of the Late 20th Century

Born Sept. 26, year unknown and unnecessary
("A woman who tells her age will tell anything.")

Founder, producer and star, Royal Palm Festival
Dinner Theatre in Boca Raton

Leading Lady

Because she's got the pep and pizazz of Auntie Mame and Dolly Levi rolled into one.

Because when she played Gypsy's Mama Rose Hovick in December 1998, she got a rave. The first line of the review in *The Palm Beach Post*: "She's a scrappy, brassy, force of nature, trying to survive in her tiny corner of show business. Could there be more dead-on casting for Jan McArt?"

Because her tiny corner of show biz is a 284-seat, four-sided stage that she's run for an amazing 23 years. It is the second-longest-running professional theater in Palm Beach County (after the Caldwell) and the only one that stays open 52 weeks a year.

Because she never intended to leave her New York singing career and open a dinner theater in Boca Raton — but while visiting her ailing mother, the light bulb of opportunity twinkled. She plunked down $25,000 on a vast space in the Royal Palm Plaza and intended to have friends from Sarasota run her dinner theater while she sat back in her Manhattan apartment counting the box-office receipts. When the money didn't flow, McArt sold the apartment, as well as a home in Connecticut, flew down here for keeps, rolled up her sequined sleeves and became a hands-on theater producer.

Because she greets the Royal Palm Dinner Theatre audience like guests in her home and occasionally saves a salary by casting herself as the female lead chanteuse.

Because over the years, McArt opened theaters in Key West, Miami Beach, Fort Lauderdale and the floor above her dinner theater, and sent out national tours of *The Pirates of Penzance*. In 1989, while juggling four stages in Florida, she set her sights on Broadway with the musical *The Prince of Central Park,* this time as a producer. As the record books note, she was the only Broadway producer in history to also understudy the star. Alas, the show closed quickly.

Because she returned to her Boca trenches and had started to relax again when an errant cigarette burned down the dinner theater in 1993. It was a dark period for her, but such is McArt's unsinkable spirit that she rallied the money and the energy to reopen the theater's doors within four months.

Because she also started a children's theater, not for its box-office potential but because "it was the right thing to do." She has always had a community-minded mentality. Last year, she made it official, restructuring her corporation as a tax-exempt, nonprofit entity, writing off an estimated $2 million she has poured into the operation over the years to ensure it will be viable into the next millennium.

Because, through good times and bum times, she's seen it all, and she's still here. And South Florida wouldn't want it any other way.

— HAP ERSTEIN

She's South Florida's First Lady of Musical Theater — and probably the hardest-working woman in show biz. Her Royal Palm Dinner Theatre serves some 1,500 meals a week, but the main dish is always McArt herself. "I love being a performer. It's so easy for me. It's what I am. It's what I do. That's the fun part."

Remembering paradise

"MY FLORIDA is the winding tropical river, heavy with the musky scent of palm blossoms, with water turkeys sunning themselves, striped necked turtles plopping from logs, grey squirrels barking and the rat-tat-tat of the pileated woodpecker resounding.

It is not a CBS, all-electric Medallion home.

MY FLORIDA is the tarpon rolling, the mullet leaping for fun, pelicans diving, red-beaked skimmer gulls skimming the surface with their bills, a manatee blowing, and an eagle stealing a fish from an osprey high in air.

It is not a four-lane highway . . .

. . . MY FLORIDA is cruising offshore in a small boat just as the sun comes up, grabbing a bending rod and boating a king mackerel, watching sea turtles and manta rays, coming back in through a boisterous inlet "on a wing and a prayer."

It is not playing shuffleboard.

MY FLORIDA is wading a sand-bottomed backwoods pond, flycasting a cork-bodied bug on a well greased GAF line, catching three or four "yearling-and-up" bass, enjoying their beauty and liking their musky smell — and then eating them fried to a tasty brown by the pond side.

It is not a Royal Castle hamburger or a Lum's frankfurter . . .

. . . MY FLORIDA is surf casting from the sea beach with no one in sight a mile either way.

It is not taking a dip in a swimming pool, covering yourself with lotion and sunbathing in a reclining chair.

MY FLORIDA is going fast."

— FROM *MY FLORIDA*,
BY ERNEST LYONS,
COPYRIGHT 1969,
STUART NEWS COMPANY

Lyons said his hobbies were his newspaper and "fishing, woods-roaming and enjoying the outdoors."

Palm Beach Post file photo

ERNIE LYONS

March 4, 1905 — April 6, 1990

Newspaper editor Ernie Lyons captured Old Florida in his columns about nature and small-town life in Stuart.

The feisty historian and author, whose prize-winning columns were collected in two books, came to Stuart in 1915 from Laurel, Miss., with his family at age 10. He worked as a writer and editor for *The Stuart News* for 44 years.

A conservationist in the days when Florida fishing still was the stuff of legends, he experienced — and wrote about — life on area waters in an era that drew rich fishermen from around the globe to Stuart, then the sailfish capital of the world.

Lyons was an early critic of a canal federal engineers built to dump water from area ranch lands and Lake Okeechobee into the St. Lucie River — and he was right. What has been an environmental disaster for the river now leads a federal and state "fix it" list of projects to re-engineer South Florida drainage.

Lyons, a founding president of the Florida Outdoor Writer's Association, wrote lyrical descriptions of the area's "jungle rivers" and abundant wildlife.

He also wrote about such local characters as Shorty Joe, who risked his life during the fierce 1933 hurricane to save a squealing lady lying behind a shed, learning only after he dragged her to safety that she was a 250-pound pig the wind blew into town. (Shorty Joe had hoisted a few during the big blow.)

Ralph Hartman Jr., a retired real estate agent whose friendship with the writer spanned six decades, used to give Lyons' books, *My Florida* and *The Last Cracker Barrel*, to people who bought houses in Martin County. Hartman introduced one new resident, a neurosurgeon, to the writer.

"Ernie asked the doctor what a neurosurgeon does," Hartman said. "The doctor explained he operates on people's brains. 'You'll make a fortune here in Martin County,' Ernie told him. 'We got hundreds of people who need their brains fixed.' "

A bridge is named for him on Hutchinson Island.

— SALLY D. SWARTZ

LAWRENCE E. WILL

Jan. 31, 1893 — Dec. 8, 1977

He left a heap of Cracker history

Lawrence E. Will came to the Glades as a pioneer and spent his last years telling the world how it was on Lake Okeechobee when the century was young.

Will came to South Florida in 1913 to clear sawgrass for farming at the first Everglades settlement, Okeelanta. Over the next 15 years, he dredged, hunted, fished, farmed, surveyed and operated canal boats. He settled down in Belle Glade and opened a combination auto dealership, service station and parts store just in time to have the roof blown off by the great 1928 hurricane.

Palm Beach Post file photo

CRACKER CHARACTER: *Lawrence Will wrote of legendary Okeechobee personalities such as William "Pogey Bill" Collins, sheriff of Okeechobee County from 1918 to 1932. Pogey Bill got the job because he was the meanest man city officials could find.*

In later years, he became fascinated with history and traveled all over the Glades. Between 1961 and 1968, he set it all down in six books, the best-known of which is *Cracker History of Okeechobee*. They were written in a folksy, backwoods dialect that made them entertaining as well as informative. They were laced with phrases such as "a heap too close for convenience" and "right smart put out."

It didn't matter that the dialect was often bogus. Will did not talk the way he wrote. His books recorded backwoods speech the way it might sound to someone who was born in Wisconsin, who went to high school in Washington, D.C., and whose father was a Harvard-educated scientist who had been president of what now is Kansas State University.

Dr. Thomas E. Will is a controversial figure in Glades history. While associated with a land-sales company, he played a role — the precise extent of which has never been clear — in production of a flawed 1911 report favoring Everglades drainage, publication of which set off a congressional investigation.

Lawrence Will spent his last years in West Palm Beach, where he died at age 84. His books are still in print and the museum attached to the library in Belle Glade bears his name.

— BILL McGOUN

James Knott wrote historical "Brown Wrappers" for The Palm Beach Post *from 1977 to 1985.*

JUDGE JAMES R. KNOTT

Jan. 8, 1910 — Jan. 5, 1999

He made history accessible

James Robert Knott was perhaps the region's best-known historian.

His grandfather was a volunteer in the Second Seminole War. His father lost a bitter campaign for governor in 1916. In 1956, Knott replaced assassinated Circuit Judge Curtis E. Chillingworth and served almost 21 years on the bench.

"All I want to do is practice law and write local history; that suits me fine," Knott said. "The history of a place is the history of the people who lived there."

The "Brown Wrappers" he wrote for *The Palm Beach Post* from 1977 to 1985 featured memories of everyday things, from when the train came to town in 1894 to square dances at Marjorie Merriweather Post's mansion in the '20s.

"One of Judge Knott's great talents was making history approachable and popularizing it," said Clemmer Mayhew III, former archivist for the Historical Society of Palm Beach County.

Knott was instrumental in restoring the name of Cape Canaveral. He also fought to save Palm Beach's Mar-a-Lago mansion and Henry Flagler's home, Whitehall. He left 22 boxes of interviews and photos to the county historical society, which named an award for him. His crowning achievement: He listened to the old-timers, then wrote their stories down.

ADA COATS WILLIAMS

Born Sept. 8, 1920

Williams wrote Florida's Ashley Gang *in 1997. She is president of the Florida Historical Society and has written eight historical dramas.*

Treasure Coast scribe

Ada Coats Williams turned a passion for pioneer history into an avocation.

Williams' grandparents — her grandmother was Robert E. Lee's cousin — came from Alabama to the Titusville area in the 1870s. They moved to Fort Pierce in 1894. Her father, William Lee Coats (known as Okeechobee Bill), was the city's first pharmacist, a real-estate salesman and a legislator. "During the boom days, he made scads of money, and after the boom, he was very broke."

An interview led her to the truth behind the deaths of the infamous Ashley gang.

John Ashley was only 18 in 1911 when he was suspected in the slaying of a Seminole trader. His gang robbed banks from Stuart to Pompano Beach and killed two lawmen.

In 1924, Ashley and three partners were stopped on the bridge over the St. Sebastian River by the St. Lucie County sheriff. Moments later, all four were dead, face down. Police insisted the Ashley gang had pulled guns — but years later, a deputy who had been on the bridge told Williams the gang members were shot unarmed.

— Stories by ELIOT KLEINBERG

In the shadow of the lighthouse

Bessie Wilson DuBois didn't just write about the history of the Jupiter Inlet area. She and her husband lived through most of its modern history.

DuBois once said the day she arrived in 1914 as an 11-year-old, she heard what sounded like people applauding in a theater. It was mullet boiling in the pristine Jupiter Inlet.

Jupiter was then a tiny town of 300 surrounding the famed lighthouse. In 1925, Bessie married John DuBois, one of four children of a pioneer couple. She wanted to be a writer, but four children came first. In 1929, she and John opened a restaurant by their home, serving fried chicken, oysters and fish from the Loxahatchee River.

World War II rationing forced them to close in 1942, but Bessie and her family awoke at 2 a.m. to bake pies for John to take to nearby Camp Murphy, now Jonathan Dickinson State Park. They also ran a fish camp until 1972.

When a daughter died of leukemia in 1955, Bessie found solace in a study of local history; she would write five small but comprehensive books about life on the Loxahatchee River, conduct many slide shows, and take part in historical groups. Even when her eyesight failed in her later years, she would still entertain visitors with lively stories of her beloved river, inlet and lighthouse.

"I wonder what's going to become of Florida?" she once asked. "Is it going to be like the Florida we once used to know?"

John DuBois died in 1987, Bessie in 1998. A nearby county park bears their name.

— ELIOT KLEINBERG

Bessie and John DuBois in the early 1980s in front of the DuBois family's 1898 home, which sits on a 20-foot shell mound built by Indians.

Everee Jimerson Clarke points out portraits to visitors at her Pleasant City Heritage Gallery. The original neighborhood "was so beautiful," she said. "I want people to remember it. I want to bring it back if I can. We don't need our young people on street corners, propping up telephone poles, selling crack cocaine and seeing drive-by shootings. It doesn't have to be like that. It wasn't like that here. I know. This is where I grew up."

JEAN HART HOWARD/Staff Photographer

PRESTON TILLMAN

Born Dec. 6, 1918

Preserving the memory of his people

He's got so many clippings in his house, it's hard to keep track. And so many stories about the important black families who changed West Palm Beach:

There was C.C. Walker, principal of Industrial High School, who revolutionized the school day for black children. Preston Tillman remembers Mr. Walker because he was in sixth grade in 1931 when Mr. Walker made a decision: Instead of starting school in September, then stopping after Christmas to pick beans, his students would go year-round like kids in the white schools.

And Tillman remembers when Harry T. Moore, the state

Frankie Tillman

head of the NAACP, stayed in West Palm Beach to help blacks get the vote. Moore and his wife were killed in a bombing in Mims, Florida, on Christmas night 1951, three years after the first black person registered to vote in Palm Beach County. That person was Frankie Tillman, Preston's wife.

And there was Dr. J.H. Terrell, who helped get the vote out as head of the local voters' league. And Johnnie Robinson, who was a caretaker in Palm Beach and helped blacks buy property. And the Rev. Randolph Washington, assistant pastor at Tabernacle Missionary Baptist, whose son started a soda factory during the Depression. And so many more. Their stories fill his West Palm Beach real estate office and his mind.

Tillman's love of history — "I've always been nosy" — led him to co-found the Black Historical Preservation Society of Palm Beach County. The society got a grant to restore the Gwen Cherry house on Division Avenue by the time of West Palm Beach's centennial in 1994, but by 1999, the society was on the verge of foreclosing on the house, once owned by Mollie Holt, grandmother of Cherry, the first black woman elected to the Florida Legislature.

Tillman's goal for the new century: To get the preservation society back on its feet and his own vast collection of photographs and clippings organized for future generations.

— JAN TUCKWOOD

Preston Tillman (third from left in plaid shirt in back row) with neighbors and supporters of the Black Historical Preservation Society in front of the Gwen Cherry house. Front row, from left: Edgar Worthy Tucker, retired teacher; Mother Irene Eagleton, who helped start the YMCA in the black neighborhood; Doris Tucker Lowe, who still lives on the same lot where she was born in this neighborhood. Back row, from left: Stan McKnight; Tommy Newberry; Preston Tillman; the Rev. J.B. Blake, 95, the presiding elder of the West Palm Beach district of the African Methodist Episcopal Church, who oversees 21 churches and 10,000 parishioners; the Rev. James Cleare, pastor of Allen Temple A.M.E. Church in Riviera Beach; the Rev. Samuel T. Grant, Church of God pastor for nearly 40 years; city commissioner James Exline; and John Clayton.

Everee Jimerson Clarke: Protector of Pleasant City's past

Hundreds of photographs and newspaper clippings have been arranged on the blue walls of Everee Jimerson Clarke's Pleasant City Heritage Gallery, which celebrates the history of what is thought to be the oldest continuously existing African-American community in West Palm Beach.

Pleasant City, a 27-block area reaching from 15th to 23rd Streets, and from Dixie Highway to the Florida East Coast tracks, forms a vital link in Palm Beach County's black history. It bridges the time and space between the old black village known as the Styx, a community of construction workers on Palm Beach who helped build Henry Flagler's Royal Poinciana Hotel in the 1890s, and the modern era.

"The Styx wasn't burned. That's a legend," Clarke said. "But it was closed up and torn down, and the people came over here, where a white developer, George Currie laid out

Pleasant City." Lots started at $140 and approximately 1,000 black families ultimately settled here.

"The talent that came from this place was incredible," Clarke said. "One family alone produced four medical doctors. Another produced three Ph.D.'s. The first black mayor of West Palm Beach, Eva Williams Mack, came from Pleasant City.

"So did the artist Preston Sampson. So did Dr. Lean Gaston Fitzhugh, first woman dean of the Interdenominational Center in Atlanta. So did Joseph Coleman, the finance officer for Bethune-Cookman college. So did Dr. Charles White, the principal of Roosevelt High School. So did Herbie Mann, a New York promoter.

"We need to motivate our children again, to be like these people."

How South Florida grew

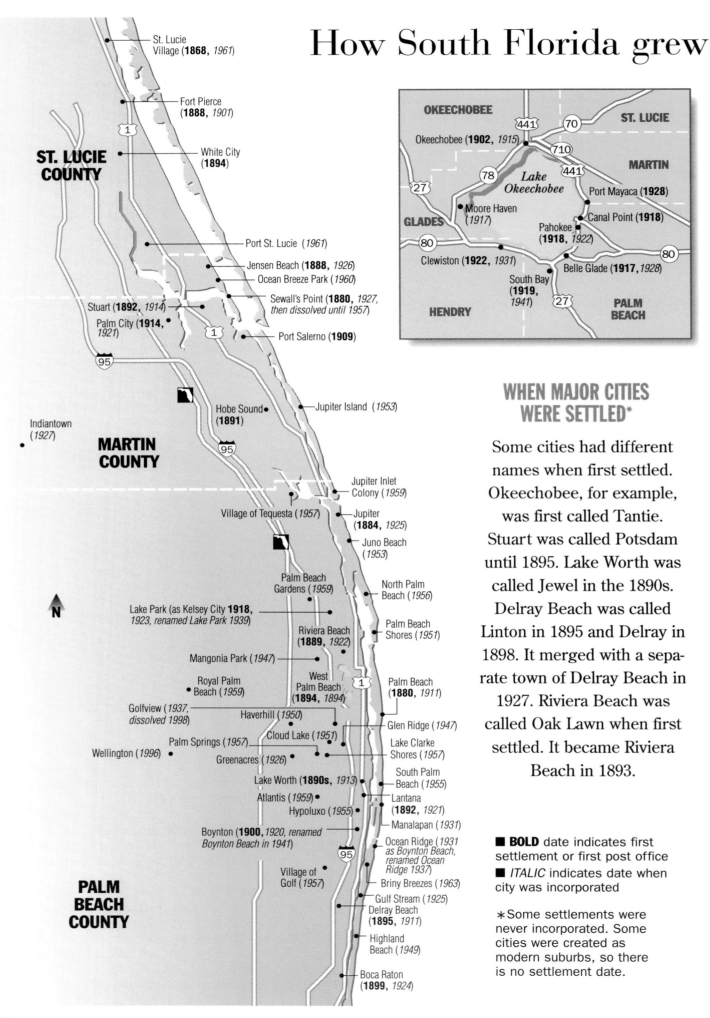

St. Lucie
Village (**1868**, *1961*)

Fort Pierce
(**1888**, *1901*)

**ST. LUCIE
COUNTY**

White City
(**1894**)

Port St. Lucie (*1961*)

Jensen Beach (**1888**, *1926*)

Ocean Breeze Park (*1960*)

Sewall's Point (**1880**, *1927,
then dissolved until 1957*)

Stuart (**1892**, *1914*)

Palm City (**1914**, *1921*)

Port Salerno (**1909**)

Jupiter Island (*1953*)

Indiantown
(*1927*)

Hobe Sound
(**1891**)

**MARTIN
COUNTY**

Jupiter Inlet
Colony (*1959*)

Village of Tequesta (*1957*)

Jupiter
(**1884**, *1925*)

Juno Beach
(*1953*)

Palm Beach
Gardens (*1959*)

North Palm
Beach (*1956*)

N

Lake Park (as Kelsey City **1918**,
1923, renamed Lake Park 1939)

Palm Beach
Shores (*1951*)

Riviera Beach
(**1889**, *1922*)

Mangonia Park (*1947*)

Royal Palm
Beach (*1959*)

West
Palm Beach
(**1894**, *1894*)

Palm Beach
(**1880**, *1911*)

Golfview (*1937,
dissolved 1998*)

Haverhill (*1950*)

Glen Ridge (*1947*)

Cloud Lake (*1951*)

Palm Springs (*1957*)

Lake Clarke
Shores (*1957*)

Wellington (*1996*)

Greenacres (*1926*)

Lake Worth (**1890s**, *1913*)

South Palm
Beach (*1955*)

Atlantis (*1959*)

Lantana
(**1892**, *1921*)

Hypoluxo (*1955*)

Manalapan (*1931*)

Boynton (**1900**, *1920, renamed
Boynton Beach in 1941*)

Ocean Ridge (*1931
as Boynton Beach,
renamed Ocean
Ridge 1937*)

**PALM
BEACH
COUNTY**

Village of
Golf (*1957*)

Briny Breezes (*1963*)

Gulf Stream (*1925*)

Delray Beach
(**1895**, *1911*)

Highland
Beach (*1949*)

Boca Raton
(**1899**, *1924*)

OKEECHOBEE

ST. LUCIE

Okeechobee (**1902**, *1915*)

MARTIN

Lake
Okeechobee

Port Mayaca (**1928**)

Moore Haven
(*1917*)

Canal Point (**1918**)

GLADES

Pahokee
(**1918**, *1922*)

Clewiston (**1922**, *1931*)

Belle Glade (**1917**, *1928*)

South Bay
(**1919**,
1941)

HENDRY

**PALM
BEACH**

WHEN MAJOR CITIES WERE SETTLED*

Some cities had different names when first settled. Okeechobee, for example, was first called Tantie. Stuart was called Potsdam until 1895. Lake Worth was called Jewel in the 1890s. Delray Beach was called Linton in 1895 and Delray in 1898. It merged with a separate town of Delray Beach in 1927. Riviera Beach was called Oak Lawn when first settled. It became Riviera Beach in 1893.

■ **BOLD** date indicates first settlement or first post office
■ *ITALIC* indicates date when city was incorporated

∗Some settlements were never incorporated. Some cities were created as modern suburbs, so there is no settlement date.

1830 POPULATION

34,730	Florida
517	Southern peninsula

1880 POPULATION

269,493	Florida
257	Dade County

1910 POPULATION

752,619	Florida
5,577	Palm Beach County
4,075	St. Lucie County
1,743	West Palm Beach
250	Delray
1,333	Fort Pierce

1940 POPULATION

1,897,414	Florida
79,989	Palm Beach County
6,295	Martin County
11,871	St. Lucie County
11,871	Okeechobee County
33,693	West Palm Beach
3,661	Delray Beach
1,326	Boynton Beach
723	Boca Raton
2,438	Stuart
1,333	Fort Pierce
1,658	Okeechobee

1970 POPULATION

6,791,418	Florida
348,993	Palm Beach County
28,035	Martin County
50,836	St. Lucie County
11,233	Okeechobee County
57,375	West Palm Beach
19,366	Delray Beach
18,115	Boynton Beach
330	Port St. Lucie
4,820	Stuart
29,735	Fort Pierce
3,715	Okeechobee

1999 POPULATION

15,307,457	Florida
1,039,814	Palm Beach County
121,514	Martin County
186,905	St. Lucie County
35,510	Okeechobee County
83,254	Port St. Lucie
81,132	West Palm Beach
69,994	Boca Raton
53,589	Delray Beach
55,483	Boynton Beach
13,846	Stuart
38,401	Fort Pierce
5,102	Okeechobee

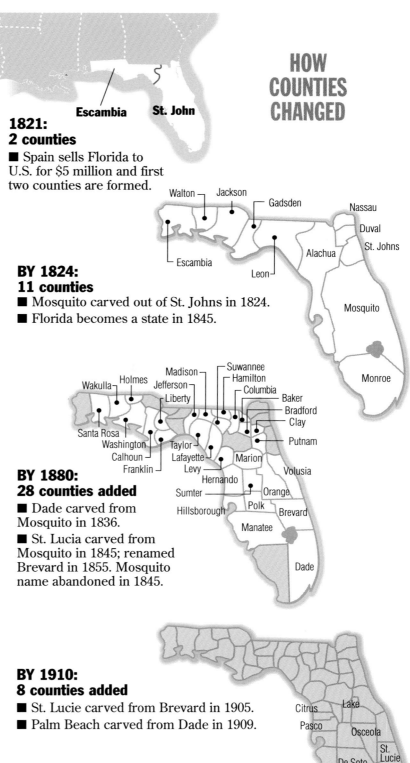

HOW COUNTIES CHANGED

1821: 2 counties
■ Spain sells Florida to U.S. for $5 million and first two counties are formed.

BY 1824: 11 counties
■ Mosquito carved out of St. Johns in 1824.
■ Florida becomes a state in 1845.

BY 1880: 28 counties added
■ Dade carved from Mosquito in 1836.
■ St. Lucia carved from Mosquito in 1845; renamed Brevard in 1855. Mosquito name abandoned in 1845.

BY 1910: 8 counties added
■ St. Lucie carved from Brevard in 1905.
■ Palm Beach carved from Dade in 1909.

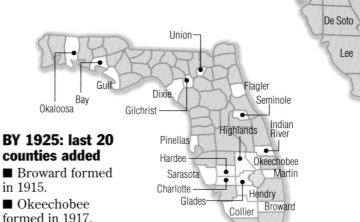

BY 1925: last 20 counties added
■ Broward formed in 1915.
■ Okeechobee formed in 1917.
■ Martin formed in 1925.

Who's the Currie behind Currie Park? Here are some namesakes behind the parks, bridges and other landmarks.

Capt. Francis Alexander Adams (Park, Stuart): The Spanish-American War veteran was a tireless patriot and downtown Stuart personality. The park at Confusion Corner was named for him May 10, 1974 — his 100th birthday. Scheduled to lead the pledge of allegiance to the nation at July 4, 1976, Bicentennial ceremonies in Philadelphia, he died at 101 in September 1975.

Nathaniel J. Adams (Park, West Palm Beach): He formed West Palm's first Boy Scout troop for blacks. He died at 73 in January 1982; the park was named in 1983.

Adams

Barley Barber (Barley Barber Swamp, Indiantown): Barber, a trapper, homesteaded the swamp in the early 1900s. He left the area in 1915; one story says he argued with an employee and stabbed him, then planted a knife in his hand, claimed self-defense and later left town. Florida Power & Light acquired the land in 1972.

John Thomas 'Jack' Barton (Barton Park, Barton Elementary School, Lake Worth): In 40 years of service to the city, he published the *Lake Worth Herald* for seven years, was a city commissioner and was twice elected mayor. He died at 64 in March 1955.

Mary Barton (Barton Park, Boynton Beach): Barton fought to clean up the area around the city's black Cherry Hill cemetery. The 5-acre park was dedicated in 1980.

L.L. Barwick (Park, Delray Beach): The prominent real-estate broker and leader in the city's financial growth moved to the area in 1913. He served on the city council and school board and was president of the Delray Beach Board of Trade.

Marshall Benjamin (The Benjamin School, North Palm Beach): Benjamin and his wife, Nancy, founded the North Palm Beach private elementary school in 1960. When its board created an upper-level school in 1974, it was named the Benjamin School. The two schools combined in 1989. Marshall Benjamin died at 61 in October 1985.

John Brooks (Park, Fort Pierce): The Fort Pierce conservationist led the fight to have the parcel bought by the state. The park was named for him in June 1988, the same month he died of a heart attack at 65.

Jake M. Boyd (Boyd Park, Palm Beach): The tiny park on North County Road was named in 1962 for the settler, 25-year town engineer and town manager.

Nathan Boynton (Boynton Beach): The retired Civil War major bought land in 1895 and planned to build a resort. He returned to Michigan and served as a U.S. congressman.

Mary Brandon (Park, West Palm Beach): Land for the park was offered by the West Palm Beach Country Club in 1959 and dedicated four years later to Brandon, a member of the city's Parks and Recreation Commission in the 1960s.

Edward and Harold Bryant (Bryant Park, Lake Worth): The Bryant family was active in the sugar industry in the Glades and their company developed thousands of acres in both Lake Worth and the Glades.

Charles Carlin (Carlin Park, Jupiter): Head of the Jupiter Lifesaving Station in 1886, he helped in many rescues. Carlin's wife was the town's postmistress for more than 20 years, and the family also ran the first hotel in the area, the Carlin House. The railroad eliminated most water traffic and the station was closed in 1896. Carlin died in 1912.

John Carroll (John Carroll High School): When the school — founded in 1916 — moved to its present site in 1965, the pope was John XXIII and the head of the Archdiocese of Miami was Bishop Coleman Carroll.

Kenneth Dale Cassens (Dale Cassens Exceptional Students Education Center, Fort Pierce): The citrus grower, a member of a pioneer family, was a state legislator and school board member who died of a heart attack in 1987, two years into his third term on the school board.

Robert Lee 'Sam' Chastain (Chastain Beach, Hutchinson Island): The family ranched in western Martin County and northwest Palm Beach County. Sam Chastain died in 1964, creating a foundation in his will that has been a large contributor to Indian River Community College, the Kravis Center for the Performing Arts and Norton Museum of Art in West Palm Beach and 1,000 Friends of Florida. Son Thomas M. Chastain bought and donated the beach property in 1973.

John Clarke (Lake Clarke, town of Lake Clarke Shores): The Pennsylvania carmaker grew pineapples and fished on the lake's shores in the early 1900s. Lake Clarke stretched from Southern Boulevard into the city of Lake Worth until the state built canals to Lake Okeechobee, creating a marsh.

Alonzo Clewis (Town of Clewiston): The Tampa banker, along with Philadelphia investors, bought land in 1920 and built a railroad to the area. He died in February 1944.

George P. Coleman (Park, West Palm Beach): Originally named Lincoln Park, it was renamed for the local community leader and founder of Coleman Funeral Home.

J.W. Connors (Connors Highway, western Palm Beach County): The Buffalo, N.Y., publisher and part-time Palm Beach resident wanted to invest in the Glades, but access was by boat only, so he spent $2 million of his own money to carve a highway through the muck to the Glades. It opened June 25, 1925. At a toll of 3 cents a mile, Connors still averaged $2,000 a day. After his death in October 1929, the road was sold to the state for $660. It is now State Road 98.

J.W. Corbett (J.W. Corbett Wildlife Management Area, Martin-Palm Beach County line): Corbett, of Fort Pierce, was a charter member of the Florida Game and Fresh Water Fish Commission in 1943 and its chairman in 1948.

Vernita M. Cox (Cox Park, South Bay): Cox was mayor from 1974 to 1975 and in 1984.

Cox

Evans Crary Sr. (Bridge, Stuart-Sewall's Point): The former state senator, speaker of the Florida House, Martin County Attorney and city judge died in 1968.

Kathryn E. Cunningham (K.E. Cunningham/Canal Point Elementary School): Cunningham was a teacher and principal for 50 years, 22 of them as principal of the school later named for her. She retired in 1990 and died in 1994.

George Graham Currie (Currie Park, West Palm Beach; Currie Commons Park, Delray Beach): Currie, a native of Quebec, arrived penniless, became a lawyer, made and lost a fortune in real estate, and was West Palm Beach mayor from 1901 to 1902. He wrote at least 18 books of poems, musical lyrics and essays and aspired to be Florida's poet laureate. Currie died in 1926, soon after the Delray Beach park was dedicated; the West Palm Beach park was dedicated in 1949. Currie's son, longtime county judge Francis Angevine "Banzai" Currie, died in 1979.

Roger Dean (Roger Dean Stadium, Jupiter): Dean was one of the top Chevrolet dealers in the country. The minor-league baseball complex, which opened in February 1998, was named for Dean after one of his daughters donated $1 million to construction costs. Dean died at 83 in April 1999.

John G. and Susan H. DuPuis Jr. (DuPuis Reserve, western Palm Beach and Martin counties): The Miami-based DuPuis dairy ranching family sold the land in 1986 for $23 million to the South Florida Water Management District , stipulating it be kept natural.

William T. Dwyer (High School, Palm Beach Gardens): Dwyer, vice president for community and government relations at Pratt & Whitney, worked there from 1962 until cancer forced his retirement in 1984. He died at 58 in January 1985. He was active in community activities. The Economic Council of Palm Beach County established the Dwyer Award for excellence in education in 1985. The school was named for Dwyer when it opened in 1991.

Lindsay Ewing (Ewing Park, Royal Palm Beach): She contracted Reyes Syndrome at 9 months. The park was dedicated in January 1996, a month before she died at 13.

C. Scott Fletcher (Fletcher Beach Park, Stuart): The Australian-born education professional spent more than three decades trying to protect beaches from development. He helped start Save Our Beaches. The former Peters beach strip, just south of Stuart beach, was named for him in March 1975. Fletcher died in 1991.

James. S. Fogleman (Park, West Palm Beach): The 27-year-old Palm Beach County deputy was killed in 1963 when his cruiser flipped into a ditch on a rain-slicked road as he raced a dying infant and his grandmother to St. Mary's Hospital.

Virginia Ransom Forrest (Virginia Forrest Beach Access, north of Stuart): Forrest, a longtime Stuart winter resident, was nationally recognized for helping save the bald eagle. She donated $30,000 to help buy the beach strip, which was dedicated in 1976. Forrest died in May 1991.

Forrest

Phil Foster (Phil Foster Memorial County Park, Riviera Beach): The pioneer, owner of one of the town's first tourist courts, lived in the area for 32 years before his death in 1917. The park was dedicated in January 1953.

A.J. Gaines Jr. (Gaines Park, West Palm Beach): The park, built in 1958, was named for the longtime city parks employee who was the black parks director when parks were separate.

Charles A. Gettler (Park, West Palm Beach): The park was named in 1965 for Gettler, a resident who worked to beautify the city.

Don Pedro Gilbert (Gilbert's Bar House of Refuge): The reef off Hutchinson Island is named for a pirate who may have hidden in the St. Lucie Inlet between raids. Hanged in 1834, Gilbert was the last of the old-time pirates to be executed in the United States.

Harvey Glascock (Beach, Jensen Beach): Glascock, then-owner of WSTU-AM, donated $25,000 for the beach access tract that shares his name. He died at 56 in 1977.

William Henry and Sarah Gleason (Park, Delray Beach): The pioneers bought oceanfront land in 1870 for $1.25 an acre. In 1899, Sarah Gleason donated land that became the municipal beach.

Genevieve Gove (Elementary School, Belle Glade): The longtime teacher conducted outdoor summer programs for children; the school was named for her in 1964.

Harry Goodmark (Park, Riviera Beach): The longtime West Palm Beach lawyer, a pioneer in workers compensation, donated several lots for the park. He retired in 1992.

Mildred Greenfield (Park, Hobe Sound): Greenfield was a longtime assistant to the Martin County Commission.

Walter R. Hooker (Hooker Highway, the Glades): Hooker was among the first businessmen to settle in the Belle Glade area, setting up a produce packing house and general store.

Edward L. Hosford (Park, Hobe Sound): Hosford, one of the original Lake Worth pioneers, was the son of a Confederate soldier. He arrived in 1891 and was a landscaper for Henry Flagler's Royal Poinciana Hotel and later settled in Sewall's Point and did landscaping there. He served on the school board from 1930 to 1938. Hosford died at 91 in February 1962.

D.D. "Dad" Howard: (Park, West Palm Beach): Howard was the city's longtime superintendent of Streets and Public Programs. The park was dedicated Dec. 23, 1934.

Ralph C. Howard (Howard Park, Lake Worth): The city director of public works from 1947 to 1959. He died in 1960; the park was dedicated in 1966.

James A. Hutchinson (Hutchinson Island). The settler received a 2,000-acre grant in March 1803 from Florida's Spanish governor for an area of mainland between Fort Pierce and Jensen Beach. He moved the grant to Jupiter Island in 1807, and after his death, it moved in 1827 to what is now Hutchinson Island.

Capt. Francis Asbury Hendry (Hendry County): The colorful Civil War leader and cattle industry pioneer established LaBelle and helped found Lee County, from which Hendry was split in 1923. Hendry died in February 1917.

A. G. Holley (Hospital, Lantana): Holley was a Panhandle hardware store owner and a longtime member of the state's tuberculosis board. Then-Rep. Wayne Mixson, later a lieutenant governor, pushed through the name change of the Southeast Florida Tuberculosis Hospital in 1965, over the objections of the Palm Beach County delegation.

Lamar D. Howard (Park, Port Salerno): The 39-year-old plumber and father of five, whose family were pioneers in the area's Golden Gate neighborhood, was killed in a motorcycle accident in 1972.

Alex Hughes (Park, Boca Raton): A pioneer in the historic Pearl City black neighborhood. He helped get the area its first black school and formed the local African Methodist Episcopal (AME) church in 1919. The park was dedicated in February 1972; he died in January 1977.

Melanie Jenkins (Jenkins Park, West Palm Beach): Jenkins was a community and church activist in the city's Northwest neighborhood. The park was named in 1993, shortly after she died at 74 in a hit-and-run accident.

Howard L. Johnson (Elementary School, Royal Palm Beach). Johnson, principal of Melaleuca Elementary in suburban West Palm Beach for 15 years, fought for an elementary in Royal Palm Beach; he died of a viral infection in 1982 and the new school he wanted opened in his name in December 1984.

Johnson

Marty Katz (Katz Field, Royal Palm Beach): Katz, president of Royal Palm Beach Colony, the original developer of the village, died in a car accident at 53 in September 1955; the park, on land he donated, was named for him in 1996.

Ulysses B. Kinsey (U.B. Kinsey/Palmview Elementary School, West Palm Beach): The longtime Palmview principal was one of the area's leading black educators for nearly 50 years.

Paul Knowles (Park, Delray Beach): Knowles was a city commissioner who pushed for the park.

Raymond F. Kravis (Kravis Center for the Performing Arts, West Palm Beach): Friends of the retired Oklahoma oilman and Palm Beach philanthropist honored his generosity by contributing almost $10 million of the $55 million to build the arts center. It was dedicated in September 1992. Kravis died at 92 in 1993.

Col. James N. Kreamer (Kreamer Island, Belle Glade): Kreamer was chief engineer for Hamilton Disston, the Philadelphia millionaire who bought four million acres of Central Florida for 25 cents an acre in June 1881 and began the state's first large drainage effort.

Richard G. Kreusler (Kreusler Park, Palm Beach): Kreusler, a Palm Beach attorney, oil executive and town council member-elect, was murdered in 1976; Mark Herman, who spent 15 years in jail for the slaying, was granted clemency in 1992.

Bobbie Jo Lauter (Park, Royal Palm Beach Town Hall): The park was dedicated in November 1970, two months after the 14-year-old was killed in an accident.

Charles Leighton/John Stewart "Jock" Leighton (Park, Palm City): Scottish settler Charles Leighton and his British wife, Rose, came to the area in 1912, starting a farm on 20 acres they bought sight unseen. The family became an institution for more than 75 years. Charles Leighton died around 1941. Rose Leighton died at 94 in 1987. One park was named for their son, Charles W. Leighton, a Martin County commissioner from the Palm City area from 1950 to 1962. Another son, entrepreneur "Jock" Leighton, died in January 1998; his estate is now negotiating to sell Martin County land for a new park.

John I. Leonard (High School, Lake Worth): He was Palm Beach County schools superintendent from 1936 to 1948, when he became first president of Palm Beach Junior College. He retired from PBJC in 1958 and died in July 1961 at 75; the school named for him opened in Greenacres four years later.

Ida Linton (Lake Ida): Delray Beach settler William Linton named the lake for his wife.

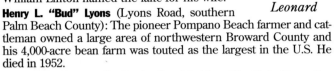

Leonard

Henry L. "Bud" Lyons (Lyons Road, southern Palm Beach County): The pioneer Pompano Beach farmer and cattleman owned a large area of northwestern Broward County and his 4,000-acre bean farm was touted as the largest in the U.S. He died in 1952.

Thomas B. Manuel (St. Lucie Canal bridge, Florida's Turnpike, Martin County): "Mr. Turnpike," a Delray Beach farmer, Fort Lauderdale mayor and banking executive, convinced state transportation officials to extend the turnpike to Miami instead of stopping at central Martin County. He died in 1987.

Gladys R. McDonald (McDonald Park, Belle Glade City Hall): The park was dedicated in 1962 to the city's parks superintendent. She died around 1985.

Leroy "Buddy" Merritt (Park, Delray Beach): The city council member and mayoral candidate died in 1979 at 47.

Robert P. Miller (Park, Delray Beach): The Chamber of Commerce officer, who had been a teacher and baseball coach at Seacrest High School, first suggested the baseball park and helped build it. It was dedicated in April 1977.

Joe C. Mitchell (J.C. Mitchell Elementary School, Boca Raton): The Boca Raton pioneer, who came in 1923, spent 15 years as mayor and 12 years as chair of the then-separate city school board. He died in 1955; the school was named for him in 1958.

John Monahan (Big John Monahan Bridge, St. Lucie Canal and State Road 76, Indiantown): Monahan, a Fort Lauderdale dry cleaner, served on the state road board. The bridge was named in 1965.

Chester Arthur Moore (Elementary School, Fort Pierce): A grocer and railroad clerk, he went back to school and became a longtime educator and principal. The school, for blacks, opened in 1959; Moore died in 1969.

Clint Moore (Clint Moore Road, Boca Raton): The longtime farmer and paving contractor sold the property to the county.

James Moore (Town of Moore Haven): The Seattle hotel owner bought 98,000 acres at the southwestern corner of Lake Okeechobee in 1915 and created the town that became the Glades County seat. He died at 67 in San Francisco in May 1929.

Dr. James Munyon (Munyon Island, Palm Beach): The man behind Paw-Paw tonic, a mixture of sulphur water and papaya juice that sold for $1 a bottle as a cure-all, bought the island in 1901 and built the five-story, 21-room Hotel Hygeia, named after the Greek goddess of health. The hotel burned down in 1911. The island, now 45 acres, is part of John D. MacArthur Beach State Park.

Robert G. Murray (Murray Middle School, Port Salerno): Murray was a teacher from 1928 to 1937 and again from 1945 to his retirement in 1958 and was principal of Stuart Training School; the school moved to Port Salerno in 1964 and was named for the Murray family.

Col. William Herbert Murphy (Camp Murphy, now Jonathan Dickinson State Park): The strategic World War II training site was named for the Signal Corps officer and radio pioneer who died in battle Feb. 3, 1942.

C.N. Newcomb (Newcomb Hall, Riviera Beach): The pioneer, who ran a fishing camp, gave three parks to the city; the community center and dance hall was built in 1959. The park was not formally named for Newcomb until 1973; it was later renamed Bicentennial Park, but Newcomb Hall is still in use.

Cardinal John Henry Newman (Cardinal Newman High School, West Palm Beach): The 19th-century British religious leader and scholar is considered the Catholic patron saint of education.

Ronald Osborne (Osborne Park, North Palm Beach): Prosperity Park was renamed in 1967 for Osborne, who died in Vietnam in 1966.

Duncan Padgett (Padgett Park, Pahokee): Part of a pioneer family that dated back to 1914 and mayor for 25 years, he died at 80 in 1986. The park was dedicated in May 1979.

Dr. Julian D. Parker (School of Science, Math and Technology, Stuart): He came to Stuart in 1924 in a Model-T Ford and would deliver more than 4,000 children; many "Parker babies" grew to be area leaders. He was Martin County's only doctor for almost a decade until World War II. Parker also served on the Martin School Board from 1939 to 1957. The school was named for him in 1960. He died at 98 in 1987.

Col. Samuel H. Peck (Peck Lake Park, Hobe Sound): The Augusta., Ga., cotton broker and banker was hit hard by an 1837 financial panic and came to the Indian River region, where he ran passengers and freight on his schooner. He left 12 years later and became a noted educator and author.

George Pendarvis (Pendarvis Cove Park, Palm City): The cove of the St. Lucie River is named for the family that homesteaded the area early in the century. The park was dedicated in 1987.

Toney Penna (Toney Penna Drive, Jupiter): He played professional golf for 32 years, winning six tournaments, and became an innovative designer of clubs, with four patents. His shop opened in 1966 on the road that bears his name. He died in 1995.

Pettway (Park, Hobe Sound): The Pettways were a pioneer black family in Gomez, north of Hobe Sound.

George Petty (Park, West Palm Beach): Originally named Royal Palm Park, it was renamed in 1990 for Petty, a millionaire who was the founder and financial backbone of the city's Good Neighbor Council and led the legal battle against airport noise.

Henry Phipps Jr. (Phipps Park, Palm Beach, West Palm Beach, Martin County): The Phipps Family (of steel, land and horse-racing fame) owned a third of Palm Beach and a large portion of coastal Martin County and built polo fields in Gulf Stream. The family gave 1,200 feet of ocean-to-lake property on Palm Beach to the county in 1948, and a park parcel on Olive Avenue to West Palm Beach in 1945. The family also donated part of its western Martin County stables for a park.

Charles A. Porter (Park, Hobe Sound): Porter, agent for a steamship line that worked the St. Lucie River, built a home in downtown Stuart that still stands.

John Prince (John Prince Park, Lake Worth): A county commissioner for 18 years, he got developers and the state to donate more than 1,000 acres in the 1930s and 1940s. Parts of the parcel became Lantana airport, Boy Scout and Girl Scout camps, Palm Beach Community College, and a rehabilitation center. The 726-acre park that bears his name is believed to be the second oldest county park in Florida.

Paul Rardin (Rardin Park, Canal Point): A Palm Beach County commissioner for two decades and publisher of the *Everglades News*, he was instrumental in establishing the west county satellite courthouse in Belle Glade. The park was dedicated in 1964.

Roy Rambo (Park, Greenacres): The retired plasterer was a volunteer and later became a city maintenance worker at 73. The park was named for him two weeks after he died in May 1979.

Todd A. Robiner (Robiner Park, Royal Palm Beach): The 21-year-old college student died of leukemia in August 1994; the park was named for him two months later.

Julius Rosenwald (Elementary School, South Bay): After getting rich as a retailer and a partner in Sears' lucrative turn-of-the-century mail-order business, he donated to black educational advancements. He died in 1932; the school opened as South Bay Elementary in 1951 and was named for him in 1956.

Donald Alexander Ross (Donald Ross Road, northern Palm Beach County): The first Lake Park resident killed in World War II was the son of Marjorie Ross, longtime principal of Lake Park Elementary School. He served as a first lieutenant in a tank battalion in the North African campaign, fought in the Anzio landing and was among the U.S. forces that battled through southern France. He was killed during the Battle of the Bulge on Dec. 18, 1944.

1910 - 1919

Burton and Annie Raulerson's Boca Raton home, built in 1914, featured plenty of windows and three porches — one on each level in the back plus a front porch. "Because there was no air conditioning, they had as many windows as they could have, and porches, because people didn't live in their back yards the way they do now," says Peggy McCall, an archivist with the Boca Raton Historical Society. Many homes of this era and the next several decades — including the Raulerson House — also sat on pilings to keep air flowing underneath the home for cooling and to prevent rot. These were pioneer days, and homes were modest, made from readily available materials such as Dade County pine and pecky cypress. The Raulerson House once sat on W. Palmetto Park Road but was moved to Southwest Second Avenue.

1920 - 1929

The great Florida land boom born of good economic times — and helped along by Henry Flagler's railroad to South Florida — led to the expansion of dozens of coastal neighborhoods. Famed architects such as Addison Mizner and Maurice Fatio designed grand Palm Beach mansions for America's nouveau riche, as well as more modest homes throughout the area. Other builders took note of the popular Mission and Mediterranean-revival styles and constructed hundreds of homes like this one, located in historic Central Park in West Palm Beach. The wood and lathe construction with stucco exterior has proved durable, as many of these homes have survived to see the new millennium.

1930 - 1939

The Depression hit South Florida hard, like everywhere else, although a few folks still built new homes. Florida remained a popular winter destination for Northerners whose wealth hadn't evaporated. One such lucky person was J.B. Evans, a businessman from the North who brokered vegetables in Florida. He built the Sandoway House on Ocean Avenue in Delray Beach, purposely keeping it modest. Other rich snowbirds did the same thing. "They didn't want a big Palm Beach mansion because it would be too ostentatious," says Carolyn Patton of Friends of the Sandoway House Nature Center. "So they were building small cottages." The home was built in a style dubbed "Resort-Colonial," a modified version of a Cape Cod-style home. Open balconies, a tile roof, breezeways and arched windows add a tropical flair.

1940 - 1949

The lean times of the Depression stretched into the war years. The '40s was not a busy time for home construction in South Florida, and almost everything that did get built was small and simple in design. Instead of whole streets of homes springing up as in the '20s, houses were built to fill in empty lots here and there in coastal neighborhoods, including this 1946 cottage in Lake Worth.

1950 - 1959

Florida's second boom started not long after World War II. As in other parts of the country, waves of returning veterans and optimistic civilians started looking for affordable homes. "We'd come a long way in how we produced materials," says Jim Anstis, an architect who served for 16 years on Palm Beach County's citizen's task force on land development. "There was more automation. That's when you started to see builders like Ross come in and build whole tracts of houses. They used the same floor plan but rotated it so it didn't look like a row of identical houses." Neighborhoods such as Lake Clarke Shores, with homes such as this one, began popping up west of the coast. The homes were basic but sturdy, employing the new concrete block with stucco construction. Concrete tiles lined the roofs and terrazzo covered the floors. They were easy to build and easy for young families to maintain, but they also signaled the end of detailed craftsmanship in average-priced homes.

1960 - 1969

The '60s saw much of the same construction styles and techniques as the '50s. CBS construction still reigned, and subdivisions continued to pop up, although homes like this one in West Palm Beach's south end also were built, filling in vacant lots or replacing smaller, poorly built homes from earlier in the century. Homes grew in size, too, as the prosperity of the '50s lingered, and air

conditioning became commonplace in new construction, a change that helped draw thousands of new residents to the state in the coming decades. Florida's popularity as a retirement destination was growing, and some of the first condominiums and apartment complexes were built, notably the city-sized Century Village in 1968. It was an inkling of things to come.

1970 - 1979

The condominium stands as the icon of South Florida homes in the '70s. Huge skyscraper-sized ones began springing up along the ocean and Intracoastal, but more noteworthy were the dozens of pod-style condo developments offering numerous pools, golf courses, activity centers and other amenities. Florida's reputation as a retirement haven was in full swing, and plenty of senior citizens from Northern cities were more than happy to trade sleet and snow for sun and surf. Condo living suited them; they were used to smallish apartments and townhomes from their years in Northern cities, says architect Jim Anstis. Also attractive was the idea of paying a monthly fee to avoid maintenance hassles such as lawn mowing. Later, condos would become increasingly popular with young families and singles.

1980 - 1989

As South Florida's population grew, so did the size of its subdivisions. Instead of a few streets, subdivisions in the '80s reached mammoth proportions. Instead of living near the golf course, you could live on it. Land-use laws passed in the '70s and early '80s paved the way for westward development. Nowhere were these changes more evident than in Wellington, a subdivision so large it was bigger than most of the county's cities. (It became a city in 1996.) Home designs, such as this one in Wellington's Wilshire Village, became more decorative, with arched windows and doorways and multi-colored barrel tile roofs. Dark colors and low roofs gave way to cathedral ceilings, bright white walls, shiny tile floors and spacious kitchens. And pools became almost standard issue, along with their screened enclosures.

1990 - 1999

The problem with the construction style of the '80s and early '90s? It seemed every new house looked the same, an effect heightened by zero-lot lines, which put houses within inches of each other. Architects and home builders began to try appealing to people tired of this homogeneous look; historic districts became popular and renovating old homes became trendy. (From the '80s to 1999, 20 historic districts were created in Palm Beach County.) That's not to say the era of the mega-subdivision ended, but the desire for "Old Florida" is apparent even in them. The Abacoa development in Jupiter ended the decade by opening its first neighborhood, New Haven, with quaint Victorian and Colonial-style homes, such as this one, featuring front porches and gabled roofs evoking the earlier part of the century.

CREDITS

RESEARCH: Lynne Palombo and Dorothy Shea of *The Palm Beach Post*

PHOTO RESEARCH: Gwyn Surface of *The Palm Beach Post*

COLOR PRODUCTION: The camera department of *The Palm Beach Post*

EDITING AND PRODUCTION: Dan Neal, Eric Weiss and the features copy desk of *The Palm Beach Post*

SPECIAL THANKS

Bobby Riggs

Cathleen McFarlane

Pat Crowley

Florida Historical Society
(Lewis N. Wynne)

Historical Association of Southern Florida
(Becky Smith)

County historical societies of Palm Beach (Kristin Gaspari & Clemmer Mayhew), Martin (Susan Duncan), St. Lucie (DeeDee Roberts and Allan King) and Okeechobee (Betty Williamson)

Historical societies of Boca Raton (Peggy McCall), Delray Beach (Dorothy Patterson), Boynton Beach (Harvey Oyer), Lake Worth (Beverly Mustaine), Belle Glade (Joseph Orsenigo) and Clewiston (Joe McCrary)

Florida History Center and Museum, Jupiter (Dorothy White)

Palm Beach County Black Historical Preservation Society (Preston Tillman, C. Spencer Pompey)

South Florida history scholars Jim Ponce, Harvey Poole Sr., Roy Simon, Sandra Thurlow and Ada Coats Williams

SOURCES

Archives of *The Palm Beach Post*

Curl, Donald, editor, *Palm Beach County, in a Class by Itself*

Curl, Donald, and John P. Johnson, *Boca Raton: A Pictorial History*

Gannon, Michael, editor, *The New History of Florida*

Hutchinson, Janet, *History of Martin County*

Lockwood, Charlotte, *Florida's Historic Indian River County*

Mahon, John, *History of the Second Seminole War*

McGoun, William E., *Southeast Florida Pioneers: The Palm and Treasure Coasts*

McIver, Stuart B., *Yesterday's Palm Beach*

Morris, Allen, *Florida Handbook*

Mustaine, Beverly, *On Lake Worth*

Simon, Sandy, *Remembering: A History of Florida's South Palm Beach County*

Tuckwood, Jan, and Eliot Kleinberg, *Pioneers in Paradise: West Palm Beach, the First 100 Years*

Van Landingham, Kyle, *Pictorial History of Saint Lucie County*

Last bites

Glad-to-meet-you Gator: Wishing you were here, 1920s

Sunday-driving Gators: Palm Beach postcard, 1910

Family portrait Gator: Gertrude Katz and Daniel Moses pose precariously around 1915.

239

BY THE BEAUTIFUL SEA: *A Delray Beach picnic, Fourth of July, early 1900s.*